The
EVERYTHING®
Classic Recipes Book

Dear Reader,

Over the past twenty-two years I have compiled many notes and recipes based on meals I have eaten both in restaurants and in the homes of family and friends, and I have absorbed information from countless cookbooks, magazines, cooking shows, and demonstrations. This passion for food knowledge led me to enter culinary school, where I learned the nuts and bolts of professional cooking from classically trained chef instructors. Creating a recipe notebook was a requirement in this education. I built upon this notebook with each professional restaurant experience, constantly expanding my repertoire. My personal and professional culinary pursuits have resulted in a valuable cooking resource.

The only problem with my culinary library is that I have to sift through all the information to find all the recipes I need every time I want to cook a meal. In the interest of saving time and space, I have written a collection of classic recipes and compiled them into one book so I no longer have to spend time searching in different files, notebooks, magazines, and cookbooks. I have synthesized my information into one volume so I can get on with the meal, from appetizer to dessert. I hope you will find this book a valuable tool in your culinary pursuits.

Lynette Rohrer Shirk

The EVERYTHING® Series

Editorial

Publishing Director	Gary M. Krebs
Director of Product Development	Paula Munier
Associate Managing Editor	Laura M. Daly
Associate Copy Chief	Brett Palana-Shanahan
Acquisitions Editor	Kate Burgo
Development Editor	Rachel Engelson
Associate Production Editor	Casey Ebert

Production

Director of Manufacturing	Susan Beale
Associate Director of Production	Michelle Roy Kelly
Series Designers	Daria Perreault
	Colleen Cunningham
Cover Design	Paul Beatrice
	Erick DaCosta
	Matt LeBlanc
Interior Layout	Brewster Brownville
	Colleen Cunningham
	Daria Perreault
	Jennifer Oliveira
Cover Artist and Interior Illustrator	Barry Littmann

Visit the entire Everything® Series at *www.everything.com*

THE

EVERYTHING®

CLASSIC
RECIPES BOOK

300 all-time favorites—
perfect for beginners

Lynette Rohrer Shirk

Adams Media
Avon, Massachusetts

With love to Zelda Shirk, Jeff Shirk,
Mary Ellen Pilgrim, and Howard Cline.

An Everything® Series Book.
Everything® and everything.com® are registered trademarks of F+W Publications, Inc.

Published by Adams Media, an F+W Publications Company
57 Littlefield Street, Avon, MA 02322 U.S.A.
www.adamsmedia.com

ISBN 10: 1-59337-690-1
ISBN 13: 978-1-59337-690-1
Printed in the United States of America.

J I H G F E D C B

Library of Congress Cataloging-in-Publication Data
Shirk, Lynette Rohrer.
The everything classic recipes book / Lynette Rohrer Shirk.
p.   cm.
ISBN-13: 978-1-59337-690-1
ISBN-10: 1-59337-690-1
1. Cookery. I. Title.
TX714.S544 2006
641.5--dc22

2006019732

Inside cover photographs © Brand X Pictures.

This book is available at quantity discounts for bulk purchases.
For information, please call 1-800-872-5627.

Contents

Acknowledgments

I would like to thank my husband, Jeff, and daughter, Zelda, for their patience as I worked on this book. Thanks also to Batavia McFarlin (Mrs. B) and Izumi Kajiyama (Ms. Izumi) at the Children's Courtyard in Lewisville, Texas, for their guidance and care for my daughter. Thanks also to Brenda Knight, June Clark, and Kate Burgo.

Introduction

The purpose of this cookbook is to provide you with a comprehensive resource for the kitchen in one book. It is more than a basic cookbook, though. It is an idea book with tidbits of information sprinkled throughout that are intended to guide and expand your cooking skills, enrich your culinary lexicon, and inspire your creativity.

In the first chapter you'll find lists of suggested kitchen supplies, explanations of a variety of cooking terms, guides to measuring, and other information that will help you know where to begin and will provide a reference point if you need clarification of any instructions in the book.

Using this cookbook, you will be able to put together whole meals of family favorites with recipes like meatloaf, mashed potatoes, and almond green beans. You will be able to satisfy cravings for a variety of whims from chocolate chip cookies to chocolate mousse. Indulge your need for comfort food with recipes for classics like macaroni and cheese and pineapple upside-down cake. Thanksgiving is covered; you don't need to leaf through several books to find recipes for dinner rolls, candied yams, turkey, or pumpkin pie when they are all here, down to the cranberry sauce.

Simple joys in life, such as a perfect chocolate cake or a steaming pot of chili, are at your fingertips in this book, along with more recipes that can be mixed and matched to create meals and snacks year-round. Peruse the party fare, kids' favorites, and sandwich classics for the next occasion that calls for you to feed and please everyone, or check out the breakfast selections before deciding whether to spend time waiting in line for brunch on Mother's Day again.

The Everything® Classic Recipes Book will give you a great start as you build your skills and cooking repertoire. You will learn techniques that enable you to go from being a novice cook to being an experienced chef, able to tackle any recipe for any occasion, all the while enjoying your time in the kitchen!

CHAPTER 1

Kitchen Basics

Cookware and Kitchen Tools

Two indispensable items you need to get started cooking are a good knife and a cutting board. Others can be improvised if necessary, such as using a wine bottle as a rolling pin, or using coffee cups for measuring when you need ratios rather than precise measurements. You will, however, need some basic cookware in order to make the simple recipes in this book.

Essential Kitchen Items

Apple corer

Baking dish (9" x 9")

Baking dish (9" x 13")

Bundt Pan

Can opener

Colander

Cookie sheets

Cooling rack

Corkscrew

Cutting board

Grater

Kitchen shears

Knives – chef's, paring, serrated

Ladle

Measuring cups (dry)

Measuring cups (liquid)

Measuring spoons

Meat thermometer

Melon baller

Mixing bowls

Muffin tin

Parchment paper (waxed paper)

Pastry brush

Essential Kitchen Items

Pastry cutter

Pie plate

Potato masher

Potholders

Ramekins

Roasting pan with rack

Rolling pin

Saucepan (2 quart)

Saucepan (4 quart)

Sauté pan (8")

Sauté pan (12")

Slotted spoon

Serving spoon

Soup pot with lid (8 quart)

Spatula (metal)

Spatula (rubber)

Springform pan

Strainer

Vegetable peeler

Vegetable steamer

Wire whisk

Wooden spoons

Zester (for citrus)

Kitchen Helpers	**Kitchen Helpers**
Basting brush	Nonstick griddle
Electric mixer	Oil pump mister
Egg separator	Pastry scraper
Fondue pot	Pizza stone
Food mill	Salad spinner
Food processor	Tongs
Hand mixer	Waffle iron
Metal skewers	Wok

Kitchen Aids

In addition to the basic tools you should have for a well-stocked kitchen, there are kitchen items that can save you time and effort when preparing dishes and are often worth the extra investment. Some helpful (but not absolutely necessary) kitchen items are listed.

How to Measure Liquid Ingredients

1. Use a liquid measuring cup—a glass or plastic cup with graduated markings on the side.

2. Place the cup on a flat, level surface.

3. View the liquid at eye level.

Tip: Liquid measuring cups can be greased with a small amount of oil or shortening before measuring thick liquids like honey.

How to Measure

Don't guess! Accurate measuring is the key to good results.

How to Measure Dry Ingredients

1. Use graduated nesting measuring cups (dry measuring cups).

2. Spoon the ingredient into the appropriate cup, or dip the cup into the container of a dry ingredient.

3. Level it off with a knife or spatula.

Exception: Brown sugar must be packed into the measuring cup, pressing firmly with the fingers. The sugar should retain the shape of the measuring cup when it is dumped.

How to Measure Soft Ingredients

1. Use graduated dry measuring cups.

2. Fresh bread crumbs, coconut, shredded cheeses, and similar soft ingredients should be lightly pressed down into the selected measuring cup.

Exception: Solid shortening must be firmly packed down into a dry ingredient measuring cup. Scoop it into the selected cup, pack with a spatula or the back of a spoon, then level it off with a spatula or knife.

How to Use Measuring Spoons

1. Use graduated measuring spoons for both liquid and dry ingredients.

2. For dry ingredients, level with a knife or spatula.

3. For liquid ingredients, pour carefully, near but not over the mixing bowl.

How to Heat, Cool, Soften, or Melt

Here you'll find basic instructions that explain the different ways a cookbook may instruct you to prepare food before adding it to the recipe.

A preheated oven has been turned on and allowed to reach the desired temperature before the food is placed inside. Unless a recipe specifies otherwise, ovens should always be preheated. In most ovens 10 to 15 minutes is adequate time to preheat.

Room temperature foods have been removed from the refrigerator about 15 minutes before use in a recipe.

Softened foods like butter or cream cheese have been allowed to stand at room temperature until they are no longer hard to the touch, usually a minimum of 15 minutes.

Melted foods have been thoroughly liquefied, either in the microwave or over heat.

Cooled foods have been allowed to stand at room temperature for a specified amount of time, or until they can be comfortably touched. Stirring food speeds its cooling time.

Chilled foods have been allowed to stand in the refrigerator for a specified amount of time, or until both the outside and inside of the food are below room temperature. Stirring food speeds its chilling time.

Thoroughly chilled foods have been allowed to stand in the refrigerator until both the outside and inside of the food have reached the refrigerator's storage temperature. Thorough chilling of heated food usually takes at least an hour or more, depending on the amount of food and shape of the container.

To soften cold butter or margarine in the microwave: Place 1 stick unwrapped or ½ cup uncovered butter or margarine on a plate. Microwave on low 30 to 45 seconds in a 1,000-watt oven. Adjust time if wattage varies.

To soften cold cream cheese in the microwave: Place unwrapped cheese on an uncovered plate. Heat on high, 15 to 30 seconds for a 3-ounce package or 30 to 45 seconds for an 8-ounce package. Adjust time if oven wattage is not 1,000.

Slicing and Dicing

It is helpful to familiarize yourself with the different cooking terms for cutting up food and what these terms mean. You can always refer back to this list if there is any question about a term.

Bias slice: to cut at a 45-degree angle.
Chop: to cut into small irregular pieces with a knife or food processor.
Core: to remove the center of a fruit like an apple or pear.
Crush: to press or smash seasonings or other foods to release their flavor, using a garlic press, heavy knife, or other implement.
Cube: to cut food into squares about ½ inch on the sides.
Cut up: to cut into small irregular pieces.
Diagonal slice: to cut at a 45-degree angle.
Dice: to cut into reasonably uniform pieces of about ¼ inch.
Grate: to rub a food such as cheese, vegetables, or spices against a sharp-edged kitchen tool called a grater, making small or fine particles.
Julienne: to cut into thin strips, about 2 inches long, that will look like matchsticks.
Mince: to chop food into very small bits.
Score: to cut through the surface of a food (usually about ¼ inch deep) to tenderize or make a pattern.
Section: to cut the pulp of a peeled citrus fruit away from the membranes that separate its segments.
Shred: to cut in narrow, thin strips, by using a kitchen shredder or a knife.
Slice: to cut into flat pieces that are usually thin and even.
Snip: to cut herbs or other food into small pieces using kitchen scissors.
Tear: to break into pieces using the hands rather than a knife.

Mixing

Beat: to stir briskly with a spoon, a whisk, a hand eggbeater, or an electric mixer.
Blend: to mix two or more ingredients until they make a uniform mixture.
Cream: to beat a fat until it is light and fluffy, often in combination with sugar or other ingredients.

Cut in: to combine a solid fat with dry ingredients, until the fat is in very small pieces about the size of small peas, by using a pastry blender or a fork. Compare cream.

Fold: to combine ingredients gently, using a spatula or spoon to lift ingredients from the bottom of the bowl and "fold" them over the top.

Knead: to work dough by continuously folding over and pressing down until it is smooth and elastic. Dough can also be kneaded with electric mixer attachments called dough hooks.

Stir: to mix ingredients at a moderate pace to combine them.

Temper: to gently heat a substance that can curdle (eggs or dairy, usually) before adding to a hot liquid by adding a bit of the hot liquid to the substance and mixing them together. This brings the temperature of the substance closer to the temperature of the hot liquid to prevent curdling.

Toss: to mix ingredients by gently lifting them from the bottom of the bowl and allowing them to tumble, usually using two forks or other utensils.

Whip: to beat rapidly with a wire whisk, hand beater, or electric mixer. Whipping increases volume because it adds air to the ingredient(s).

Food Preparation

Baste: to spoon or pour broth, sauce, or other liquid over food while cooking to prevent dryness or add flavor.

Blacken: to cook Cajun-seasoned foods over a very high heat.

Bread: to coat foods before cooking in bread crumbs or cracker crumbs.

Caramelize: to coat the top of a food with sugar and then broil it quickly until the sugar is melted. Or, to melt sugar in a saucepan over a low heat until it turns into a golden syrup. Caramelizing can also mean melting the sugar in a certain food (onions or beef, for example) to give it a brown color and bring out its slightly sweet flavor.

Deglaze: to add liquid to a skillet in which meat has been cooked, stirring to loosen meat bits and make a broth. The broth can be used to make a sauce.

Dot: to place pieces of butter randomly on top of a food.

Drizzle: to pour a liquid topping in thin, irregular lines over a food.

Dust: to sprinkle a dry ingredient lightly and fairly evenly over a food.

Glaze: to spread a thin coating such as jelly on food, making it appear glossy.

Grease: to coat the surface of a pan with shortening or cooking spray to prevent foods from sticking while they bake. To "grease and flour" is to dust the pan lightly with flour after applying the shortening.

Marinate: to let food stand in a special liquid to flavor it or tenderize it. The liquid is called a marinade.

Purée: to make into a thick liquid, usually by using a blender or food processor.

Reduce: to boil a liquid until some of it evaporates, thus concentrating the flavor.

Roux: a combination of melted butter, flour, and seasonings over heat to use as a thickening base for sauces, gravies, soups, and stews.

Sift: to process dry ingredients through a kitchen sifter or sieve. Sifting adds air to dry ingredients that have been compressed in storage and also removes any lumps.

Skim: to remove fat or foam that has accumulated on the surface of a liquid, usually using a spoon.

Bake

Cooking Techniques

Bake: to cook food with the indirect dry heat of an oven. Covering food while baking it preserves moistness; leaving food uncovered results in a drier or crisp surface.

Barbecue: to cook with barbecue sauce or spices, or to cook slowly on a grill or spit, usually outdoors.

Blanch: to cook fruits, vegetables, or nuts very briefly in boiling water or steam, usually to preserve the color or nutritional value or to remove the skin. Also called parboiling.

Boil: to cook a liquid at a temperature at which bubbles rise and break on the surface. To bring to a boil means to heat just until bubbling begins.

Boil

In a full or rolling boil, the bubbles are larger and form quickly and continuously.

Braise: to cook food slowly in a tightly covered pan in a small amount of liquid. Usually, food is first browned in a small amount of fat. Braising tenderizes food and can be done either on the stovetop or in the oven.

Broil: to cook food directly under a direct source of intense heat or flame, producing a browned or crisp exterior and a less well-done interior.

Deep-Fry: to cook food in hot, liquefied fat (usually kept at 350° to 375°F) that is deep enough to cover and surround the food completely.

Fry: to cook in hot fat or oil, producing a crisp exterior.

Grill: to cook foods directly above a source of intense heat or flame. Foods can be pan-grilled on a stovetop by using a specially designed pan with raised grill ridges.

Oven-Fry: to cook food, usually breaded, in a hot oven with a small amount of fat, usually dotted or drizzled on top of the food.

Pan-Fry: to fry with little or no added fat, using only the fat that accumulates during cooking.

Parboil: see Blanch.

Poach: to cook in a simmering (not boiling) liquid.

Roast: to cook meat or poultry in the indirect heat of the oven, uncovered. Roasted foods are not cooked in added liquid (compare braise), but are often basted with liquids for flavor and moistness.

Sauté: to cook in a small amount of fat over high heat.

Scald: to heat a liquid to just below the boiling point, when small bubbles begin to appear around the edges of the pan. When milk is scalded, a film will form on the surface.

Sear: to brown on all sides over high heat to preserve juiciness.

Simmer: to keep a liquid just below the boiling point; a few bubbles will rise and break on the surface.

Steam: to cook food above (not in) boiling or simmering water.

Stew: to cook food, covered, very slowly in liquid.

Stir-Fry: to cook small pieces of food in a hot wok or skillet, using a small amount of fat and a constant stirring motion.

Simmer

Stir-Fry

Common Ingredients

Baking powder is a leavening, or an ingredient that makes a mixture expand or rise by releasing (harmless) carbon dioxide bubbles.

Baking soda is a leavening that works in the presence of acidic ingredients.

Cornstarch is a thickener made from corn. It takes only about half as much cornstarch as flour to achieve the same amount of thickening.

Cream of tartar is used primarily to add stability to candies, frostings, and egg whites.

Yeast is a leavening that makes a mixture rise or expand in the presence of warmth, sugar, and liquid. If baking soda or baking powder is used as leavening in a recipe, yeast is not used.

Chocolates

These **chocolates** should not be substituted for one another without making other adjustments. (See Appendix A for substitutions.)

Baking cocoa (a powder) is made from the pure "liquor"—the liquid substance—of the cocoa bean. It contains no cocoa butter, sweetener, or other product.

Bittersweet, semisweet, sweet, and milk chocolate have cocoa butter, sugar, and sometimes milk added to the cocoa bean liquor.

Unsweetened baking chocolate contains cocoa butter but no sugar.

Creams

Creams result when milk butterfat is separated from milk liquids.

Half-and-half or light cream is a mixture of milk and cream. It can be substituted for heavy cream, which has more fat and calories, when the cream is used as a liquid in a recipe. It cannot be substituted for heavy cream that must be whipped, however, because the fat content of heavy cream is what allows successful whipping.

Sour cream is cream cultured with lactic acid to make it thick and tangy. Low-fat and nonfat varieties are available, but only the low-fat version should be substituted for full-fat sour cream in cooked recipes.

Whipping or heavy cream has a very high fat content. When whipped, it doubles in volume.

Fats and Oils

Butter, a saturated fat made from cream, is usually considered the best-tasting fat. Unless otherwise specified, recipes calling for butter require stick or cube butter. Do not use whipped butter as a substitute.

Lard is shortening made from animal (pork) fat. It is a saturated fat. Some cooks believe that the flakiest biscuits and pie crusts are made with lard.

Margarine is an unsaturated fat that is a substitute for butter and contains at least 80 percent fat. Only the sticks (not the tubs or squeezable liquids) should be used in preparing recipes.

Oils are fats from nuts, seeds, or vegetables that remain liquid at room temperature. Sesame oil and some nut oils have a distinctive flavor and should not be substituted for regular cooking oil unless the flavor is acceptable in the recipe.

Shortening is vegetable oil that remains solid at room temperature. Plain and butter-flavored varieties are interchangeable.

Flours

All-purpose flour is a blend of wheat that can be used for all general cooking and baking. It is usually enriched with vitamins but has no wheat bran or germ. Bleached and unbleached varieties are interchangeable.

Cake flour, bread flour, and pasta flour are made from different kinds of wheat and perform differently when cooked or baked. Substituting a specific-purpose flour for another flour in recipes will lead to different and usually unsatisfactory results.

"Instant" flour has a fine, powdery texture that dissolves easily for sauces and gravies.

Self-rising flour has salt and leavening added to it. Do not substitute for all-purpose flour without making other adjustments. (See Appendix A for substitutions.)

Whole-wheat or graham flour is made from the entire wheat kernel and thus includes the bran and germ. It can be substituted for up to half the amount of all-purpose flour called for in most baked goods. However, the resulting product will be denser and flatter, and will have a nuttier flavor.

Milks

Buttermilk is low-fat milk that is cultured with lactic acid to give it a tangy flavor and thicken it. Despite its name, it is actually lower in fat than whole milk.

Condensed milk is made from whole or part skim milk with part of the water removed and sugar added. It cannot be substituted for **evaporated milk**, which has had 60 percent of the water removed and is not sweetened. Evaporated milk, when prepared by mixing with an equal amount of water, can be substituted for whole milk.

Whole, 2 percent or low-fat, and skim milk can all be substituted for each other in recipes.

Sugars and Sweeteners

Brown sugar is usually made by adding molasses to granulated sugar. Darker brown sugars contain more molasses and have a more intense flavor. Brown sugar is always measured by packing it into the measuring cup unless a recipe specifies otherwise.

Corn syrup is a liquid sweetener made from corn. Light corn syrup and dark corn syrup can be substituted for each other, but corn syrup should not be substituted for other sweeteners.

Granulated sugar is standard white sugar made from sugar cane or beets. When a recipe calls for sugar, use granulated sugar.

Honey is a sweetener that bees make from the nectar of flowers. It is almost twice as sweet as sugar. It cannot be substituted for sugar in a recipe without making other adjustments (because honey is a liquid).

Maple syrup is a thick liquid sweetener made from the sap of maple trees. Most commercial syrups are a blend of maple syrup and corn syrup.

Molasses is a sweetener made from sugar cane. Dark molasses can be substituted for light molasses, although the dark has a more intense flavor. Blackstrap molasses, however, contains almost no sugar and is not used as a sweetener. It should not be substituted for regular molasses.

Powdered or confectioners' sugar, usually used for icing, is pulverized granulated sugar. It cannot be substituted for granulated sugar in baking.

Raw sugar is produced when molasses is removed from sugar cane.

Synthetic sugars or artificial sweeteners differ, and some cannot be used successfully in cooking. They should be used only in accordance with the manufacturers' directions.

Vinegars

Balsamic vinegar is made from grapes. It is sweet, dark, and more strongly flavored than cider vinegar.

Fruit and herb vinegars are flavored cider or wine vinegars.

Rice vinegar is made from rice wine.

White vinegar is made from grain alcohol. It is not often used in recipes and should not be substituted for cider vinegar.

Wine vinegars are made from different varieties of wine.

Herbs and Spices

Don't buy too large of a quantity of dried herbs unless you will use them within one year, because they lose their potency over time. Spices lose potency too, although they are a little more robust. Fresh herbs can be kept as a living plant in a pot on a windowsill, or in the garden in temperate climates. Fresh herbs, which can also be purchased at the grocery store, are best stored wrapped in a slightly damp paper towel and sealed in a plastic bag. Some fresh herbs, such as cilantro and mint, are not worth using in dried form because their flavor is too delicate. Strong herbs, such as tarragon and oregano, can be used successfully in dried form and should be used sparingly in fresh form. They can be preserved in vinegar for winter use.

The form in which you should buy spices depends on the individual spice. Spices such as nutmeg and coriander are best if purchased whole and grated before each use rather than bought in powder form. Ground ginger and fresh gingerroot have different personalities; the first is dry, and the second is wet. On page 14 is a list of herbs and spices in their preferred forms. Keep in mind that when substituting fresh herbs for dried, or vice versa, the quantity should change—use twice as much fresh as dried.

Vinegars are acidic condiments and preservatives. When no special vinegar is specified, use cider vinegar, which is made from apple cider.

Herbs and Spices

Basil	fresh and dried
Bay Leaves	dried
Black Pepper	ground and whole peppercorns
Cayenne Pepper	dried ground
Chives	fresh and dried
Cilantro	fresh only
Cinnamon	ground and stick
Cloves	whole, ground
Coriander	whole, ground
Cumin	ground
Curry	powder
Dill Weed	fresh and dried
Dry Mustard	ground
Ginger	fresh root and dried ground
Lavender	dried blossoms
Mint	fresh only
Nutmeg	whole, ground
Oregano	dried
Paprika	ground
Parsley	fresh and dried
Rosemary	fresh and dried
Sage	fresh and dried
Tarragon	dried
Thyme	fresh and dried

Nutrition

Recent research indicates that many serious diseases, such as heart disease, certain cancers, diabetes, and high blood pressure, are diet-related. The typical American diet contains far more fat than is healthy, and surprisingly, about twice as much protein as is necessary.

Proteins are the "building blocks" of the body. They are necessary for the growth, maintenance, and rebuilding of every cell. The most concentrated sources of protein are animal products. Animal proteins, which include meat, fish, eggs, and milk, contain all of the nine essential amino acids that proteins can provide. They are called complete proteins. Vegetable proteins are present in nuts, seeds, whole grains, and legumes. All vegetable proteins, however—with the one exception of soy—are incomplete. If animal sources of protein are not included in the diet, vegetable proteins must be combined carefully to supply the body with all essential amino acids. This is why many vegetarians take supplements to achieve a well-balanced diet.

Carbohydrates provide most of the body's energy. Simple carbohydrates include all kinds of sugars and are sweet. Complex carbohydrates include grain products and some fruits and vegetables, such as beans and potatoes. Because complex carbohydrates must be split apart during the digestive process before they can be absorbed by the body, they supply energy over a longer period of time than do simple carbohydrates. Complex carbohydrates also contain vitamins, minerals, and dietary fiber. Fiber is the part of a plant that cannot be digested by humans. Water-insoluble fiber, found in fruits, vegetables, and grains, stimulates and regulates the digestive tract. Water-soluble fiber, present in fruits, vegetables, oat bran, and beans, may slow the absorption of sugar into the bloodstream and reduce blood cholesterol levels.

Although they have a deservedly bad name, fats are necessary to good health in appropriate amounts. They provide body insulation, cushioning, and energy reserve, and allow the body to use fat-soluble vitamins. In addition, fats make the body feel full or satisfied after eating.

Cholesterol is not a fat, but is a substance that is present in some fats. It is necessary for proper functioning of nerves and hormones. The human liver can manufacture all the cholesterol the body needs. However, dietary cholesterol is also present in some foods. A high level of cholesterol in the blood is related to cardiovascular disease.

Fats contain both saturated and unsaturated essential fatty acids. Saturated fats not only contain dietary cholesterol but also encourage the body to produce more than it needs. All animal fat is saturated fat. Two plant fats—palm and coconut oils—are also heavily saturated. Both are used extensively in processed and packaged bakery products, sweets, snacks, and other junk foods.

Unsaturated fats, which include most vegetable fats, are believed to actually reduce blood cholesterol levels when they replace saturated fat in the diet. Monounsaturated fats include fish oils and olive, canola, and peanut oils. Polyunsaturated fats are found in tuna and salmon, and in sunflower, corn, and sesame oils. However, partially hydrogenated vegetable oils (although unsaturated) contain trans-fatty acids, which research indicates may raise blood cholesterol. Partially hydrogenated oils are used in many shortenings and margarines.

Dietary Guidelines

The American Heart Association recommends a diet in which not more than 30 percent of total caloric intake is from fats. The nutrition labels that now appear on most cans, milk cartons, and other food packages show how much protein, carbohydrate, and fat a serving contains in gram weight. A calorie measures the energy value of food, not its fat content.

A calorie is actually the amount of heat needed to raise 1 kilogram of water 1° centigrade. Using a 30 percent guideline, the average 2,000-calorie-per-day diet should contain no more than 600 calories from fat.

Nutrition labels also show the percentage of recommended daily nutrient intake contained in a serving of food. These percentages are based on the U.S. Department of Agriculture (USDA) Food and Nutrition Service estimate of 2,000 calories per day for the average daily diet. Actual caloric intake will and should vary with age, gender, weight, and activity level. In general, men and young adults need more calories than do women and older adults. Pregnant and breastfeeding women need more calories, as well.

Based on 2,000 calories per day, the USDA suggests the following nutrient levels:

Total fat	Less than 65 grams
Saturated fat	Less than 20 grams
Cholesterol	Less than 300 milligrams
Sodium	Less than 2,400 milligrams
Total carbohydrate	300 grams
Dietary fiber	25 grams

The USDA also recommends:

- maintaining a diet high in grains, vegetables, and fruits
- maintaining a diet low in fat, saturated fat, and cholesterol
- maintaining a diet with a moderate intake of sugar, salt, and sodium
- eating a variety of foods

Conversion Chart

1 pint	=	16 ounces
1 cup	=	8 ounces
½ cup	=	4 ounces
¼ cup	=	2 ounces
1 ounce	=	2 tablespoons
1 tablespoon	=	3 teaspoons

Basic Cooking Tips

1. Always wash hands before preparing food.

2. Always use pot holders to take a pan from the oven. To indicate that a pan is hot from the oven, carefully mark it with flour or a pot holder on the edge of the pan.

3. Keep handles of pots and pans on the stove turned in from the edge.

4. Prevent steam burns by opening pot lids away from you.

5. Never leave knives in the sink. Knives should be hand-washed after each use.

6. Always use a timer when baking.

7. Use an oven thermometer for accurate oven temperature.

8. Use a meat thermometer to check internal temperature of foods.

9. Keep a fire extinguisher close by for emergencies.

10. Never throw water on a grease fire. Smother it with a pot lid if possible.

11. Wipe up spills on the floor right away. Sprinkle salt on the floor where there has been a greasy spill.

CHAPTER 2
Appetizers

8 slices French bread
2 cloves garlic, peeled and
    halved
1 teaspoon olive oil
2 tablespoons minced onion
1 tomato, diced
6 fresh basil leaves, sliced
    thinly
pinch of pepper
2 tablespoons grated
    Parmesan cheese

Tomato Bruschetta

Bruschetta is a classic light Italian appetizer that is especially delicious in the summer, when made with flavorful, ripe tomatoes and fragrant fresh basil.

• • •

1. Toast the bread on both sides. Rub one side of each piece of toast with the cut side of the garlic. Keep bread warm by placing it on a baking sheet in an oven set to warm.

2. Heat the oil in a medium-sized nonstick skillet over medium-high heat. Add the onion and cook, stirring until tender, about 10 minutes. Remove from the heat and stir in the tomato, basil, and pepper.

3. Preheat broiler. Spoon the tomato mixture over garlic-rubbed side of the toast, dividing evenly. Sprinkle with the cheese and brown slightly under preheated broiler for 1 minute. Serve immediately.

Eggplant Bruschetta

Toasts with toppings are a popular appetizer, and the Mediterranean flavors in this bruschetta are a satisfying way to start a light meal of soup and salad. Serve with Minestrone (page 52) and a green salad with Balsamic Vinaigrette (page 74).

• • •

Serves 6

1 baguette loaf French bread, sliced into ¼-inch rounds
½ cup olive oil
6 cloves garlic, peeled (2 cloves left whole for rubbing, 3 or 4 minced for eggplant mixture)
1 medium eggplant
2 tablespoons red wine vinegar
2 tablespoons minced capers (optional)
1 teaspoon salt
1 roasted red bell pepper, peeled and diced
¼ cup fresh parsley, chopped after measuring

1. Preheat oven to 350°F. Lay the baguette rounds on an ungreased cookie sheet. Brush both sides with olive oil and set aside the rest of the oil. Toast rounds in the oven until lightly browned; then turn and toast the other side. Remove from oven. Rub one side of each warm toast with garlic; set aside.

2. Place a piece of aluminum foil on the bottom oven rack. Prick eggplant all over with a fork. Place the eggplant directly on top oven rack and bake for about 1 hour, until tender. Test tenderness by inserting a fork into the flesh of the eggplant. If the fork slides easily in and out, the eggplant is tender. Remove from oven and let the eggplant cool enough to handle. Cut the eggplant in half and scoop the flesh into a bowl. Discard skin and stem.

3. Mince 3 or 4 cloves of the garlic, according to your taste, and add to cooked eggplant along with ¼ cup olive oil, red wine vinegar, capers, and salt. Mix thoroughly.

4. Spread each toast with eggplant mixture. Top with diced roasted red bell pepper, and sprinkle with parsley.

How to Roast a Pepper
Preheat broiler on high. Cut pepper in half and remove seeds. Rub the outside with oil, put on a baking dish, and broil in the oven until skin is charred. Pick up the broiled pepper with tongs and put it in a paper bag to steam for 10 minutes. Remove pepper from bag, and scrape skin off with a paring knife.

2 bunches green onions
16 ounces cream cheese,
*   softened*
8 ounces sour cream
¼ cup salsa
¼ cup black olives, chopped
½ teaspoon garlic powder
8 ounces Cheddar cheese,
*   grated*
¼ bunch fresh cilantro,
*   chopped*
10 large (burrito size) flour
*   tortillas*

Tortilla Pinwheels

These festive hors d'oeuvres are also called Mexican Sushi because of their
ingredients and their appearance. They resemble the California Rolls you may
get at a sushi bar but they taste like a deluxe taco treat!

• • •

1. Set aside 10 whole green onions. Chop the remaining green onions (green and white parts) and put into a mixing bowl.

2. Add cream cheese, sour cream, salsa, olives, garlic powder, Cheddar cheese, and cilantro to the chopped green onions and mix together thoroughly.

3. Lay a tortilla flat and spread 4 tablespoons of the cream cheese mixture over it. Put a whole green onion on the edge of the tortilla and roll tortilla into a log, squeezing firmly as you roll. Repeat with remaining tortillas, green onions, and filling.

4. Wrap each log in plastic wrap and refrigerate for 4 hours.

5. Unwrap logs and cut each one into 1-inch-thick slices. Arrange on a platter, and serve.

Honey Gorgonzola Toasts

Offer these creamy toasts as an appetizer before a casual dinner party or serve them as an accompaniment to a salad of baby mixed greens.

• • •

Serves 4

1 baguette loaf French bread
8 ounces Gorgonzola cheese
2 tablespoons heavy cream
¼ cup honey

1. Preheat oven to 350°F. Slice the baguette into ¼-inch rounds and lay them out on an ungreased cookie sheet. Toast them in the oven for about 5 minutes, then turn them over and toast the other side. Remove from oven and set aside.

2. In a bowl, combine Gorgonzola and heavy cream and mix well to a spreadable consistency. Add more cream if necessary.

3. Spread each toast round with 1 tablespoon of the Gorgonzola mixture, and then drizzle honey on top of them.

4. Turn the oven to "broil" and broil the toasts just until they are browned, about 3 minutes.

Gilding the Lily
Pears are a perfect companion to blue cheeses, like Gorgonzola. Top the Honey Gorgonzola Toasts with peeled, diced pears before drizzling them with honey. Broil and serve them as a cheese and fruit course.

1 bunch fresh asparagus
    spears
1 sheet frozen puff pastry,
    thawed
4 ounces Swiss cheese, grated
1 egg

Asparagus Puffs

*Tender asparagus tips, creamy cheese, and flaky pastry make
these elegant hors d'oeuvres irresistible. You could also use Jarlsberg cheese
for this recipe, and frozen asparagus may be substituted for fresh.
Puffs may be assembled ahead and frozen before baking.*

• • •

1. Preheat oven to 400°F. Bend a few asparagus spears at the base to snap off the tough ends. Using the lengths of the tops of these spears as a guide, cut off the tough ends of the remaining spears. Discard tough pieces. Cut the asparagus spears in 2-inch pieces and set aside.

2. Roll pastry on a floured board to an 8" × 10" rectangle. Use a pizza wheel or a sharp knife to cut twenty 2-inch squares in the pastry by making a row of five squares (along the 10" side) and a row of four squares (along the 8" side).

3. Make egg wash by mixing beaten egg with 2 tablespoons of water. Brush egg wash on the pastry squares, and then sprinkle with the cheese. Place one piece of asparagus diagonally, from corner to corner, on each pastry square.

4. Fold the left corner of pastry across the middle of the asparagus, then the right corner to make a blanket for the asparagus. Pinch pastry together in the middle and place filled pastries on a cookie sheet in rows so they are not touching. Brush egg wash on each pastry.

5. Bake for 12–15 minutes. Serve warm.

Stuffed Mushrooms

Classic stuffed mushrooms can be jazzed up with a variety of ingredients. Try adding crabmeat, bacon, cream cheese, pesto, blue cheese, or cooked sausage to the filling in this recipe. Or you could wrap the (unbroiled) stuffed mushrooms in puff pastry or phyllo dough and bake 15 minutes for a more substantial appetizer with a dramatic presentation.

• • •

Serves 6

16 ounces fresh mushrooms
3 tablespoons butter
½ cup finely chopped onion
1 tablespoon chopped fresh thyme
¼ cup cream
¾ cup dry bread crumbs
¼ cup grated Parmesan cheese
½ teaspoon salt
¼ teaspoon pepper

1. Wipe the mushrooms clean with a tea towel. Remove the stems and set the caps aside. Chop the stems in a fine dice.

2. Melt butter in a sauté pan, add the onions and sauté for a minute. Add the mushroom stems and thyme and cook for about 4 minutes. Add cream, stir to combine, and then transfer mixture to a bowl.

3. Add bread crumbs, half of the Parmesan cheese, salt, and pepper to the bowl and mix well with mushroom mixture. Set aside.

4. Put the mushroom caps on a baking sheet, gill sides up. Stuff each cap with a teaspoon of the mushroom stem mixture. Sprinkle with remaining Parmesan.

5. Broil mushrooms in the oven for about 5 minutes, until stuffing is nicely browned. Serve warm.

Duxelles

Duxelles is a mushroom stuffing traditionally used in the classic dish Beef Wellington. Chopped mushrooms are twisted in a tea towel to squeeze out excess moisture. Then they are sautéed in butter with shallots, seasoned with parsley, salt, and pepper, and cooled. This simple, delicious concoction can be added to rice pilaf, stirred in sauces, or spread on toasts.

Serves 6

9 eggs
¼ cup mayonnaise
1 tablespoon mustard, yellow
*   or Dijon*
2 tablespoons sour cream
*   (optional)*
1 teaspoon salt
½ teaspoon pepper
2 teaspoons dried dill weed
¼ teaspoon cayenne
*   pepper sauce*
paprika

Deviled Eggs

Picnics and backyard barbecues aren't complete without this staple.
Surprise your guests with the addition of crabmeat under the filling,
or for an elegant gathering cut the eggs in quarters instead of halves and
put the filling in a piping bag with a star tip for stuffing.

• • •

1. Put the eggs in a saucepan and cover them with water. Bring water to a boil, then reduce heat so that the water is simmering. Set the timer for 15 minutes.

2. When the timer goes off, pour the hot water out of the saucepan and run cold water over the eggs.

3. Crack and peel eggs carefully. Cut peeled eggs in half, carefully remove yolks, and set aside white halves. Put yolks in a bowl and mash with a fork.

4. Add mayonnaise, mustard, and sour cream to yolk mixture and mix together with fork to a smooth paste, then season with salt, pepper, dill weed, and cayenne pepper sauce.

5. Scoop about 1 tablespoon of the yolk filling into each white. Cover and refrigerate until chilled.

6. Sprinkle deviled eggs with paprika before serving.

Snack Mix

*Snack mix is a standard appetizer at most parties that is
fast and easy to make. Prepare it a day in advance and store in a zippered
plastic bag to save some time the day of an event.*

• • •

1. Preheat oven to 250°F. Combine cereals, peanuts, cashews, and pretzels in a large roasting pan.

2. In a small bowl, combine melted butter, Worcestershire sauce, garlic powder, onion powder, and seasoned salt.

3. Drizzle the butter mixture over the cereal mixture and toss to distribute.

4. Bake in the oven for 15 minutes. Stir. Continue baking for 45 more minutes, stirring every 15 minutes, so that total cooking time is 1 hour.

5. Remove from oven. Spread mix out on cookie sheets and let cool.

Serves 12

6 cups corn and rice cereal
   (Crispix)
3 cups wheat cereal
   squares (Chex)
6 tablespoons butter, melted
2 tablespoons Worcestershire
   sauce
1 teaspoon garlic powder
½ teaspoon onion powder
1 teaspoon seasoned salt
1 cup salted peanuts
1 cup honey-roasted cashews
1 cup mini pretzel sticks or
   twists

Serves 6

1 cup water
8 tablespoons unsalted butter
½ teaspoon salt
1 cup flour
4 eggs
1½ cups grated Gruyere
    cheese

Gougeres (Cheese Puffs)

*Puffs of cheesy pastry (pâtée a choux) make a classic
hors d'oeuvre that can be served as is, or filled with Tuna Salad (page 95).
You can also make these with Cheddar or Parmesan.*

• • •

1. Preheat oven to 400°F. Lightly grease a cookie sheet.

2. Put the water, butter, and salt in a saucepan over medium-high heat and bring to a boil. When butter is melted turn heat to medium and add the flour all at once. Stir constantly with a wooden spoon over medium heat until the mixture is the consistency of mashed potatoes.

3. Remove from heat and beat in eggs one at a time, using a wooden spoon or an electric mixer. Stir in 1 cup grated cheese.

4. Scoop dough with two spoons onto greased cookie sheet into 1-inch mounds, evenly spacing them about two inches apart. Sprinkle them with remaining cheese.

5. Bake 15 minutes, reduce heat to 350°F, then bake 15 minutes more. Serve warm or at room temperature.

Dates and Parmesan

*This is a delicious combination of cheese and fruit that
makes a great appetizer or dessert. Medjool dates and Parmigiano-Reggiano
cheese are the best choices for this recipe.*

• • •

1. Pit the dates (if they have seeds) by making a lengthwise slit and prying out the pit.

2. Shave slices of Parmesan with a vegetable peeler. They will curl and be irregularly shaped.

3. Arrange pitted dates and shaved Parmesan beside each other on a plate.

Serves 4

*20 fresh dates, whole
4-ounce piece of Parmesan
cheese*

Spiced Almonds

*Sweet, spicy, and salty nuts are a refined snack to munch on before or after
dinner. These also make a great afterschool snack for kids.*

• • •

1. Preheat oven to 350°F.

2. Toss nuts with oil in a bowl, sprinkle remaining ingredients over nuts, and toss to coat.

3. Bake for 15 minutes.

Soup to Nuts

*Nuts are often served before or after dinner, but they are also perfect for
serving in salads and can even be turned into soup. Colonial Americans in
Virginia and Georgia made a unique and delicious soup out of peanuts.*

Serves 4

*8 ounces whole almonds,
    skin on
2 tablespoons vegetable oil
¼ cup sugar
1 teaspoon salt
1 teaspoon cumin
¼ teaspoon cayenne pepper*

Serves 6

15 red-skinned new potatoes
2 cups rock salt
1 cup grated Cheddar cheese
6 slices bacon, cooked crisp
    and crumbled
black pepper
½ cup sour cream
¼ cup chopped fresh chives

New-Potato Cups

*Bite-sized red-skinned potatoes make a perfect shell for
filling with sour cream and chives. Serve these mini baked potatoes anchored
in a plate of rock salt to prevent them from rolling around.*

• • •

1. Preheat oven to 350°F. Wash potatoes and bake until tender, about 30 minutes. Remove from oven and let cool slightly so you can handle them.

2. Cut each potato in half. Scoop out a hole in the center of each half with a melon baller to make a cup. Discard the part you have scooped out or save it for another use.

3. Line a tray with rock salt and nestle the potato cups in it. Alternately, you can cut a tiny slice off the bottom of each potato half so the cups will stand up and not roll around.

4. Put a large pinch of cheese and a few pieces of bacon in each potato cup, sprinkle with black pepper, and bake until cheese melts, about 5 minutes. Top each potato cup with a teaspoon of sour cream and garnish with chives. Serve warm.

Endive Petals

Belgian endive is a slightly bitter lettuce grown in a mound of earth to control photosynthesis so that its color is a pale shade of red or green. If you can't find Belgian endive, feel free to use romaine, radicchio, butter lettuce, or any other green that can serve as a cuplike container.

• • •

1. Separate the individual leaves of the endive by cutting off the bottoms of the stalks.

2. Mix together the chicken, green onions, hoisin sauce, ¼ cup of the peanuts, bell pepper, sesame oil, and cilantro.

3. Put a teaspoon of chicken filling onto the bottom end of each endive leaf. Sprinkle a pinch of the remaining peanuts onto the filling.

4. Serve chilled or at room temperature. You want the endive to remain crisp and not get limp.

Petal Possibilities
You can alternately fill your endive petals with bay shrimp and basil mayonnaise, chunky ham salad, or bleu cheese, currants, and walnuts. If your endive leaves are ragged around the edges, give them a trim with scissors before filling them. Dress up a salad with a julienne of the smaller inner leaves.

Serves 6
_____

4 heads Belgian Endive lettuce
1 cup minced cooked chicken
¼ cup minced whole green onions
¼ cup hoisin sauce
½ cup chopped roasted peanuts
¼ cup diced red bell pepper, seeds removed
1 teaspoon sesame oil
2 tablespoons minced fresh cilantro

CHAPTER 3
Dips

Serves 6

4 cloves garlic
¼ teaspoon salt
1 cup mayonnaise
1 teaspoon lemon juice
1 tablespoon olive oil

Quick Aioli

This garlicky mayonnaise is delicious served with grilled asparagus, chilled arti-choke leaves, boiled fingerling potatoes, or Fried Calamari (page 142). You can also spread it on a Grilled Vegetable Sandwich (page 100).

• • •

1. Mince the garlic, sprinkle it with the salt, and continue mincing. Turn the knife blade parallel to the cutting board and mash the garlic and salt into a paste.

2. Put garlic paste in a bowl with the mayonnaise and whisk together. Add lemon juice and whisk again.

3. Pour oil in a stream while whisking it into the mayonnaise mixture.

Rouille
Add puréed roasted red bell pepper and a little heat, like cayenne pepper, to aioli and you have Rouille, a garlicky sauce served on bread croutons with bouillabaisse, the Provençal fish stew. Substitute Roasted Garlic (page 178) for half the garlic cloves in the aioli for more flavor depth.

Roasted Red Bell Pepper Dip

Serve this dip chilled in hollowed-out green, yellow, and red bell pepper bowls in the middle of a platter of fresh celery and carrot sticks, steamed broccoli florets, yellow summer squash, cherry tomatoes, and radishes.

. . .

1. In a food processor or blender, purée the roasted peppers and garlic.

2. Add the cream cheese and process until smooth, scraping down the sides of the bowl at least once.

3. Add the sour cream and basil and process until smooth again.

4. Season with salt, white pepper, and cayenne pepper sauce (if you like it spicy). Mix to incorporate. Pour into a bowl and chill for 4 hours.

5. Spoon into serving bowl and serve chilled.

Serves 12

3 red bell peppers, roasted and peeled
1 clove garlic
16 ounces cream cheese, softened
½ cup sour cream
3 fresh basil leaves, chopped
1 teaspoon salt
3 drops cayenne pepper sauce
½ teaspoon white pepper

Serves 6

8 ounces sharp Cheddar
  cheese, grated
3 cloves garlic, peeled
1 teaspoon salt
2 ounces cream cheese,
  softened
2 tablespoons unsalted
  butter, softened
1 tablespoon Dijon mustard
2 tablespoons yellow mustard

Cheddar Pretzel Dip

Serve this garlicky cheese spread with honey mustard to accompany breadsticks, pretzel rods, or warm, soft pretzels. Pack the cheese dip in a crock, cover surface with a piece of waxed paper, and store in the refrigerator for up to 3 weeks.

• • •

1. Mince garlic with salt. In a bowl, combine garlic mixture and cream cheese. Mix until smooth.

2. Add shredded Cheddar cheese and mix, or blend in a food processor until smooth.

3. Add butter and mustards and mix again until smooth. Scrape down the sides of the bowl and mix or blend one more time.

4. Serve at room temperature or slightly warmed.

Breadsticks

Roll out one recipe of Pizza Dough (page 221) and cut into 1-inch-wide strips. Brush with olive oil, then dip them in 1 cup grated Parmesan cheese and 2 tablespoons chopped fresh herbs. Sprinkle them with coarse salt, twist them, and put them on a cookie sheet lined with parchment paper (which is the same as waxed paper). Bake in a preheated 350°F oven for 12–15 minutes.

Artichoke Dip

Serve this baked dip hot from the oven accompanied by crusty French bread slices or slices of Focaccia (page 220).

• • •

1. Preheat the oven to 325°F.

2. Mix together all ingredients except ¼ of the Parmesan cheese.

3. Sprinkle the remaining Parmesan cheese over the top of mixed ingredients and bake in a 9" × 9" baking dish or 1½ quart casserole dish for 45 minutes or until golden brown. Serve with crackers or bread.

Serves 4
___

2 15-ounce cans artichoke
  hearts, drained and
  rinsed
1 red bell pepper, chopped
  finely
1 green bell pepper, chopped
  finely
3 cloves garlic, minced
2 cups mayonnaise
white pepper
1 pound Parmesan cheese,
  grated

Spinach Dip

For a gathering, you can serve this tasty dip in a bread bowl. Take an unsliced sourdough loaf and hollow it out. Then cut the bread you removed from the center of the loaf into bite-sized pieces. Serve the Spinach Dip inside the hollowed-out loaf with the bite-sized bread pieces on the side for dipping.

• • •

1. Squeeze out water from thawed spinach.

2. Add all other ingredients and mix. Chill well and serve with raw vegetables, bread, or crackers.

Serves 6
___

10-ounce package frozen
  spinach, thawed
2 cups sour cream
1 cup mayonnaise
1 envelope vegetable
  soup mix
1 small white onion, peeled
  and chopped
8-ounce can water chestnuts,
  drained and chopped
2 tablespoons grated
  Parmesan cheese

4 ounces cream cheese,
    softened
1 cup cooked shrimp,
    chopped or popcorn size
1 cup canned crabmeat,
    drained and squeezed dry
1 cup diced celery
2 tablespoons minced onion
2 tablespoons chopped fresh
    parsley
¼ cup mayonnaise
2 teaspoons fresh lemon juice
¼ teaspoon sugar
¼ teaspoon pepper
⅛ teaspoon salt
2 drops cayenne pepper
    sauce

Shrimp Crab Dip

Serve this chunky dip chilled with crackers or use it as a filling in Gougeres (page 28) or Endive Petals (page 31).

. . .

1. With a mixer, beat the cream cheese until soft and fluffy.

2. Add the rest of the ingredients and mix thoroughly.

3. Chill for at least 2 hours before serving.

6 cloves garlic, peeled
½ teaspoon salt
1 can garbanzo beans
⅓ cup tahini (sesame seed
    paste)
2 tablespoons fresh
    lemon juice
2 tablespoons olive oil
½ teaspoon ground cumin
    (optional)

Hummus

This Middle Eastern dip is made from cooked garbanzo beans, which are also known as chickpeas. It is served topped with olive oil and parsley, and tastes best with warmed pita bread wedges for dipping.

. . .

1. Purée garlic and salt in food processor or blender. Add garbanzo beans and purée to a paste.

2. Add the remaining ingredients and blend until smooth.

3. Serve finished dip in a bowl or spread out on a platter. Drizzle with more olive oil and serve with raw vegetables and warmed pita wedges.

Cheese Fondue

Served hot, this dip is hearty and satisfying, and can be rich and sinful or light and healthy depending on the cheese you use, the flavorings you add, and the dippers you serve with it. Try substituting shredded Swiss cheese and adding sautéed mushrooms. Use bamboo skewers to dip bread into the fondue.

• • •

1. Remove rind on Brie, cut into cubes, and toss with flour. Set aside.

2. Sauté shallots in butter for 3 minutes, add juices, and reduce (thicken) the liquid at a simmer for about 15 minutes. Turn heat to medium low.

3. Whisk in cheese cubes, a few at a time, until they are all melted. Remove from heat.

4. Pour into fondue pot over heat source and serve with bread cubes for dipping.

Dippers
Some of the many foods you can use as dippers for fondue include bread cubes (French, sourdough, rye, multigrain, pumpernickel), soft bread sticks, boiled new potatoes, blanched broccoli, asparagus, cauliflower, baby carrots, cooked shrimp, smoked sausage, fresh mushrooms, and endive leaves.

Serves 6

2 pounds Brie cheese
2 tablespoons flour
3 tablespoons minced shallots
1 tablespoon butter
1 cup white grape juice
½ cup cranberry juice
1 loaf French bread, cut into cubes

Serves 12

16 tablespoons unsalted
    butter, softened
8 ounces cream cheese,
    softened
¼ cup chopped sun-dried
    tomatoes
½ cup Pesto (page 154)
cheesecloth (which can be
    purchased at a gourmet
    cooking store)

Pesto Torta

Spread this creamy tri-color dip on crackers, toasts, breadsticks, or bagels.

• • •

1. Line a quart bowl or mold with 2 layers of dampened cheesecloth.

2. Combine butter and cream cheese thoroughly.

3. Spread ⅓ of the cheese mixture in the bottom of the mold. Layer all of the dried tomatoes next, then ⅓ cheese mixture, all of the pesto, and last ⅓ of cheese.

4. Fold cheesecloth over cheese and refrigerate at least 1 hour to firm.

5. To serve, fold back the cheesecloth and put a platter over the exposed cheese. Invert so the platter is on the bottom and mold is on top. Take off mold, peel off cheesecloth, and garnish with fresh basil. Serve with crackers.

Chile con Queso

*This classic Tex-Mex favorite is served hot with corn tortilla chips
and Tomato Salsa (page 42).*

* * *

Serves 6

⅓ cup cream
3 ounces cream cheese,
   chunked
8 ounces Monterey jack
   cheese, shredded
½ cup canned green chiles,
   chopped

1. Preheat the cream in a pan. Add cream cheese piece by piece and stir until it all melts.

2. Add jack cheese over low heat and stir until creamy and melted.

3. Stir in green chiles, remove from heat, and spoon into ramekins or cups to serve.

Hot Taco Dip

In an ungreased 9" x 9" baking dish, mix together 1 cup refried beans, ½ cup sour cream, ½ cup taco salsa, ¼ cup chopped green onions, ¼ cup chopped black olives, and ¼ cup chopped banana peppers. Top with shredded Cheddar cheese and bake at 350°F for 25 minutes. Serve with corn chips or broken taco shells.

Serves 4

2 cups diced, seeded
   tomatoes
1 cup diced onion
1 jalapeño pepper, seeds
   removed, chopped finely
1 clove garlic, minced
¼ cup chopped cilantro
1 tablespoon lemon juice
1 teaspoon red wine vinegar
1 tablespoon olive oil
½ teaspoon ground cumin
   (optional)
salt to taste

Tomato Salsa

*This is chunky and crunchy salsa, not cooked or puréed.
Serve it with tortilla chips and Guacamole (page 43). Remember to
wash your hands after chopping the jalapeño so that you don't accidentally
transfer hot pepper juice residue to your eye!*

• • •

Toss all ingredients together in a bowl and chill for 1 hour.

Serves 4

¾ cup tomato ketchup
¼ cup chili sauce
¼ cup grated horseradish
   (bottled; not creamy
   sauce)
1 teaspoon Worcestershire
   sauce
2 tablespoons lemon juice
5 drops cayenne
   pepper sauce
¼ teaspoon celery seeds
   (optional)
pepper to taste
salt to taste

Shrimp Cocktail Sauce

*When you make this simple dipping sauce from scratch,
the bright flavors complement the sweet meat of boiled shrimp
instead of masking it. Cocktail sauce isn't just for shrimp, though.
Try it with crab, oysters, fried fish, and other seafood.*

• • •

Combine all ingredients and chill. Serve in individual dipping cups.

Guacamole

Guacamole is best made with a knife and fork rather than a food processor. This standard version allows for a range of "hotness" with the optional addition of jalapeño pepper. Serve crispy beef taquitos, chicken flautas, or tortilla chips to dip in guacamole, along with sour cream and Tomato Salsa (page 42).

• • •

Serves 6

¼ small red onion
1 tomato, seeded
2 large avocados, peeled
1 or 2 cloves garlic, chopped
1 tablespoon olive oil
3 tablespoons fresh lime juice
salt and pepper to taste
1 fresh jalapeño pepper,
    seeded and chopped
    (optional)

Cut the onion, tomato, and avocado flesh into rough ½-inch chunks and mash them in a bowl with a sturdy fork. Add the remaining ingredients and serve with tortilla chips.

Avocado Salsa

Cut an avocado in half, remove the pit, and score the flesh in a crosshatch pattern. Scoop out the flesh with a large serving spoon and mix it with 2 tablespoons fresh lime juice and 2 tablespoons diced red bell pepper. Add avocado mixture to 1 cup fresh tomato salsa. Serve on fish, or with tortilla chips.

CHAPTER 4
Soups

Serves 8

2 large onions
3 tablespoons unsalted butter
½ cup apple cider
32 ounces chicken broth
    (low salt)
32 ounces beef broth
    (low salt)
2 sprigs fresh thyme or 1
    teaspoon dried thyme
1 bay leaf
salt to taste
pepper to taste
Cheese Croutons (see sidebar)
¼ cup chopped fresh parsley

French Onion Soup

This soup is a bistro classic. Serve in a crock, topped with cheese croutons and sprinkled with parsley.

• • •

1. Slice the onions and sauté them in the butter until they caramelize. (This means the natural sugars in them will cook to a light brown caramel color.) Cook a little longer to a rich mahogany color.

2. Add the cider and deglaze the pan, with the onions still in it, by scraping up all the browned bits. Cook until the caramelized onion mixture thickens.

3. Add chicken and beef broth and stir to combine into a soup consistency. Add thyme, bay leaf, salt, and pepper, and simmer for 45 minutes.

4. Remove the bay leaf and thyme sprigs and ladle soup into individual crocks. Top each with cheese croutons.

5. Sprinkle with parsley.

Cheese Croutons
Slice French bread 1–2 inches thick. Lay slices out on a cookie sheet, brush them with olive oil, and toast them in the oven under the broiler on both sides. Top each toast with shredded Swiss cheese; return to oven until brown and bubbly.

Chili

Chili is a classic dish that can be made in large quantities to feed a group. If you're not feeding a crowd, freeze the leftovers in serving sizes so you can heat up a single bowl on a cold evening. Serve with crackers, corn chips, crusty French bread, or Corn Bread (page 218).

• • •

1. Spread cornmeal out in a pie pan and bake at 350°F for 5 minutes to toast. Set aside.

2. In a large soup pot, brown ground beef. Drain and set aside.

3. Sauté onions, garlic, green pepper, celery, and carrots in olive oil until translucent.

4. Add browned meat to the pot and stir. Add tomato paste, chopped tomatoes, tomato juice, and water. Stir and bring to a simmer.

5. Add chili powder, cumin, paprika, cayenne pepper sauce, oregano, black pepper, and cornmeal. Simmer uncovered for 1 hour.

6. Add kidney beans and season with salt to taste. Serve with cheese, green onions, and sour cream.

Serves 6

16 ounces ground beef
2 tablespoons olive oil
1 onion, chopped
2 cloves garlic, chopped
¼ cup chopped green bell
    pepper
¼ cup diced celery
¼ cup diced carrot
2 tablespoons tomato paste
1 can peeled, chopped
    tomatoes, with juice
1 cup tomato juice
1 cup water
2 tablespoons chili powder
1 teaspoon ground cumin
½ teaspoon paprika
¼ teaspoon cayenne
    pepper sauce
1 teaspoon dried oregano
½ teaspoon black pepper
¼ cup cornmeal
1 can kidney beans, drained
salt to taste
shredded Cheddar cheese
chopped whole green onions
sour cream

¾ cup chopped onion
2 tablespoons olive oil
2 cups peeled, chopped
    tomatoes
3 cups chicken broth
½ cup heavy cream
salt and pepper to taste

Tomato Soup

*Pure and basic, classic tomato soup is perfect for dipping a Grilled Cheese Sandwich
(page 300) on a chilly day. Use a sharp paring knife to peel the tomatoes.*

· · ·

1. Sauté onions in oil. Add tomatoes and sauté 2 minutes.

2. Add chicken broth and simmer for 25 minutes.

3. Purée in blender, add cream, and season with salt and pepper.

3 potatoes, peeled and diced
1 leek (white part only), diced
2 cups water
1 cup heavy cream
salt and pepper to taste
chopped chives

Vichyssoise

*This velvety chilled potato-leek soup is puréed,
but if served hot it can be left chunky.*

· · ·

1. Boil potatoes and leeks in water until tender, about 25 minutes.

2. Purée leek, onion, and water mixture in blender; add cream, salt, and
   pepper, and blend well.

3. Chill thoroughly before serving. To serve, thin out with more cream if
   necessary and garnish with chopped chives.

Origin of Vichyssoise
*Chef Louis Diat's creation of chilled potato-leek soup was inspired by
the soup his mother made him for breakfast as a child in France. Diat
invented this classic while working at the Ritz-Carlton Hotel in New
York City.*

Corn Chowder

Fresh corn cut off the cob is featured in this chunky chowder made with hearty pieces of potato, carrot, and celery and accented with the smoky flavor of bacon. For a cheesy soup, whisk 1 cup shredded Monterey jack or Cheddar into the hot soup before serving.

. . .

1. Sauté the bacon in a large soup pot until crisp. Add onions, carrots, and celery. Sauté until vegetables are tender.

2. Add the corn kernels and sauté 5 minutes. Add potatoes and chicken broth and bring to a boil.

3. Simmer 45 minutes, until potatoes are cooked.

4. Dissolve cornstarch in ¼ cup cold water. Add milk to soup pot and bring to a boil. Stir in the cornstarch mixture and cook, stirring, until thickened. Remove from heat.

5. Season with salt and pepper. Serve with oyster crackers.

Mirepoix

The combination of carrots, celery, and onion is called mirepoix in classic French culinary terminology. This trinity of vegetables is the foundation for many recipes, such as stocks, sauces, soups, and stews. It contributes aroma, flavor, and body to braised dishes, roasts, and stuffing. In Creole cooking, green bell pepper replaces the carrot part of the equation.

Serves 6

6 slices bacon, diced
1 small onion, diced
1 carrot, peeled and diced
1 stalk celery, sliced
4 ears corn, kernels cut from cob
1 large potato, peeled and diced
32 ounces chicken broth (low salt)
1 tablespoon cornstarch
¼ cup cold water
2 cups milk
salt and pepper to taste

Serves 6

1 small onion, diced
2 tablespoons olive oil
½ cup diced green chiles
    (canned)
1 cup diced, peeled tomatoes
32 ounces chicken broth
2 cups chopped, cooked
    chicken meat (leftover
    Oven-Roasted [page 132]
    is good)
3 corn tortillas, cut in ¼ inch
    strips
1 teaspoon ground cumin
2 limes
salt and pepper to taste
cayenne pepper sauce
¼ cup chopped cilantro
2 avocadoes, peeled
    and diced
1 cup shredded Monterey jack
    cheese
1 cup crushed tortilla chips

Tortilla Soup

*A staple of Tex-Mex and Southwestern cuisine, corn tortillas are
sliced and simmered like noodles in this soup, which is a clean, bright broth
accented with lime juice. Chunky pieces of chicken, tomato, and avocado
round out the body of the soup; cheese and crispy tortilla chips top it off.*

• • •

1. In a soup pot, sauté the onion in olive oil until translucent. Add green chiles, tomatoes, and chicken broth.

2. Bring mixture to a boil. Add chicken meat, tortilla strips, and cumin, and simmer for 15 minutes. Remove from heat.

3. Cut one lime in half and add the juice to the soup pot. Cut the other lime in wedges to serve with each bowl.

4. Season the soup with salt, pepper, cayenne pepper sauce, and cilantro.

5. Put diced avocado in soup bowls, ladle soup into bowls, garnish with cheese and tortilla chips, and serve with lime wedges.

Butternut Squash Soup

*Autumn is the time to start enjoying the harvest, and this soup is
a great place to start. Crisp bacon bits, crème fraîche and chives, dried
cranberries, herb butter, croutons . . . the list of what to garnish it with is
endless. Serve it on Thanksgiving Day before the turkey and stuffing.*

•   •   •

1. In a soup pot, sauté onions in butter until translucent.

2. Add chicken broth, squash, and apples.

3. Bring to a boil; then turn down heat and simmer until squash and apple
   are tender, about 45 minutes.

4. Purée soup in a blender until smooth.

5. Season with salt and white pepper.

Quatre Epices Crème

*Ginger powder, ground cloves, nutmeg, and white pepper make up the
classic pâté spice called quatre epices (four spices). Mix 1 teaspoon of
this spice mixture into ½ cup of sour cream and serve a dollop of the
spicy cream in Butternut Squash Soup.*

Serves 4

½ cup chopped onion
2 tablespoons butter
4 cups chicken broth
2 cups peeled and chopped
    butternut squash
½ cup peeled and chopped
    Granny Smith apple
salt to taste
white pepper to taste

Minestrone

Serves 6

½ cup chopped onion
½ cup chopped carrots
¼ cup chopped celery
2 tablespoons olive oil
2 cloves garlic, minced
¼ cup chopped spinach
1 cup chopped cabbage
32 ounces chicken broth
2 cups chopped zucchini
1 cup chopped, peeled
    tomatoes
½ cup cut green beans
½ cup broken spaghetti
salt and pepper to taste

*Serve this classic Italian vegetable and pasta soup with Pesto (page 154),
Parmesan cheese, and crusty bread.*

• • •

1. Sauté the onions, carrots, and celery in the olive oil over medium heat for 15 minutes.

2. Add garlic, spinach, and cabbage, and cook until greens are wilted.

3. Add chicken broth, zucchini, tomatoes, and green beans. Bring to a boil.

4. Simmer for 15 minutes. Add the spaghetti and simmer 15 minutes more.

5. Season soup with salt and pepper.

Black Bean Soup

Serves 6

¼ cup onion, diced
1 clove garlic, minced
2 tablespoons olive oil
1 large potato, peeled
    and diced
32 ounces chicken broth
    (low salt)
1 cup chopped, peeled
    tomatoes
2 cups cooked black beans
    (canned)
1 teaspoon dried thyme
½ teaspoon ground cumin
½ teaspoon ground coriander
1 tablespoon red wine
    vinegar
2 teaspoons salt
5 drops cayenne
    pepper sauce
2 tablespoons chopped
    fresh cilantro
⅓ cup sour cream
1 cup Tomato Salsa (page 42)

*Garnish this southwestern soup with a swirl of sour cream and Tomato Salsa
(page 42). It's also delicious served with warm Corn Bread (page 218).*

• • •

1. Sauté onions and garlic in olive oil. Add potatoes and chicken broth; simmer uncovered for 30 minutes.

2. Add tomatoes, black beans, thyme, cumin, and coriander; simmer 45 minutes more.

3. Purée ⅓ of the soup in a blender, and then return it to the pot.

4. Stir in the vinegar, salt, cayenne pepper sauce, and cilantro.

5. Serve with a garnish of sour cream and tomato salsa.

Carrot Ginger Purée

Serves 6

1 large onion, chopped
2 tablespoons butter
8 carrots, peeled and sliced
4 cups chicken broth
2-inch piece fresh gingerroot,
    peeled and minced
salt to taste
white pepper to taste
½ teaspoon ground cumin
5 drops cayenne
    pepper sauce

This is a brightly colored and flavored soup that can be enjoyed warm or cold. Possible garnishes include crème fraîche, sour cream, chopped chives, cilantro, Ginger Butter, fresh dill, croutons, or Roasted Garlic (page 178).

• • •

1. Sauté onion in butter until translucent. Add carrots and sauté for 10 minutes.

2. Add chicken broth and gingerroot, and bring to a boil.

3. Cook until carrots are tender, about 25 minutes.

4. Purée soup in blender. Return to heat.

5. Add seasonings and heat for 5 minutes to blend the flavors.

Ginger Butter

This butter melts into carrot soup, creating a flavorful "sauce." Whip 4 ounces of soft butter with 1 tablespoon lemon juice, 1 tablespoon grated fresh gingerroot, 1 teaspoon minced parsley, ¼ teaspoon salt, and ⅛ teaspoon white pepper. Roll into a log, wrap in plastic wrap, and chill until firm. Cut into pats; float them on top of soup.

½ cup diced onion
¼ cup diced leeks (white and
    light green parts only—
    discard dark green)
¼ cup diced celery
2 tablespoons butter
1 tablespoon tomato paste
4 cups chicken broth
¼ cup rice
1 tablespoon Worcestershire
    sauce
1 bay leaf
pinch nutmeg
1 cup lump crabmeat
½ cup cream
salt to taste
pepper to taste

Crab Bisque

Named after the Bay of Biscay in France, bisque is a rich, creamy soup that is thickened with rice and often contains seafood. In this recipe, sweet crabmeat is the seafood addition. Other seafood to turn into bisque include crayfish, shrimp, lobster, and oysters. Vegetables, such as tomatoes, mushrooms, asparagus, or pumpkins, can also be turned into bisque.

• • •

1. Sauté onions, leeks, and celery in butter until soft. Mix in tomato paste. Add chicken broth and rice, and bring to a boil.

2. Add Worcestershire sauce, bay leaf, and nutmeg. Simmer uncovered for 45 minutes.

3. Remove bay leaf; purée liquid in a blender.

4. Return bisque to low heat and stir in crabmeat and cream.

5. Season bisque with salt and pepper.

Relish the Bisque

Garnish your crab bisque with lump crabmeat and a relish of diced red bell peppers, cucumbers, lemon zest, olive oil, and lemon juice. Or top it with blanched asparagus tips, crabmeat, and a dab of Hollandaise Sauce (page 200) spiked with cayenne pepper.

Beef Stew

*Hearty beef stew with chunky potatoes, carrots, and peas
is satisfying comfort food that is simple to prepare and contains no "exotic"
ingredients to keep you from making it, no matter what your budget.*

• • •

Serves 6

1 pound stewing beef cubes
¾ cup diced onions
2 tablespoons olive oil
¼ cup flour
4 cups beef broth
½ cup sliced carrots, cut in
    ½" pieces
1 potato, peeled and diced
1 teaspoon dried thyme
1 tablespoon Worcestershire
    sauce
½ cup frozen peas
salt to taste
pepper to taste

1. Brown the beef cubes and onion in olive oil. Dust meat with flour; stir to coat and distribute. Add beef broth, carrots, potatoes, thyme, and Worcestershire sauce.

2. Bring liquid to a boil; reduce heat and simmer, covered, for 1½–2 hours, until beef is tender.

3. Add peas and season with salt and pepper. Cook 10 minutes longer.

Browning Meat

When browning meat for a recipe such as stew, do not flour the meat first, because the idea is to caramelize the natural juices in the meat. To add flour for thickening, sprinkle it over the meat after it has been browned.

4 cups water
4 cups chicken broth
1 4-pound chicken, cut in 8
pieces
4 carrots, peeled and sliced
into ½" pieces
1 large onion, diced
2 stalks celery, sliced into ½"
pieces
1 clove garlic, sliced
3 peppercorns
1 bay leaf
½ teaspoon turmeric
salt to taste
chopped fresh parsley

Chicken Soup

This is the base for comfort food like chicken noodle and matzo ball soup, and a generations-old remedy for the common cold. For the chicken, you can either purchase a chicken already cut into parts—at the meat counter of the supermarket or in the refrigerated meat section—or you can buy a whole chicken and cut it up yourself (see diagram on page 130 for instruction).

• • •

1. Put the water, chicken broth, chicken, vegetables, peppercorns, and bay leaf in a large soup pot. Bring to a boil and simmer uncovered for 2 hours.

2. Using a slotted spoon, remove the chicken from the broth and set aside until it is cool enough to handle.

3. Remove bay leaf and peppercorns from soup broth and add turmeric and salt to taste.

4. Remove the bones and skin from the chicken meat and discard. Chop the meat into bite-size pieces and return it to the soup broth.

5. Serve soup sprinkled with parsley.

Matzo Balls
Using a fork, mix 4 eggs and 2 tablespoons olive oil in a bowl. Add 2 tablespoons water, 2 teaspoons salt, and 2 teaspoons chopped dill; mix. Add 1 cup matzo meal; mix. Cover; refrigerate 15 minutes. Scoop walnut-size balls with wet fingers and drop into boiling water or broth. Cook for 35 minutes. Serve in chicken soup.

Asian Broth

Use this soup as a base for won ton or noodle soup or enjoy with thinly shredded carrots, sliced mushrooms, and peas.

. . .

Combine all ingredients and simmer 45 minutes. Strain and serve in a bowl with thinly sliced green onions.

Serves 4

4 cups chicken broth
1 bulb Roasted Garlic (page 178)
3-inch piece of lemongrass
2-inch piece fresh gingerroot, cut in ½" slices
1 tablespoon soy sauce
1 tablespoon rice vinegar
3 roughly chopped whole green onions
1 small onion, chopped
1 diced jalapeño pepper
3 peppercorns
1 teaspoon sesame oil

Cream of Potato Soup

You can turn this into "baked potato" soup by topping it with bacon bits, shredded Cheddar cheese, sour cream, and green onions, or serve it plain with just a scattering of chives. Dress it up with smoked salmon and caviar or stir in a purée of roasted bell peppers for a hearty broth.

. . .

1. Sauté the shallots in butter until translucent, 5–10 minutes.

2. Add the chicken broth to the shallots; then add the potatoes.

3. Bring to a boil. Reduce heat and simmer uncovered until potatoes are cooked, about 25 minutes.

4. Purée in a blender, return to low heat, and add milk.

5. Add cream, salt, and pepper; stir and remove from heat.

Serves 6

3 shallots, minced
2 tablespoons butter
4 cups chicken broth
5 large potatoes, peeled and diced
1 cup milk
½ cup heavy cream
salt to taste
½ teaspoon white pepper

Serves 4

1 can unsweetened
    coconut milk
4 cups chicken broth
½ cup lemon juice
½ teaspoon lime zest (use
    only the colored outer
    skin and not the bitter
    white pith)
2 thinly sliced boneless,
    skinless raw chicken
    breasts
2 minced shallots
1 teaspoon grated fresh
    gingerroot
1 teaspoon Worcestershire
    sauce
¼ cup chopped fresh cilantro
1 sliced jalapeño (optional)

Thai Chicken Soup

Coconut milk, lemon juice, and cilantro accent this classic chicken soup.

• • •

Combine all ingredients and simmer for 20 minutes. Season with salt and pepper.

Miso Soup

Miso is a paste made from fermented soy beans (and sometimes barley and/or rice) and salt used in Japanese cuisine. Mix together 1 tablespoon miso, ¾ cup chicken broth, 2 ounces cubed tofu, and 1 shredded spinach leaf. Combine, heat, and serve immediately.

Serves 4

½ cup diced onions
½ cup diced carrots
¼ cup diced celery
2 tablespoons olive oil
¼ cup diced ham
1 tablespoon tomato paste
4 cups chicken broth
2 cups cooked white beans
    (canned)
1 sprig fresh thyme
salt and pepper to taste

White Bean Soup

Smoky ham, diced carrots, and white beans make up this hearty and stewlike soup. Serve with freshly ground black pepper, a drizzle of olive oil, a slice of feta cheese, and pita bread.

• • •

1. Sauté onions, carrots, and celery in oil for 15 minutes.

2. Add ham and tomato paste and stir to combine.

3. Add chicken broth, beans, and thyme. Bring to a boil; reduce heat and simmer for 25 minutes.

4. Remove thyme sprig. Purée half of the soup in a blender.

5. Return purée to the pot, stir, and season with salt and pepper.

Split Pea Soup

*Hearty and thick, this soup gets its satisfying ham flavor from a ham bone.
If you don't have a ham bone, substitute ¾ cup diced ham.
Add diced ham to the soup for the last 15 minutes of cooking time, and either
remove it before serving or leave it in for additional taste.*

•   •   •

Serves 6

*8 cups water
2 cups dried split peas
1 ham bone
½ cup diced carrots
¼ cup diced celery
1 cup diced onions
salt to taste
pepper to taste*

1. Simmer water, split peas, and ham bone for 1 hour.

2. Add vegetables and simmer for 1 hour more.

3. Remove ham bone and season with salt and pepper.

Fresh Pea Soup

*Cook 2 cups fresh or frozen peas in 4 cups chicken stock for 15 minutes.
Purée in blender, return to pan, and add 1 cup heavy cream, 1 teaspoon
salt, ½ teaspoon white pepper, and 1 tablespoon chopped fresh mint.*

Serves 8

½ cup chopped onion
¼ cup leeks (white and light
    green parts only—
    discard dark green part)
½ cup sliced celery stalks (½"
    pieces)
2 tablespoons olive oil
½ cup peeled and sliced
    carrots (½" pieces)
½ cup parsnips, peeled and
    sliced into ½" pieces
1 clove garlic, minced
½ cup chopped cabbage
½ cup peeled, cubed potatoes
½ cup peeled, chopped
    tomatoes
½ cup green beans, cut in
    1" pieces
1 tablespoon tomato paste
6 cups chicken broth
2 tablespoons chopped
    parsley
salt and pepper to taste

Vegetable Soup

*Packed with vegetables in a tomato broth, this essential soup
is satisfying all year long and is a great way to eat vegetables.*

• • •

1. Sauté onions, leeks, and celery in olive oil 15 minutes.

2. Add carrots, parsnips, and garlic, and cook another 10 minutes.

3. Add cabbage, potatoes, tomatoes, green beans, tomato paste, and chicken broth. Bring to a boil; reduce heat, and simmer uncovered 45 minutes.

4. Season with parsley, salt, and pepper.

CHAPTER 5
Salads

Pesto Pasta Salad

Serves 4

1 cup Pesto (page 154)
4 cups cooked penne pasta
¼ cup diced red onion
¼ cup sliced black olives
½ cup cherry tomatoes
¼ cup diced roasted red bell
    peppers
¼ cup chopped artichoke
    hearts
4 ounces cubed salami
4 ounces cubed provolone
    cheese
1 clove minced garlic

This is an antipasto salad with salami and provolone cheese.
You may use other shapes of pasta, such as corkscrew or tortellini,
and vary the vegetables to suit your taste.

• • •

Combine all ingredients and chill.

Macaroni Salad

Serves 6

4 cups cooked macaroni
½ cup thinly sliced celery
1 tablespoon minced
    pimiento
1 cup mayonnaise
¼ cup sliced green olives
2 tablespoons chopped fresh
    parsley
salt and pepper to taste
4 eggs
paprika

Serve this classic with hot dogs and hamburgers from the
backyard grill, pack it in a basket for a picnic in the park, or take in a cooler to
the beach and serve it in a clean plastic sand pail.

• • •

1. Place eggs in a saucepan with cold water that rises about an inch above the eggs. Bring the water to a boil and cover the saucepan. Boil eggs for 20 minutes, then run under cold water. Remove shells and thinly slice eggs.

2. Mix all ingredients except eggs in a bowl. Chill for 1 hour.

3. Cover the surface with sliced eggs, sprinkle with paprika, and serve.

Retro Salad
Mix 1 can of drained tuna into 1 recipe of macaroni salad and top it with tomato wedges for a popular lunch salad from the past.

Potato Salad

This potato salad features potatoes with the skin on and the robust flavors of mustard seeds and pickles. Adjust the consistency with more mayonnaise if it gets dry after being chilled.

• • •

1. Quarter the potatoes and put in a bowl.

2. Cut the pickles into fine dice and add to the potatoes.

3. Chop the hard-boiled egg; add it to the potatoes.

4. Add the rest of the ingredients to the bowl and stir until well mixed.

5. Chill and adjust seasoning before serving.

Serves 6

30 boiled baby red-skinned potatoes
3 baby dill pickles
1 hard-boiled egg
¼ cup diced red onion
2 tablespoons coarse brown mustard
2 tablespoons Dijon mustard
¾ cup mayonnaise
¼ teaspoon paprika
½ teaspoon salt
¼ teaspoon pepper
1 tablespoon dill pickle juice
2 tablespoons chopped chives

Sour Cream Potato Salad

This is a creamy potato salad with no potato skins. It requires chilling overnight in the refrigerator, so it can be prepared the day before it is needed, freeing up the kitchen to make other things.

• • •

Combine all ingredients and chill 8–24 hours.

Serves 8

8 medium potatoes, peeled, cubed, and boiled for 15 minutes
1½ cups mayonnaise
1 cup sour cream
1½ teaspoons grated, bottled horseradish
1 teaspoon celery seed
½ teaspoon salt
½ cup dried parsley flakes
2 medium onions, minced

Serves 6

6 medium potatoes, peeled
  and boiled for 15 minutes
3 sliced whole green onions
4 slices fried bacon, crumbled
2 tablespoons lemon juice
2 tablespoons white wine
  vinegar
1 tablespoon olive oil
salt and pepper to taste

Warm Potato Salad

*Sometimes called German Potato Salad, this is a warm
alternative to traditional potato salad.*

• • •

1. Cube the potatoes.

2. Toss everything else in a bowl with the potatoes.

3. Serve warm.

Sweet Potato Salad

*Mix together 1 cup Oven-Roasted Sweet Potatoes (page 196), ½ cup
Oven-Roasted Red Potatoes, cubed (page 195), ½ cup diced apples; 2
tablespoons malt vinegar; and 1 tablespoon olive oil. Season with 1
teaspoon minced fresh rosemary, and salt and pepper to taste.*

Serves 8

3 cups shredded cabbage
¼ cup shredded purple
  cabbage
¼ cup shredded carrot
¼ cup whole green onion,
  chopped
½ cup mayonnaise
1 tablespoon milk
1 teaspoon sugar
1 tablespoon cider vinegar
1 teaspoon celery seed
salt and pepper to taste

Coleslaw

*Serve coleslaw on a barbecued pork sandwich, or as a side with BBQ Ribs
(page 120) or Oven-Fried Chicken Nuggets (page 295).*

• • •

1. Mix all ingredients together.

2. Refrigerate at least 15 minutes before serving.

Pea Salad

For extra crunch add 1 cup salted peanuts and ¼ cup chopped celery to this salad, and sprinkle it with crisp bacon bits before serving.

• • •

Mix everything in a bowl; season with salt and pepper to taste.

Carrot Slaw
Some people add raisins and mayonnaise to shredded carrots to make carrot slaw, but you could instead add sliced whole green onions and honey mustard for a more savory version of carrot slaw.

Serves 4

2 cups fresh peas or thawed
   frozen peas
½ cup diced red onions
1 cup shredded Cheddar
   cheese
1 chopped hard-boiled egg
1 tablespoon diced red bell
   pepper
1 tablespoon diced green bell
   pepper
2 tablespoons chopped fresh
   dill
¼ cup sour cream
½ cup mayonnaise
1 teaspoon lemon juice
salt and pepper to taste

Cold Peanut Noodles

This noodle salad is a slightly exotic addition to any summertime barbecue or potluck dinner.

• • •

1. Toss noodles with 1 tablespoon sesame oil and let cool.

2. Purée remaining sesame oil, peanut butter, soy sauce, water, vinegar, honey, ginger, and garlic in the blender.

3. Add dressing to noodles; toss.

4. Toss in fresh vegetables right before serving.

5. Top with chopped peanuts or sesame seeds.

Serves 4

12 ounces spaghetti noodles,
   cooked
2 tablespoons sesame oil
½ cup creamy peanut butter
¼ cup soy sauce
¼ cup water
2 tablespoons rice vinegar
2 teaspoons honey
1 tablespoon grated fresh
   gingerroot
2 cloves garlic, crushed
1 stalk celery, thinly sliced
2 whole green onions, thinly
   sliced
½ cup peeled and seeded
   cucumber slices
¼ cup shredded carrots
chopped peanuts or
   sesame seeds

Serves 4
_____

1 pint fresh strawberries, sliced
½ cup sugar
1 tablespoon poppy seeds
2 teaspoons minced onion
¼ teaspoon Worcestershire sauce
¼ teaspoon paprika
¼ cup cider vinegar
½ cup canola oil
salt and pepper to taste
2 bunches baby spinach leaves
¼ red onion, sliced

Strawberry Spinach Salad

Here is a healthier spinach salad than the usual hot bacon dressing version.

• • •

1. Purée ¼ of the strawberries in a blender.

2. Add sugar, poppy seeds, minced onion, Worcestershire sauce, paprika, and vinegar to the blender. Mix well.

3. Add oil in a stream with the blender running. Season dressing with salt and pepper.

4. Toss spinach, remaining strawberries, and red onion.

5. Serve with freshly ground black pepper.

Wilted Spinach Salad

Old-fashioned hot bacon dressing warms and wilts the spinach in this salad. Mix together ¼ cup cider vinegar, 2 tablespoons hot bacon fat, ½ cup olive oil, a pinch of sugar, 1 teaspoon minced onion, and salt and pepper to taste. Toss warm dressing with spinach and crumbled bacon. Top with chopped hard-boiled egg and sliced mushrooms.

Caesar Salad

This is the authentic version of Caesar salad, with dressing made in the bowl just before serving. A wooden salad bowl is nice for making this classic of tableside restaurant service, but you can make it using any bowl.

. . .

1. With the heel of your palm, press on the peeled, whole garlic clove to bruise it and bring out its juice and flavor. Rub the garlic around the inside of the bowl with a fork. Remove garlic clove.

2. Add egg, mustard, salt, and pepper; stir with fork.

3. Add 2 anchovies, mashing them into the egg mixture. Add vinegar, oil, Worcestershire sauce, and cayenne pepper sauce; stir with fork or whisk to combine. Adjust seasoning with salt and pepper.

4. Add hearts of romaine leaves to the dressing in the bowl. Squeeze the juice of ½ lemon onto the lettuce; add croutons.

5. Toss lettuce and croutons with dressing and top with grated Parmesan cheese, remaining 2 anchovies, and black pepper.

Serves 2

1 clove garlic
1 coddled egg (which is an egg boiled for three minutes in the shell)
1 teaspoon Dijon mustard
salt and pepper to taste
4 anchovies
1 tablespoon white wine vinegar
¼ cup olive oil
3 dashes Worcestershire sauce
dash cayenne pepper sauce
3 hearts of romaine lettuce (The heart is the tender center section of a head of romaine. Discard tough outer leaves.)
1 lemon
Croutons (page 76)
Parmesan cheese

Greek Salad

Use kalamata olives and Greek olive oil in this salad to capture the authentic taste of Greece.

. . .

1. Make the salad dressing by whisking together oregano, oil, and vinegar. Season with salt and pepper.

2. Toss lettuce with dressing and put in a serving bowl.

3. Scatter vegetables and cheese over the dressed lettuce.

Serves 4

1 teaspoon dried oregano
½ cup olive oil
3 tablespoons red wine vinegar
salt and pepper to taste
1 head romaine lettuce, chopped
1 large tomato, chopped
¼ red onion, sliced
¼ cup black olives
½ cucumber, sliced
4 ounces feta cheese, crumbled

Serves 4

6 ripe red tomatoes
6 ounces fresh mozzarella
* cheese*
10 fresh basil leaves
¼ cup olive oil

Tomato, Mozzarella, and Basil

This salad is called Caprese in Italy and features fresh mozzarella.
It is an especially wonderful salad in the summer, when a light
and flavorful supper is refreshing.

• • •

1. Slice tomatoes and mozzarella.

2. Stack the basil leaves, roll them up, and slice them into ribbons.

3. On a platter, alternate layers of tomatoes and mozzarella, drizzle with olive oil, and sprinkle with basil.

Serves 6

1 head iceberg lettuce,
* chopped*
½ cup Balsamic Vinaigrette
* (page 74) or bottled*
* Italian dressing*
2 diced tomatoes
½ cup diced cooked chicken
1 diced avocado
½ cup crumbled blue cheese
¼ cup bacon bits (bottled
* or freshly fried and*
* crumbled bacon)*
3 hardboiled eggs, chopped
½ cup whole chopped green
* onions*

Cobb Salad

This is a California-born classic. It is a hearty salad that includes a
variety of ingredients for a depth of flavor and texture.

• • •

1. Toss lettuce leaves with dressing. Mound dressed lettuce on an oval platter.

2. Top dressed lettuce with all the other ingredients arranged in separate stripes.

Brown Derby
The Cobb Salad was invented at the Brown Derby restaurant in Los Angeles, a famous hangout of stars and gossip columnists since its opening in 1926.

CHAPTER 6
Dressings

5 teaspoons anchovies
1 clove garlic, minced
1 teaspoon Dijon mustard
3 tablespoons lemon juice
2 coddled egg yolks
1 cup olive oil
dash Worcestershire sauce
2 tablespoons grated
    Parmesan cheese
salt and pepper to taste

Caesar Dressing

This is a make-ahead dressing to be added to romaine lettuce, croutons, and Parmesan cheese for Caesar salad. Egg yolks are partially cooked with heat and then chemically cooked with lemon juice.

• • •

1. Using a fork, mash anchovies in a bowl. Mix in garlic and mustard.

2. Whisk in lemon juice and egg yolks.

3. Drizzle oil in slowly while whisking to emulsify.

4. Stir in Worcestershire sauce and Parmesan cheese.

5. Season with salt and pepper to taste.

Coddling Eggs

To make coddled eggs, gently drop raw eggs into boiling water. Cook for 3 minutes in boiling water to firm the yolks, then remove. Allow to sit without immersing in cold water for another two minutes. Whites will be cooked and yolks will be partially cooked but still runny.

Vinaigrette

This is a versatile, basic oil and vinegar dressing.

• • •

1. Combine mustard, shallots, and vinegar in a bowl with a whisk.

2. Drizzle in olive oil while whisking, and season with salt and pepper.

3. Store in a jar and shake to combine before using.

Serves 8

½ teaspoon Dijon mustard
1 tablespoon minced shallots
¼ cup red wine vinegar
1 cup olive oil
salt and pepper to taste

Sesame Dressing

This can be used for dressing a chicken and cabbage salad, cooked and chilled vegetables, or basic salad greens. It is also a great marinade for grilling.

• • •

Combine ingredients in a blender or a bowl with a whisk. Adjust seasoning with salt and pepper.

Serves 8

1 cup peanut oil
½ cup sesame oil
1 tablespoon peeled,
    chopped fresh gingerroot
1 tablespoon minced whole
    green onions
1 teaspoon minced garlic
½ cup rice vinegar
1 tablespoon honey
1 tablespoon soy sauce
2 tablespoons sesame seeds
salt and pepper to taste

2 tablespoons orange juice
1 teaspoon lemon juice
1 teaspoon lime juice
1 tablespoon chopped
    shallots
1 cup olive oil
salt and pepper to taste

Citrus Vinaigrette

*Any citrus juice can be used in this, but remember that orange
is sweet, grapefruit is bitter, lemon is sour, and lime is tart.
This recipe uses a combination of citrus juices.*

• • •

1. Combine juices and shallots in a bowl.

2. Drizzle oil in while whisking.

3. Season with salt and pepper.

Vinegars
*Experiment with different vinegars and citrus juices to create dressings
with unique personalities to complement the ingredients of your salad.
Some different acids include champagne vinegar, red wine vinegar,
white wine vinegar, rice vinegar, cider vinegar, tarragon vinegar, blueberry vinegar, raspberry vinegar, sherry vinegar, balsamic vinegar,
lemon juice, lime juice, grapefruit juice, and orange juice.*

Buttermilk Dressing

This is what is commonly called "ranch" dressing, made with buttermilk and herbs. If using dried herbs, use half the amount called for in the recipe.

• • •

1. Whisk together the mayonnaise and buttermilk until smooth.

2. Add remaining ingredients and combine well.

3. Adjust seasoning with salt and pepper.

Serves 8

1 cup mayonnaise
1 cup buttermilk
1 teaspoon lemon juice
pinch sugar
¼ teaspoon onion powder
¼ teaspoon garlic powder
½ teaspoon chopped
    fresh oregano
½ teaspoon chopped
    fresh dill
½ teaspoon chopped
    fresh chives
½ teaspoon chopped
    fresh thyme
1 teaspoon chopped
    fresh parsley
½ teaspoon chopped
    fresh tarragon
salt and pepper to taste

Blue Cheese Dressing

This is a creamy dressing that is perfect for topping a wedge of iceberg lettuce or serving with celery and carrot sticks for dipping with hot buffalo wings.

• • •

1. Whisk together mayonnaise and sour cream until smooth.

2. Add lemon juice and vinegar, and whisk again.

3. Stir in blue cheese to desired chunk consistency.

4. Season with onion powder, salt, and pepper.

Serves 8

1 cup mayonnaise
½ cup sour cream
1 tablespoon lemon juice
1 tablespoon red wine
    vinegar
4 ounces blue cheese,
    crumbled
¼ teaspoon onion powder
salt and pepper to taste

Herbs

Add fresh or dried herbs to a basic vinaigrette recipe to create herb vinaigrette. Some good herbs to use are basil, oregano, thyme, rosemary, chives, parsley, dill, or tarragon. Experiment with different combinations to create your signature herb vinaigrette.

Serves 8

1 clove garlic, crushed
½ teaspoon kosher salt
1 teaspoon Dijon mustard
2 tablespoons balsamic
  vinegar
1 tablespoon red wine
  vinegar
1 cup olive oil
pepper to taste

Balsamic Vinaigrette

There are many different kinds of balsamic vinegar, and they vary in price. The oldest and most expensive ones are thick and sweet from aging in oak barrels. For this dressing use a moderately aged (and priced) one.

• • •

1. Combine garlic and salt in a wooden bowl and smash to a paste with a wooden spoon (or combine in a blender).

2. Add mustard and vinegars and whisk together.

3. Drizzle in the oil while whisking.

4. Season with pepper.

Serves 8

½ cup chicken broth
½ cup salad oil
2 tablespoons Dijon mustard
1 tablespoon honey
2 tablespoons white wine
  vinegar
1 teaspoon minced onion
salt and pepper to taste

Honey Mustard Dressing

This dressing is lower in fat than others, because part of the oil is replaced by chicken broth.

• • •

Combine ingredients in a blender until smooth. Adjust seasoning to taste with salt and pepper.

Oils

Try using different oils in vinaigrette to vary the flavor and weight of the dressing. Extra-virgin olive oil is more flavorful than pure olive oil, which is lighter in taste. Oils to experiment with include canola, sunflower, peanut, safflower, grape seed, corn, and vegetable. Accent oils include sesame, walnut, hazelnut, and chile.

Raspberry Vinaigrette

*This is a tangy, tart, and slightly sweet dressing that
adds a touch of fruit to salad greens.*

• • •

Combine ingredients in a blender until smooth. Adjust seasoning with
salt and pepper.

Serves 8

¼ cup fresh raspberries,
   puréed and strained
1 cup salad oil
2 tablespoons raspberry
   vinegar
1 tablespoon minced shallots
1 teaspoon sugar
1 teaspoon Dijon mustard
salt and pepper to taste

Sun-Dried Tomato Vinaigrette

*This dressing can be puréed in a blender or left chunky.
It also makes a good dip for artichokes.*

• • •

1. Combine garlic and vinegars in a bowl with a whisk.

2. Drizzle in the oil while whisking until all of it has been incorporated.

3. Stir in tomatoes and basil. Season with salt and pepper.

Serves 8

1 teaspoon minced garlic
3 tablespoons red wine
   vinegar
1 tablespoon balsamic
   vinegar
1 cup olive oil
¼ cup minced sun-dried
   tomatoes
1 tablespoon chopped fresh
   basil
salt and pepper to taste

1 loaf bread, crust removed,
  cut into cubes
5 cloves garlic, minced
8 tablespoons unsalted
  butter, melted
1 tablespoon kosher salt
1 teaspoon pepper

Croutons

Any bread can be used in this recipe, though a hearty bread, such as levain or sourdough, makes croutons that hold up better in salads.

• • •

1. Preheat oven to 350°F.

2. Put bread cubes in a large bowl with garlic.

3. Pour butter over bread cubes and toss them to distribute the butter and garlic evenly.

4. Sprinkle salt and pepper on bread cubes; toss to distribute seasoning.

5. Bake seasoned bread cubes on an ungreased cookie sheet 15–25 minutes, until toasted. If cubes brown unevenly, stir on the sheet halfway through cooking time. Cool and store in an airtight container.

Salad Toppers

Croutons aren't your only choice for a crunchy addition to salad. Top salads with toasted nuts, sunflower seeds, or bacon bits for flavor and crunch. Candied nuts add depth, and various cheeses and fruits give salads dimension.

CHAPTER 7
Breakfast

Serves 12

2 cups all-purpose flour
⅔ cup sugar
1 tablespoon baking powder
½ teaspoon salt
2 eggs
1 cup milk
6 tablespoons butter, melted
1 teaspoon vanilla extract
1½ cups fresh or frozen
    blueberries

Blueberry Muffins

This basic muffin recipe can be used to make different muffins by substituting blackberries, raspberries, cranberries, chocolate chips, peaches, or pecans for the blueberries. Add orange zest to the cranberry, lemon zest to the blueberry, or chopped hazelnuts to the chocolate chip for more variety.

•   •   •

1. Preheat oven to 400°F. Grease a 12-cup muffin tin or line it with fluted paper cups.

2. Combine flour, sugar, baking powder, and salt in a large bowl using a whisk.

3. Combine eggs, milk, butter, and vanilla in another bowl using a whisk.

4. Stir the wet ingredients into the dry ingredients; then fold in blueberries with a spatula. Fill muffin cups with the batter, distributing the batter evenly.

5. Sprinkle tops with sugar. Bake 15 minutes.

Strawberry Scones

These directions call for shaping the scones like drop biscuits,
but you can make them in triangles by forming the dough into one large circle
and then cutting the circle into wedges before baking.
Scones also can be frozen before baking for use at a later date. Bake frozen
scones in a preheated oven for about 45 minutes.

• • •

Serves 6

1½ cups all-purpose flour
3 tablespoons sugar, plus
   more for sprinkling
½ teaspoon salt
1⅛ teaspoons baking powder
6 tablespoons cold, unsalted
   butter, cut in pieces
2 eggs
⅔ cup heavy cream
½ teaspoon vanilla extract
1 cup sliced fresh strawberries

1. Preheat oven to 400°F. Line a cookie sheet with parchment paper, or brush lightly with oil. (You could alternately spray the cookie sheet with cooking spray.)

2. Combine flour, sugar, salt, baking powder, and butter in a food processor with a metal blade, or use two butter knives to mix dry ingredients while chopping up butter into smaller pieces. Cut butter until mixture resembles cornmeal.

3. In a large bowl combine eggs, cream, and vanilla using a whisk. Stir in strawberries with a spatula or wooden spoon.

4. Fold in dry ingredients with a spatula. Drop scones into rounds onto prepared cookie sheet.

5. Sprinkle scones with sugar and bake for 15 minutes.

Stilton Scones

To make Stilton Scones, leave out the strawberries and vanilla in the Strawberry Scones recipe, and add 3 ounces crumbled blue cheese. Season with a few drops of cayenne pepper sauce; do not sprinkle with sugar before baking. Bake for the same amount of time as the Strawberry Scones recipe.

Serves 12

2 puff pastry sheets, thawed
    if frozen
4 tablespoons unsalted
    butter, melted
1 cup sugar
¼ cup cinnamon

Cinnamon Rolls

You can drizzle these cinnamon rolls with a glaze made from 2 tablespoons butter, melted; ¼ cup powdered sugar; and a few drops of water.

• • •

1. Preheat oven to 375°F. Unfold and lay flat on pastry sheet. Brush pastry with melted butter.

2. Sprinkle sugar and cinnamon on the melted butter. Beginning at one end, roll up the pastry tightly. Repeat with the second sheet. Cut each log into six pieces.

3. Place cinnamon rolls cut side down on an ungreased cookie sheet, spacing them evenly. Bake 15 minutes.

Serves 12

12 Cinnamon Rolls (above),
    unbaked
4 tablespoons butter, cut into
    12 pats (12 teaspoons
    butter)
½ cup dark brown sugar
½ cup chopped pecans

Sticky Buns

These are made from cinnamon rolls that have not been baked yet. They are baked in muffin tins in a pecan caramel sauce, then turned upside down so the caramel glazes the buns.

• • •

1. Preheat oven to 375°F. Place 1 teaspoon butter, 2 teaspoons brown sugar, and 1 teaspoon pecans in the bottom of each of 12 muffin tin cups.

2. Place 1 unbaked cinnamon roll in each cup, on top of the sugar mixture.

3. Bake 15 minutes, then immediately invert the muffin pan onto a clean cookie sheet to un-mold sticky buns.

Coffeecake

Fruit can be added to the batter of this recipe for a variety of different-flavored coffee cakes. Try fresh or frozen blueberries or dried apricots and cranberries. Nuts can be added too.

• • •

Serves 12

½ cup dark brown sugar
2 teaspoons cinnamon
3⅓ cups all-purpose flour
1 cup cold butter
1½ cups sugar
3 eggs
2 teaspoons baking powder
1 teaspoon baking soda
½ teaspoon salt
1 cup sour cream

1. Preheat oven to 350°F. Butter a bundt pan.

2. Make filling by combining the brown sugar, cinnamon, ⅓ cup of the flour, and ¼ cup of the butter with fingertips until crumbly. Set aside.

3. For the batter: Cream together ¾ cup butter and sugar until fluffy. Add eggs one at a time and beat them in to form a smooth batter. Separately, mix together 3 cups flour, baking powder, baking soda, and salt, using a whisk.

4. Add flour mixture alternately with sour cream to the butter/egg mixture until all is incorporated. Layer half the batter in the bundt pan; sprinkle it with the filling mixture. Layer the rest of the batter on top.

5. Bake 50 minutes, or until a toothpick inserted in the middle comes out clean. Sprinkle with powdered sugar before serving in slices.

Breakfast Burrito
Wrap scrambled eggs, crumbled cooked sausage, shredded Cheddar cheese, sliced green onions, salsa, sour cream, and black olives in a large flour tortilla and serve warm for an on-the-go hearty breakfast. For a different taste, add crisp Home Fries (page 88) and substitute bacon for sausage.

8 slices white bread, cubed

½ cup cooked,
    crumbled bacon

6 eggs

2 cups shredded Monterey
    jack cheese

2 cups skim milk

1 teaspoon dry mustard

½ teaspoon salt

¼ teaspoon pepper

1 tablespoon butter (for
    buttering the pan)

Omelet Casserole

Make this the night before you need it and bake it fresh in the morning.
Leftovers can be wrapped individually and frozen to save
for a quick gourmet breakfast any time you want.

• • •

1. Butter a 9" x 13" baking dish (brownie/lasagna pan). Lay bread cubes on bottom of pan. Sprinkle bacon over bread.

2. Using a whisk, combine eggs, milk, mustard, salt, and pepper in a bowl. Pour this mixture over bacon and bread. Sprinkle cheese over top of everything.

3. Cover and refrigerate overnight.

4. Preheat oven to 350°F. Bake casserole uncovered for 25 minutes.

French Toast

French toast, known in France as pain perdue ("lost bread") is delicious served with warm maple syrup and powdered sugar. Use white bread, challah, French bread, sourdough, or brioche for variety. A Monte Cristo (page 97) is an entire sandwich "French toasted."

. . .

Serves 4

6 eggs
1½ cups milk
1 teaspoon vanilla extract
½ teaspoon cinnamon
8 tablespoons butter
8 slices day-old bread
¼ cup powdered sugar

1. Combine eggs, milk, vanilla, and cinnamon in a shallow, flat bowl (like a soup or pasta bowl), using a whisk. Melt butter in a frying pan over medium heat, being careful not to let it burn.

2. Dip both sides of each slice of bread in the custard mixture and immediately pan-fry in melted butter on both sides.

3. Cut French toast in triangular halves and sprinkle with powdered sugar.

4. Serve with butter and warm maple syrup.

Croissant French Toast

To make croissant French toast, use 1 croissant per person. Freeze croissant to make slicing easier. Using a serrated bread knife, slice croissant horizontally into 3 slices. Dip in regular French Toast custard (egg and milk mixture—above) to which 1 teaspoon orange zest has been added. Fry in butter in a nonstick pan. Serve with fresh strawberries and powdered sugar.

1 blind-baked half-recipe Pie
    Dough crust (page 222),
    baked in 9-inch tart pan
    with removable bottom
½ cup diced leeks, white
    part only
1 tablespoon olive oil
1 cup shredded smoked
    gouda cheese
¼ cup baby spinach
    leaves, packed into
    measuring cup
2 tablespoons julienned sun-
    dried tomatoes
3 eggs
1½ cups heavy cream
1⁄16 teaspoon nutmeg
½ teaspoon salt
3 drops cayenne
    pepper sauce
¼ teaspoon white pepper
2 tablespoons chopped
    fresh chives

Quiche

Quiche, a savory egg tart, is a custard with cheese and various add-ins baked in a pastry shell. The classic Quiche Lorraine has sautéed onions and bacon, but no cheese. Broccoli, ham, roasted red bell peppers, and sautéed mushrooms make good quiche add-ins. The cheese can be any kind you like.

• • •

1. Preheat oven to 375°F.

2. Sauté leeks in olive oil until tender. Spread them on the bottom of the prebaked pastry shell. Sprinkle cheese on top of leeks. Tuck spinach leaves here and there in the cheese. Distribute the tomatoes evenly on top.

3. Combine eggs, cream, nutmeg, salt, cayenne pepper sauce, and white pepper. Stir in chives.

4. Pour egg mixture over the ingredients in the tart shell, gently pressing down on anything that floats to the top so that everything stays submerged.

5. Bake for 30 minutes, until set. Serve warm. If you like, you also can chill, slice, and reheat the quiche in an oven or toaster oven.

Eggs Benedict

This brunch classic is a combination of English muffins, Canadian bacon, poached eggs, and Hollandaise Sauce (page 200). A lighter version can be made by replacing the Canadian bacon with fresh tomato slices. Other delicious variations include smoked salmon, avocado slices, prosciutto, or sautéed spinach. Eggs can be poached the night before, kept in the refrigerator, and reheated in hot water when ready to use.

• • •

1. Split the English muffins, put them on a plate, and cover with aluminum foil. Keep muffins in a warm oven until you are ready to use them.

2. In a medium saucepan, simmer water with a teaspoon of distilled white vinegar. Break eggs into a tea cup or bowl and gently slide them into the water. Poach eggs in simmering water until the eggs hold their shape, but still have runny yolk centers. Remove poached eggs from simmering liquid with a slotted spoon and lay them on several layers of paper towel. Trim any straggling pieces of egg white from the poached eggs.

3. Brown the Canadian bacon in a skillet.

4. Heat the hollandaise sauce in a water bath if it has been made ahead of time. It can be made and kept warm in a Thermos with no need to reheat.

5. Each serving begins with 2 English muffin halves. On each half put a piece of Canadian bacon, then a poached egg. Spoon or pour hollandaise sauce to cover each egg. Top each egg with an olive half and sprinkle with paprika and chopped parsley. Serve immediately.

Biscuit Breakfast

Biscuits (page 214) can be eaten solo with honey, or used to make breakfast sandwiches. Mini biscuits with crispy Oven-Fried Chicken Nuggets (page 295) is a tasty breakfast. Regular biscuits with bacon, scrambled eggs, and cheese is another.

Serves 2

2 English muffins
4 eggs
1 teaspoon distilled white vinegar
4 slices Canadian bacon
½ cup Hollandaise Sauce (page 200)
2 black olives, sliced in half lengthwise
1 teaspoon paprika
1 tablespoon chopped fresh parsley

Serves 6

1¾ cups all-purpose flour
1 tablespoon baking powder
1 tablespoon sugar
½ teaspoon salt
3 eggs
8 tablespoons unsalted
    butter, melted
1½ cups milk
vegetable oil for waffle iron
½ cup maple syrup
2 tablespoons salted butter

Belgian Waffles

Belgian waffles are thick, square waffles with deep, large indentations where syrup and melted butter pool together for a luscious flavor. Belgian waffles are great for topping with ice cream to make dessert waffles, but this recipe can be used for any shape of waffle.

• • •

1. Preheat waffle iron and oil it with vegetable oil.

2. Combine flour, baking powder, sugar, and salt in a bowl, using a whisk.

3. Combine eggs, melted butter, and milk in another bowl, using the whisk.

4. Stir egg mixture into flour mixture until just combined; don't overmix.

5. Pour or ladle about ½ cup waffle batter onto preheated and oiled waffle iron; cook according to manufacturer's instructions.

6. Heat maple syrup and 2 tablespoons unsalted butter together in a small pitcher or bowl in the microwave and serve warm with waffles.

Buttermilk Pancakes

These basic cakes can be embellished with many delicious ingredients. Blueberries, bananas, chocolate chips, pecans, bacon, green onions, and grated cheese are just a few possible variations. Adding a little cornmeal will give the pancakes some texture.

• • •

Serves 4

1½ cups all-purpose flour
3 tablespoons sugar
1½ teaspoons baking powder
½ teaspoon baking soda
½ teaspoon salt
2 eggs
3 tablespoons butter, melted
1½ cups buttermilk

1. Combine flour, sugar, baking powder, baking soda, and salt in a large bowl, using a whisk.

2. Combine eggs, melted butter, and buttermilk in another bowl with whisk.

3. Add just enough vegetable oil to a frying pan to coat the bottom. If you're using a griddle that isn't nonstick, lightly oil it to prevent pancakes from sticking. Heat pan or griddle over medium heat.

4. Stir egg mixture into the flour mixture until combined, but don't overmix.

5. Pour about ⅓ cup batter onto hot, oiled griddle or pan for each pancake. Flip pancake when bubbles have formed and started to pop on one side. Cook on other side for a minute or two.

6. Serve hot with butter and syrup or fresh fruit, whipped cream, and powdered sugar.

Pigs in a Blanket

Make silver-dollar-sized buttermilk pancakes. Place one cooked breakfast sausage link on the bottom edge of one pancake and roll up so the sausage is in the middle of the pancake roll. Repeat to make as many as desired. Freeze for a quick breakfast at a later date. Serve with warm maple syrup for dipping.

Hash Browns

Serves 4

4 tablespoons olive oil
2 large potatoes, peeled and
    grated
¼ cup grated onion
salt and pepper to taste

These breakfast potatoes are both crunchy and tender, like a potato pancake.

. . .

1. Heat oil in a skillet over medium-high heat.

2. Wrap potatoes in a clean dishtowel and squeeze out excess moisture. Carefully add potatoes to the oil in the pan, forming one large circle. Sprinkle onion, salt, and pepper over potatoes.

3. Cook potatoes until a golden brown crust forms, then turn them over with a spatula and continue cooking until potatoes are tender.

Home Fries

Serves 4

¼ cup olive oil
1 cup diced onion
3 cups diced, parboiled
    potatoes
½ teaspoon dried rosemary
1 teaspoon salt
½ teaspoon pepper

These breakfast potatoes are chunky, with pieces of caramelized onion and herbs, and are a delightful addition to a brunch buffet.

. . .

1. Heat oil in skillet over medium heat. Sauté onions in oil for 3 minutes.

2. Add potatoes, rosemary, salt, and pepper to the pan and cook, pushing potatoes and onions around with a spatula until onions caramelize and some potatoes get crunchy.

Granola

This crunchy oat cereal is delicious with milk or yogurt, or by itself. Any dried fruit may be mixed in, and various nuts and seeds can be combined to create your own signature mix.

• • •

1. Preheat oven to 350°F. Toss oats, almonds, orange zest, nutmeg, cinnamon, vanilla, maple syrup, and melted butter together in a big bowl. Spread the mixture onto an ungreased cookie sheet and bake for 10 minutes, uncovered.

2. Stir, add sunflower and sesame seeds, and stir again. Bake for 15 minutes more.

3. Stir, add coconut, and stir again. Bake 10 minutes more.

4. Remove from oven, and set aside until pan is cool. Then break up large chunks with your hands.

Yogurt Fruit Parfait

Layer granola, vanilla yogurt, and fresh fruit, such as sliced strawberries, blueberries, raspberries, and sliced peaches, in a glass. Make 2 or 3 stripes of each to make a healthy, crunchy, and tasty breakfast.

Serves 6

4 cups old-fashioned rolled oats
1 cup whole almonds
1 tablespoon chopped orange zest
⅛ teaspoon nutmeg
¼ teaspoon cinnamon
1 teaspoon vanilla extract
¼ cup maple syrup
8 tablespoons butter, melted
½ cup raw sunflower seeds
¼ cup sesame seeds
¼ cup shredded, unsweetened coconut

CHAPTER 8
Sandwiches

2 boneless, skinless chicken
    breasts
4 cups chicken broth
1 cup diced red apple
1 cup diced celery
½ cup halved seedless grapes
½ cup chopped pecans
1 cup mayonnaise
4 large flour tortillas
8 leaves tender green lettuce

Chicken Waldorf Roll-Up

This sandwich is a twist on the classic Waldorf Salad. Pecans are used in place of walnuts in this recipe. Yogurt can be substituted for some or all of the mayonnaise for a lighter version. If you don't have chicken broth on hand, use water and add a few slices of carrot, celery, onion, and a peppercorn for the poaching liquid. For a heartier sandwich, serve this chicken salad on Focaccia (page 220).

• • •

1. In a 4-quart saucepan, bring chicken broth to a boil. Poach chicken breasts by cooking in the boiling chicken broth for 20 minutes. Refrigerate and let cool completely in poaching liquid (overnight if necessary).

2. Remove chicken breasts from poaching liquid. Dice chicken breasts and combine with apple, celery, grapes, pecans, and mayonnaise in a bowl to make filling.

3. Lay out tortillas and line each with 2 pieces of lettuce.

4. Spoon filling onto lettuce and roll up like a burrito: Tuck the side in, roll up from the bottom, and finish by rolling to the top to form a log.

5. To serve, slice in half diagonally through the center of each roll.

The Original Waldorf Salad

The original Waldorf Salad was invented by the chef of the Waldorf-Astoria hotel in the 1890s and quickly became the height of dining fashion. It has survived in variations, including some that call for miniature marshmallows and whipped cream.

Gourmet BLT

*Bacon, lettuce, and tomato make this sandwich classic,
and basil mayonnaise and focaccia make it gourmet.*

• • •

1. Slice the focaccia horizontally. Cut the bacon pieces in half.

2. Mix basil and mayonnaise together and spread on underside of the top half of the focaccia.

3. Layer the lettuce, tomato, and bacon on the bottom piece of focaccia. Top with the focaccia spread with the basil mayonnaise, and slice the sandwich on the diagonal into 2 triangles.

Serves 1

1 4-inch square piece of
   focaccia, store-bought or
   homemade (page 220)
2 pieces cooked bacon
1 basil leaf, chopped
1 tablespoon mayonnaise
2 butter lettuce leaves
3 slices tomato

Gourmet Peanut Butter and Jelly

*Sliced strawberries and chopped peanuts elevate this perennial favorite.
It's great for adults and kids alike!*

• • •

1. Spread peanut butter on one slice of bread and jam on the other.

2. Arrange strawberry slices on the jam and peanuts on the peanut butter.

3. Put bread together with the filling in the middle and serve whole.

Serves 1

2 thick slices white bread
4 tablespoons peanut butter
2 tablespoons strawberry jam
¼ cup sliced fresh
   strawberries
2 tablespoons chopped
   peanuts

3 hardboiled eggs
2 tablespoons diced celery
1 tablespoon whole chopped
    green onions
¼ cup mayonnaise
1 tablespoon plain yogurt
2 tablespoons Dijon mustard
2 teaspoons honey
¼ teaspoon curry powder
salt and pepper to taste
¼ cup chopped roasted
    cashews

Curried Egg Salad

*Crunchy cashews and a dash of curry powder turn ordinary egg salad
into a flavorful entrée. Serve this egg salad on bread with
honey mustard, chopped cashews, and green lettuce.*

• • •

1. Peel and chop the hardboiled eggs and put in a bowl with celery and green onions. Toss to mix briefly.

2. Add mayonnaise, yogurt, mustard, honey, and curry powder to the bowl and mix well.

3. Season with salt and pepper to taste.

4. Sprinkle the cashews over the egg salad and fold them into the mixture.

Hero

A submarine sandwich made with various sliced meats, cold cuts, and cheeses is sometimes called a hero. When served hot, a hero can have steak, meatballs, or even hamburger patties lined up on the bun. Italian beef sandwiches from Chicago qualify as heroes.

Tuna Salad

Use soft white bread and lettuce when making this lunchbox classic, or dress it up on a croissant with alfalfa sprouts, mayonnaise mixed with a bit of fresh lemon juice, and tomato slices. Tuna salad also makes a good snack served on Gougeres (page 28).

• • •

1. Combine all ingredients in a bowl with a spatula.

2. Adjust seasoning with salt and pepper.

Serves 4

1 6-ounce can tuna packed in
   water, drained
¼ cup diced red onion
2 tablespoons diced celery
1 tablespoon sweet pickle
   relish
¼ cup mayonnaise
1 tablespoon chopped
   parsley
1 tablespoon lemon juice
salt and pepper to taste

Club Sandwich

This double-decker sandwich combines a BLT with a turkey sandwich and is best eaten with potato chips, carrot sticks, and pickle slices, lunch-counter style.

• • •

1. Put mayonnaise on all three pieces of toast.

2. Put lettuce, tomato, and bacon on one piece of toast, and turkey and cheese on another piece of toast. Stack the toast with the turkey on the bottom and the third piece of toast on the top.

3. Slice sandwich into 4 triangles and insert toothpicks in each quadrant. Top each toothpick with an olive.

Serves 1

3 pieces white bread, toasted
2 tablespoons mayonnaise
2 leaves lettuce
2 slices tomato
2 pieces cooked bacon, cut
   in half
3 thin slices roast turkey
1 slice American cheese
   (optional)
4 toothpicks
2 black olives
2 green olives

Smoked Salmon Bagel

Serves 1

1 plain bagel, sliced
4 tablespoons whipped
    cream cheese
3 slices smoked salmon
1 slice red onion
1 teaspoon drained capers
    (optional)

*A fresh, chewy bagel is a must for this deli favorite. Smoked salmon or lox
may be used, and additions of avocado, tomato, and/or sprouts build up the
classic bagel-and-cream-cheese combination.*

• • •

1. Spread the cream cheese on the cut sides of the bagel.

2. Top cream cheese on the bottom half with smoked salmon, onion, and
   capers.

3. Top with the other half of the bagel, and cut sandwich in half.

Grinder
*A submarine sandwich made with sliced meat and cheese is sometimes called
a grinder. Other names are gondola, torpedo, bomber, zeppelin, and hoagie.*

Cheesesteak

Serves 2

½ cup sliced onions
¼ cup green pepper slices
1 tablespoon olive oil
1 pound strip steak,
    sliced thin
1 tablespoon butter
1 cup shredded provolone
    cheese
1 12-inch-long sub bun

*There is controversy over which cheese is best in this hot hero sandwich,
so feel free to use your favorite cheese instead of shredded provolone.
Red cherry peppers and sautéed mushrooms are a tasty addition.*

• • •

1. Sauté onions and peppers in olive oil; set aside.

2. Sauté steak in butter until cooked through.

3. Toss onions and peppers in with the meat.

4. Top the meat with the provolone.

5. Scoop meat with everything on it onto bun. Cut sandwich in half.

Monte Cristo

A double-decker turkey and ham sandwich is dipped in French toast custard
mixture and pan-fried in butter to make this heavenly brunch sandwich.
Fresh melon slices, a sprinkle of powdered sugar, and warm maple syrup
in a ramekin complete the plate.

• • •

1. Spread a thin film of butter on each slice of bread. (This will help hold it together in addition to adding flavor.)

2. Put Cheddar cheese and turkey on 2 slices of bread and Swiss cheese and ham on 2 more slices of bread.

3. Stack the turkey layer on the ham layer and top with last piece of bread, butter side in, for each sandwich. Cut off the crusts, then cut each sandwich in half diagonally to form two triangles.

4. Mix together the eggs, milk, vanilla, and cinnamon to make the custard. Melt remaining butter in skillet.

5. Dip all sides of each sandwich triangle into the custard mixture and cook in skillet, browning on all sides. Serve warm.

Serves 2

6 slices buttermilk bread
4 tablespoons butter
2 slices Cheddar cheese
6 slices smoked turkey
2 slices Swiss cheese
6 slices ham
2 eggs
⅓ cup milk
¼ teaspoon vanilla extract
pinch cinnamon

Serves 2

1 12-inch-long sub bun
6 slices deli ham
6 slices salami
6 slices provolone cheese
1 cup shredded lettuce
5 slices tomato
¼ cup sliced hot banana
   peppers
2 tablespoons bottled Italian
   dressing

Italian Submarine Sandwich

This sandwich can be served cold, or heated open-face in the oven, minus the salad ingredients, which are then added after the sandwich is taken out of the oven. Cut sub in smaller pieces to serve as appetizers for more people.

•   •   •

1. Slice the sub bun lengthwise, but not all the way through. Open it up flat like a book.

2. Cover the bread with the slices of ham. Lay the salami on top of the ham. Line up the cheese on top of the salami. Layer the lettuce, tomato, and banana peppers on the meats and cheese.

3. Drizzle dressing on the lettuce, and fold the sandwich closed.

4. Cut sandwich in half with a serrated knife.

Muffaletta
A famous New Orleans sandwich is the muffaletta, which is made with olive salad on a round loaf of bread with sliced lunchmeat and cheese.

Meatball Sandwich

You can make your own meatballs and sauce for this or go with prepared meatballs and tomato sauce for a quicker meal. You can also include green peppers, onions, black olives, or Parmesan cheese on your meatball sandwich.

• • •

Serves 2

6 2-inch meatballs (page 161)
1 cup Marinara Sauce
   (page 152)
2 6-inch sub buns
4 slices provolone cheese
½ cup shredded mozzarella
   cheese

1. Heat the meatballs in the sauce.

2. Open the buns flat and line them with provolone cheese.

3. Put 3 meatballs with sauce on each sandwich.

4. Sprinkle mozzarella cheese on top of meatballs.

5. Heat sandwiches in the oven at 350°F until cheese melts.

Po'Boy

A po'boy is a sandwich on a submarine bun, sometimes filled with fried oysters, shrimp, or catfish. Originally a French-fried potato sandwich, it was invented in New Orleans in the 1920s to keep striking workers ("poor boys") fed. Outside of Louisiana, a po'boy is often a sub sandwich with sliced meats.

Serves 2

4 slices rye bread
2 tablespoons butter,
    softened
2 slices Swiss cheese
8 ounces thinly sliced corned
    beef brisket
½ cup drained sauerkraut
¼ cup Russian or Thousand
    Island dressing

Reuben

*Perhaps invented in Omaha, but made famous in the
delicatessens of the Lower East Side of Manhattan, this combination
of corned beef, sauerkraut, and Russian dressing perfectly balances
salty and tangy flavors. Serve with a garlic pickle spear.*

• • •

1. Butter one side of each slice of bread.

2. For each sandwich, layer one slice of bread, butter side out, with
    cheese, corned beef, sauerkraut, dressing, and another slice of bread,
    butter side out.

3. Grill sandwich in a skillet or on a griddle until toasted.

4. Cut in half and serve warm.

Serves 1

2 half-inch slices eggplant
3 half-inch slices zucchini
3 half-inch slices yellow
    squash
1 teaspoon olive oil
¼ cup sliced onions
pinch of sugar
Quick Aioli (page 34)
Focaccia (page 220)
2 sun-dried tomatoes
5 one-inch strips roasted red
    bell pepper

Grilled Vegetable Sandwich

*Any combination of grilled or roasted vegetables can be used to create your
sandwich. You can also try using different condiments and sauces to change
the flavor of your grilled sandwich, such as pesto, or tapenade.*

• • •

1. Brush the eggplant, zucchini, and squash with olive oil. Toss the onion
    with a pinch of sugar.

2. Grill eggplant, zucchini, squash, and onions until tender and
    browned.

3. Spread aioli on the focaccia. Then build on top of the aioli with grilled
    vegetables, sun-dried tomatoes, and roasted red pepper.

Grilled Chicken Sandwich

The chicken in this recipe can also be sliced and served cold or warm on top of Caesar Salad (page 67).

• • •

1. Marinate chicken in garlic, oil, rosemary, salt, and pepper for at least 1 hour.

2. Grill marinated chicken on preheated grill or grill pan on both sides until juices run clear.

3. Put aioli on top of the bun, and grilled chicken and lettuce on the bottom half.

Gyro

A gyro is a Greek sandwich made with pita bread, lamb, tomatoes, onions, and yogurt-garlic-cucumber sauce (tziziki). The meat for the sandwich is usually cooked on a revolving spit, from which the person preparing the gyro slices the meat to put on the warm pita. The gyro (which means "to turn" in Greek) is named after this spit.

Serves 2

2 boneless, skinless chicken breasts
1 clove garlic, minced
2 tablespoons olive oil
1 teaspoon fresh rosemary, minced
¼ teaspoon salt
⅛ teaspoon pepper
2 tablespoons Quick Aioli (page 34)
2 kaiser rolls or hamburger buns
4 lettuce leaves

CHAPTER 9
One-Dish Meals (Casseroles)

Serves 4

4 cups water
1 cup coarse cornmeal
1 teaspoon salt
2 tablespoons butter

Basic Polenta

Polenta is a classic Italian dish that has withstood the ages, perhaps because it is so versatile. You can serve warm polenta with almost any vegetable or sauce, mix it with freshly grated Parmesan cheese, or simply serve it plain as a creamy and satisfying side dish.

• • •

1. Put water and salt in a medium-sized saucepan and bring to a boil.

2. Turn heat down to medium-low. Gradually add cornmeal, stirring constantly, until it has thickened; about 15 minutes. Polenta should be thick without becoming stiff, and should have large bubbles rising and popping on the surface.

3. Stir in butter.

4. Serve immediately for soft polenta, or pour into a greased 9" x 13" baking dish and allow to cool. When cool it can be sliced and grilled, fried or baked.

Polenta Bake

When using precooked polenta that has been chilled and molded solid in a loaf pan for this recipe, cut polenta in slices and lay them down on the bottom of the casserole dish instead of pouring hot, creamy polenta (cooked cornmeal) into it. Proceed as directed for the remaining steps.

• • •

1. Preheat oven to 350°F.

2. Over medium heat, cook cornmeal in salted water and milk, stirring with a wooden spoon or whisk until cooked and creamy, about 10 minutes.

3. Add egg and beat in completely, followed by butter, cream cheese, Parmesan cheese, and half of the mozzarella.

4. Grease a 9" x 13" baking dish with olive oil; pour in polenta mixture.

5. Drizzle 1 tablespoon olive oil over polenta, and then pour tomato sauce over it. Sprinkle garlic, herbs, and remaining mozzarella over top. Bake 25 minutes.

Serves 6

1 cup uncooked coarse-ground cornmeal
3 cups water
1 teaspoon salt
1 egg
½ cup milk
2 ounces cream cheese
¼ cup grated Parmesan cheese
1 cup shredded mozzarella cheese
1 tablespoon butter
1 tablespoon olive oil
1 8-ounce can tomato sauce
3 cloves garlic, sliced
½ teaspoon dried oregano
2 fresh basil leaves, chopped

Serves 6

3 boneless, skinless chicken
    breasts, cubed
½ cup olive oil
1 large onion, diced
1 cup diced green bell pepper
½ cup diced red bell pepper
½ cup diced yellow bell
    pepper
5 cloves garlic, minced
1 tablespoon turmeric
3 cups white long-grain rice,
    uncooked
4 cups chicken broth
¾ cup chopped green olives
2 bay leaves
salt and pepper to taste

Chicken with Rice

*This is a basic meal made in one pot from a cut-up chicken and uncooked
rice, simmered together with aromatic vegetables and chicken broth.
A variety of ingredients can be added, such as sausage or seafood,
which will make it resemble jambalaya or paella.*

· · ·

1. Brown chicken in oil in a large pot. Remove chicken and set aside.

2. Add onion, peppers, garlic, and turmeric to the pot, and sauté until onions are translucent.

3. Add rice and cook for 5 minutes, stirring occasionally. Add chicken broth, browned chicken, olives, and bay leaves. Stir to combine, bring mixture to a simmer over medium heat, and cover pot with a lid.

4. Simmer 20 minutes or until rice is cooked.

5. Remove bay leaves. Season with salt and pepper.

Arroz con Pollo

Arroz con Pollo is Spanish for "rice with chicken." It is a meal in itself, but when served with black beans and fried plantains it becomes a feast. The rice itself is colored vibrant yellow with annatto seeds, similar to the paella of Spain.

Easy Jambalaya

This is a quicker version of the traditional Creole/Cajun spicy chicken and rice dish, which is made with tomatoes, andouille (pork sausage), and shrimp.

• • •

Stir together all ingredients in the pot the chicken and rice were made in, and cook over medium-low until all ingredients are heated through.

Serves 6

1 recipe Chicken with Rice
    (page 106)
½ cup chicken broth
1 smoked sausage, sliced
½ cup diced ham
½ cup canned diced tomatoes
1 cup cooked, peeled small
    shrimp (you can purchase
    these frozen)
1 teaspoon cayenne
    pepper sauce

Shrimp Prep

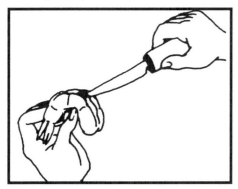

To devein a shrimp:
Use the tip of a knife to make a cut along the back of a peeled shrimp. Use the knife tip to pull out the vein.

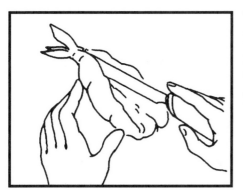

To butterfly a shrimp:
Laying the peeled shrimp on its side, make a deep cut along the curl of the shrimp. Using your fingers, open the shrimp.

Pie Dough (page 222)
1 egg
½ medium onion, diced
1 celery stalk, diced
1 leek, diced (white and
*   light green parts only—*
*   discard dark green part)*
2 carrots, peeled and diced
2 tablespoons butter
¼ cup all-purpose flour
3 cups chicken broth
1 large potato, peeled and
*   cubed*
1 cup cubed butternut squash
2 parsnips, diced
½ cup cut green beans
1 sprig fresh thyme or
*   ¼ teaspoon dried*
1 bay leaf
½ cup frozen peas
½ cup heavy cream
salt and pepper to taste
¼ cup chopped fresh chives

Potpie

This recipe is for open-top potpies with vegetable filling.
The filling can also be made from chicken, beef, or seafood in the same sauce,
using chicken, fish, or beef broth to match the appropriate filling.
It can be made vegetarian with vegetable broth.

• • •

1. Preheat oven to 400°F. Roll out pie dough and cut into 2-inch circles with a round cookie cutter. You will need 4 circles for each serving.

2. For each potpie "cup" turn one ramekin upside down, oil it, and over-lap four circles of pie dough around it, leaving an open hole in the bottom for juice to flow through when served. Attach dough circles to each other with egg wash (1 egg beaten with 2 tablespoons water). Bake pastry cups for about 15 minutes. Let cool and remove them from ramekins. Set aside.

3. Sauté onion, celery, leek, and carrots in butter until onion, celery, and leek are translucent. Dust with flour; stir and cook a few minutes. Add chicken broth, then add potato, squash, parsnips, and green beans. Bring to a boil, add thyme and bay leaf, and simmer for 40 minutes, until the vegetables are cooked and the liquid is thickened.

4. Stir in peas and cream and remove from heat. Remove thyme sprig and bay leaf; season with salt and pepper. Add chives. To serve, place a pastry cup on a plate and spoon vegetables and sauce into it.

Pasties

Pasties are little pocket pies made from meat and vegetable stew wrapped in pie pastry like a turnover. These portable potpies originally went down the shafts with Welsh coal miners to be enjoyed for their subterranean lunch. Immigrants spread the traditional miner's lunch to mining communities in Michigan, Kentucky, and West Virginia.

Shepherd's Pie

Shepherd's Pie is basically stew with a top crust of mashed potatoes. Lamb is a traditional filling, but you can fill it with chili, or you can make it with all vegetables, like Potpie (page 108).

. . .

1. Preheat oven to 400°F.

2. Sauté onion, carrots, and celery in oil. When the onion and celery are translucent, add the beef and cook until browned.

3. Sprinkle meat mixture with flour; stir. Add broth. Simmer until the mixture is thickened, season with salt and pepper, and pour stew into ungreased 9" x 13" casserole dish.

4. Spread mashed potatoes over the meat mixture, drizzle with melted butter, and sprinkle with paprika.

5. Bake for 20 minutes.

Serves 4

1 small onion, diced
2 carrots, peeled and diced
1 celery stalk, sliced into ½-inch slices
2 tablespoons vegetable oil
1 pound ground beef
2 tablespoons all-purpose flour
1½ cups beef broth
salt and pepper to taste
2 cups Mashed Potatoes (page 188)
2 tablespoons butter, melted
paprika

Tortilla Lasagna

Serves 8

½ cup chopped onion
1 clove garlic, minced
1 teaspoon olive oil
1 pound ground turkey
¼ teaspoon cumin
3 cups enchilada sauce
12 corn tortillas
2 cups shredded Monterey
    jack cheese

This southwestern version of lasagna tastes like baked enchiladas but doesn't require the labor-intensive rolling.

• • •

1. Preheat oven to 400°F. Sauté onions and garlic in oil. Add turkey and cook until it is browned. Stir in cumin. Set aside.

2. Spoon a layer of enchilada sauce on the bottom of a 9" x 13" casserole dish. Layer tortillas, meat mixture, and cheese; then sauce, tortillas, meat, and cheese again. Top with a layer of tortillas, sauce, and cheese.

3. Bake 15–20 minutes.

Quick Paella

Serves 6

1 recipe Chicken with Rice
    (page 106)
1 cup frozen peas
1 smoked sausage, sliced
½ cup calamari, cut into
    1-inch slices
½ cup diced canned clams
1 cup (about ½ pound)
    uncooked cocktail shrimp
    in the shell

A quicker version of the traditional Spanish rice dish, which is made with saffron, peas, chicken, chorizo (spicy pork sausage), and shellfish. Dress up this recipe by adding cooked lobster claws and crab legs at the end.

• • •

1. Preheat oven to 375°F.

2. Combine everything except mussels and put in a 9" x 13" shallow baking dish. Cover with foil and bake 20 minutes.

3. Arrange mussels on top and return to the oven uncovered for 15 minutes.

Tamale Pie

Tamale Pie is similar to the Polenta Bake (page 105), but with southwestern flavors instead of Italian flavors.

• • •

1. Boil 3 cups water in a medium saucepan. Add 1 teaspoon salt to boiling water, followed by the coarse cornmeal. Over medium heat, cook, stirring, until mixture thickens.

2. Preheat oven to 400°F. Brown meat in a skillet; add onion and cook until translucent, about 5 minutes. Add tomato sauce and chili powder and simmer for 10 minutes. Set aside.

3. Stir corn into cooked cornmeal. Layer half the cornmeal mixture on the bottom of an ungreased 9" x 13" casserole dish. Spoon meat filling on top of this layer. Spread remaining cornmeal on top of meat mixture.

4. Sprinkle cheese on top and bake for 20 minutes.

Quick Cassoulet
For this rustic French dish, put 2 cans of cannelini beans in a 9" x 13" casserole dish that has been rubbed with bacon fat or olive oil. Add 2 turkey legs, 1 sliced smoked sausage, ¼ cup diced onion, 1 tablespoon tomato paste, 1 clove garlic, and seasonings (thyme, salt, and pepper to taste). Sprinkle top with bread crumbs and bake for 40 minutes at 375°F.

Serves 8

1 cup coarse-ground cornmeal
3 cups water
1 teaspoon salt
1 pound ground beef
½ cup chopped onion
1 8-ounce can tomato sauce
1 tablespoon chili powder
1 cup corn (frozen kernels)
1 cup shredded Cheddar cheese

Serves 6

8 ounces egg noodles, cooked
1 cup sliced mushrooms
2 tablespoons butter
2 tablespoons
    all-purpose flour
2 cups milk
2 cans tuna, drained
¾ cup frozen peas
salt and pepper to taste
1 cup crushed potato chips

Tuna Noodle Casserole

This recipe is the real thing from scratch! It is just as easy as a packaged mix, and you get to control the seasonings and quality of ingredients. This recipe uses crushed potato chips for a topping, but you can use bread crumbs instead for a more elegant presentation. Enrich the recipe with 1 cup shredded Cheddar cheese stirred in before baking.

• • •

1. Preheat oven to 375°F and butter a 9" x 13" casserole dish. Lay cooked noodles in the dish.

2. Sauté mushrooms in butter, sprinkle with flour, and cook for a few minutes. Add milk, and cook until thickened. Stir in tuna and peas. Season with salt and pepper.

3. Pour mushroom sauce mixture over noodles and gently toss if necessary to distribute evenly.

4. Sprinkle potato chips over the top and bake for 20 minutes.

Stuffed Peppers

*This can be made with red, yellow, or orange bell peppers,
and the filling can be made with other meats, such as lamb or turkey.
Tofu can be substituted for a meatless version.*

• • •

Serves 4

*4 green peppers
1 pound ground beef
¼ pound ground pork
½ cup white long-grain rice,
    uncooked
½ cup diced onion
1 16-ounce can tomato sauce*

1. Preheat oven to 350°F.

2. Cut peppers in half through the stem and discard seeds, stem, and membrane. Lay pepper cups in an ungreased 9" x 13" casserole dish.

3. In a bowl mix together the meat, rice, onion, and ½ cup tomato sauce. Season mixture with a bit of salt and pepper.

4. Stuff each pepper half with a ball of meat mixture, mounding it on top.

5. Pour tomato sauce over tops of stuffed peppers, cover with foil, and bake 45 minutes to 1 hour.

Choux Farci
Choux farci is French for "stuffed cabbage." The same filling in stuffed peppers can be used to stuff blanched (quickly boiled, then immersed in cold water) cabbage leaves, which are rolled up after the filling is added. Bake cabbage rolls covered in tomato sauce for a taste of home-cooked comfort food.

Serves 6

dough for Biscuits (page 214)
1 Oven-Roasted Whole
  Chicken (page 132)
1 cup diced onion
1 cup sliced, peeled carrots
½ cup sliced celery
4 tablespoons butter
¼ cup all-purpose flour
4 cups chicken broth
salt and pepper to taste
½ cup frozen peas

Chicken and Dumplings

In this dish the dumplings are steamed floating on top of the stew, but you can instead drop thinly rolled squares of dumpling dough into boiling water to cook them first and then add them to the finished stew. A roasted chicken adds depth of flavor and also makes this recipe easier than using a raw chicken, which would need to be boiled first.

• • •

1. Remove chicken meat from the skin and bone, cut into bite-size pieces, and set aside.

2. In a large soup pot, sauté onion, carrot, and celery in butter until translucent. Sprinkle flour over vegetables and stir, cooking for a few minutes.

3. Add chicken broth and chicken meat and cook until thickened.

4. Season with salt and pepper, and add peas.

5. Drop 1-inch pieces of biscuit dough onto the stew, put a lid on the pot, and simmer 15 minutes.

CHAPTER 10
Meat

Serves 2

2 filet mignon steaks
1 tablespoon olive oil
2 tablespoons butter
1 shallot, minced
1 cup red wine (Bordeaux
    style)
1 tablespoon beef broth
1 teaspoon ketchup
1 dash Worcestershire sauce
salt and pepper to taste
2 steak-sized Croutons made
    out of toasted bread
    rounds (page 76)

Steak with Red Wine Sauce

This sauce is a quicker version of the French classic Steak Bordelaise, also known as Wine Merchant's Steak. It is made in the same pan the steak was seared in to utilize the browned flavor bits left behind. Serve this with Sour Cream and Chive Mashed Potatoes (page 191) and broccoli.

• • •

1. Preheat oven to 400°F. Sear steaks on both sides in a sauté pan with oil and 1 tablespoon of the butter. Transfer steaks to a baking dish and cook them in the oven while you are making the sauce in the pan; about 8 minutes.

2. Sauté shallots in pan for a few minutes, then add wine, broth, ketchup, and Worcestershire sauce. Cook to reduce by half. Season with salt and pepper.

3. Put one crouton on each plate and top it with the steak.

4. Swirl remaining butter in the pan sauce to make it glossy, and pour sauce over steak.

Pot Roast

*There are different variations for this meal, including Swedish,
which incorporates spices, and Italian, which adds tomatoes, garlic, and wine.
This recipe is a basic meat-and-potatoes version that can be expanded on
with whatever flavor elements you like. Use the leftover meat for sandwiches,
or turn the meat and vegetables into potpie.*

* * *

Serves 4

*1 large onion
1- to 2-pound beef roast
3 carrots, peeled
2 celery stalks
2 large potatoes, peeled
1 cup beef broth
½ teaspoon salt
¼ teaspoon pepper
1 tablespoon chopped
    parsley*

1. Preheat oven to 325°F.

2. Cut onion into large chunks and scatter them on the bottom of a roasting pan.

3. Put the meat on top of the onions.

4. Cut the carrots, celery, and potatoes into 2-inch chunks and scatter them around the meat. Pour the broth over the meat. Sprinkle the salt, pepper, and parsley over the meat and vegetables.

5. Cover and roast in the oven for 2–2 ½ hours.

Italian Pot Roast

Make your pot roast with tomato juice and red wine instead of beef broth and add canned diced tomatoes, oregano, and basil. Poke holes in the meat with a paring knife and insert garlic slices before cooking. Serve sliced pot roast and vegetables over creamy polenta (page 104).

Smoked Sausage with Apples

*The sweet, tart flavors of apples and sauerkraut complement
the smoky sausage in this easy meal. Serve it with vegetables and
Cheddar Mashed Potatoes (page 190) for a hearty fall supper.*

• • •

1. Preheat oven to 350°F.

2. Line a 9" x 13" baking dish with sauerkraut, then sprinkle the caraway seeds over it. Lay the sausage in the middle, on top of the sauerkraut, and scatter the apple slices around.

3. Bake uncovered for 35 minutes.

Creamed Ham on Toast

*This recipe uses a ham steak, but any ham will do, including lunchmeat or
leftover baked ham. This is an easy, comforting dish.*

• • •

1. Heat the ham in the butter in a skillet until it is warmed throughout.

2. Sprinkle with flour, cook a few minutes, and then add the milk and the seasonings.

3. Cook until sauce thickens. Spoon over toast.

Stuffed Pork Loin

*This roast is delicious served hot with Rice Pilaf (page 169)
and asparagus, or sliced thin and served cold with coarse mustard, cheese,
and cornichon pickles. This recipe uses dried fruit as a stuffing, but stuffing
with corn-bread (page 282) makes an excellent alternative (for a hot meal
accompanied by sweet potatoes and parsnips).*

• • •

Serves 6

1 3-pound boneless pork
   loin roast
½ cup dried whole apricots
½ cup whole prunes
1 tablespoon butter, softened
½ teaspoon salt
¼ teaspoon pepper
1 cup apple cider or juice

1. Preheat oven to 450°F.

2. Make a T-shaped cut in the meat by cutting halfway through the roast down its whole length. Then make a cut to the left and another one to the right. This will form the pocket to hold the fruit filling. Lay the meat out flat with the inside of the cut part facing up.

3. Lay the fruit in the middle of the meat extending all the way to either end.

4. Put the roast back together by folding it over the fruit. Tie it with kitchen twine (or any clean, unused cotton string) in several places to make a roast shape.

5. Set the stuffed roast in a baking dish and rub it with butter. Season the roast with salt and pepper and pour apple cider or juice over it. Bake uncovered for 10 minutes, then reduce oven temperature to 250°F and continue roasting for about 1½ hours. Baste a few times during the roasting for a flavorful outer layer of meat.

2 tablespoons paprika
1 clove garlic, minced
2 teaspoons salt
1 teaspoon sugar
1 teaspoon pepper
1 teaspoon dried oregano
1 teaspoon dried thyme
1 slab baby back pork ribs
½ cup barbecue sauce

BBQ Ribs

This is a method for making barbecued ribs in your oven instead of the grill so you can make them any time of the year. Serve ribs with barbecue sauce, Twice-Baked Potatoes (page 197) or Potato Salad (page 63), Boston Baked Beans (page 172), and Coleslaw (page 64).

• • •

1. Preheat oven to 350°F.

2. Mix dry ingredients together in a bowl, and then rub the mixture on both sides of the ribs.

3. Place ribs in a roasting pan, cover, and bake for 2 hours.

4. Remove cooked ribs from oven. Brush on barbecue sauce, and bake uncovered for 10 minutes.

5. Cut slab in half to serve two.

Serves 4

1 cup teriyaki sauce
1 flank steak
1 tablespoon honey
1 tablespoon peeled, grated
    fresh gingerroot
½ cup sliced whole green
    onions
1 clove garlic, minced
½ teaspoon sesame oil

Teriyaki Flank Steak

Take advantage of bottled teriyaki sauce and add different flavors to it to personalize your marinade. Corn on the cob and Mashed Potatoes (page 188) round out the meal, and a warm Apple Crisp (page 261) with vanilla ice cream makes a good ending.

• • •

1. Combine ½ cup of the teriyaki sauce with all ingredients except the steak.

2. Marinate the steak for 1 hour or more (up to overnight) before grilling.

3. Grill both sides of flank steak, basting with remaining teriyaki sauce (not the marinade).

4. Serve sliced thin and on the diagonal.

Rosemary-Crusted Lamb Chops

*Mint jelly traditionally accompanies lamb, but mint hollandaise sauce
is a touch more elegant and is easily made by simply stirring
chopped fresh mint into Hollandaise Sauce (page 200). Serve with Ratatouille
(page 181) and Oven-Roasted Red Potatoes (page 195).*

• • •

1. Combine bread crumbs, herbs, and olive oil. Set aside.

2. Season lamb chops with salt and pepper. Sauté them in butter until medium-rare; transfer to a broiler pan. Heat the broiler.

3. Mound 2 tablespoons of bread-crumb mixture on each lamb chop.

4. Broil chops until crust is sufficiently browned.

Ragout

A ragout is a combination of meat and vegetables in juices that are braised together to make a sauce-based stew. The vegetables in an Italian pot roast become a ragout with a tomato sauce base, and when the beef is chunked and added, it is like a stew.

Serves 4

1½ cups dry bread crumbs
1 tablespoon chopped fresh
    rosemary
4 basil leaves, minced
2 tablespoons olive oil
12 lamb chops
salt and pepper
4 tablespoons butter

⅔ pound ground beef
⅓ pound ground pork
¼ cup shredded carrots
¼ cup minced onion
½ teaspoon celery salt
1 tablespoon Dijon mustard
1 tablespoon ketchup
1 teaspoon Worcestershire
   sauce
1 egg
1 tablespoon chopped fresh
   parsley
salt and pepper
¼ cup oatmeal
¼ cup bread crumbs
3 slices bacon

Meatloaf

Meatloaf can be cooked with a variety of toppings, such as ketchup, barbecue sauce, brown sugar, mustard, onions, or beef broth. Serve it with Mashed Potatoes (page 188), Onion Gravy (page 202), and Almond Green Beans (page 179) for a satisfying meal. Leftovers can be turned into hot or cold sandwiches.

• • •

1. Preheat oven to 350°F.

2. In a bowl, using your hands, combine all ingredients except for the bacon.

3. Shape into a loaf and press into a loaf pan.

4. Line the top of the meatloaf with bacon slices.

5. Bake until meat thermometer inserted in the center of the meatloaf reads 160°F, which should be after about 1¼ hours.

Gyro Meat Loaf

Use half beef and half lamb in the meatloaf recipe and season with 1 teaspoon dried oregano to make a meat similar to the kind used in gyro sandwiches. Let the loaf cool, slice thin, and then grill the slices on a griddle to serve on pita bread. Add tomatoes, onions, and yogurt-garlic-cucumber sauce.

Beef Wellington

This recipe is for individual Wellingtons. Beef Wellington is thought to be named after the first Duke of Wellington, Arthur Wellesley, who became a British war hero after defeating Napoleon at Waterloo in 1815. He loved a version of this tasty dish made with pâté and Madeira wine.

• • •

1. Season filets with salt and pepper and sauté them in butter until they are browned but still pink inside (medium). Chill filets.

2. Roll out and cut puff pastry into 4 squares. Spread ¼ cup duxelles in the middle of each pastry square. Place a chilled filet on top of the duxelles. Spread pâté evenly divided on top of the filets. Wrap the pastry around the filet, sealing with egg wash to make a package. Chill until ready to bake.

3. Preheat oven to 400°F. Brush Wellingtons with egg wash, and bake for 35 minutes.

Serves 4

4 filets mignon
salt and pepper
4 tablespoons butter
1 sheet puff pastry
1 cup mushroom Duxelles
    (page 25)
2 ounces pâté de foie gras
egg wash (egg beaten with
    about 2 tablespoons of
    water)

City Chicken

City Chicken is not chicken at all, but chunks of veal or pork (or both) on a wooden skewer. It resembles a chicken leg, but is less messy to eat.

• • •

1. Season meat cubes with salt and pepper.

2. Thread meat cubes onto skewers, alternating veal and pork.

3. Brush meat with oil, and then grill, broil, or bake until done. If you choose to bake the meat, bake at 350°F for 20 minutes. To grill, grill for 12 minutes. To broil, broil for 8 minutes.

Serves 4

1 pound pork, cubed
1 pound veal, cubed
salt and pepper
8 wooden skewers, presoaked
    in water
vegetable oil

CHAPTER 11
Poultry

Serves 4

2 cloves garlic, minced
2 tablespoons olive oil
1 teaspoon Dijon mustard
1 teaspoon red wine vinegar
salt and pepper
4 skinless, boneless chicken
   breasts

Grilled Chicken Breasts

Serve these chicken breasts hot or cold as an entrée, or in a salad or a sandwich.

• • •

1. Season chicken with salt and pepper. Combine all remaining ingredients except chicken. Pour marinade over chicken; marinate for 1 hour.

2. Remove chicken from marinade. Cook 4 minutes on each side on a grill or grill pan.

3. Internal temperature should be 165°F when chicken is cooked.

Serves 4

1 cold roasted chicken, bones
   and skin removed (see
   note)
1 cup mayonnaise
¼ cup diced celery
½ cup diced canned artichoke
   hearts
½ cup chopped walnuts
salt and pepper to taste

Chicken Salad

This recipe takes advantage of the rotisserie chicken that is available in grocery stores already cooked for you. Instead of purchasing a chicken, you could also cook your own chicken using the recipe for Oven-Roasted Whole Chicken (page 132). Serve on a croissant with lettuce or by itself with carrot sticks.

• • •

1. Dice chicken.

2. Combine all ingredients and season with salt and pepper.

How to Bone a Chicken Breast

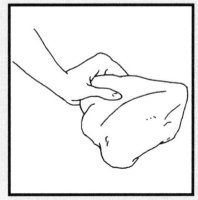

1 Place the breast skin-side down on a clean cutting board. The wider end should be nearest you.

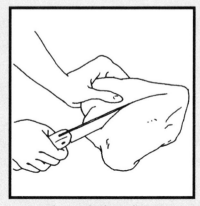

2 Cut through the white cartilage, starting from the V at the neck end.

3 Pick the breast up in both hands and bend the sides back to pop out the keel bone.

4 Loosen the meat from the bone. Run your thumbs around both sides and pull out the keel bone and cartilage.

5 Cut the breast meat from the bone by inserting the tip of the knife close to the long rib bone. Work one side at a time.

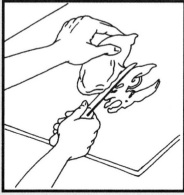

6 Cut and scrape all meat from the bone. Work from the ends of the wishbone.

Serves 4

2 boneless, skinless chicken
    breasts, diced
4 garlic cloves, sliced
1 teaspoon sesame oil
¼ cup sliced whole
    green onion
1 teaspoon cornstarch
1 tablespoon soy sauce
¼ cup hoisin sauce
1 teaspoon sugar
2 teaspoons sherry
2 tablespoons peanut oil
½ cup chicken broth
¼ cup diced fresh mushrooms
¼ cup diced canned water
    chestnuts
¼ cup frozen peas
8–12 lettuce cups, iceberg or
    butter lettuce
1 cup sliced almonds

Stir-Fried Lettuce Chicken Cups

*The cold crunch of lettuce contrasts with the warm, chunky filling
of juicy chicken bits in this recipe, once found only in Chinese restaurants.
It is messy to eat, but worth every moment!*

• • •

1. Preheat oven to 350°F. Lay the almonds out in an even layer on an ungreased baking sheet pan; bake for 10 minutes. Set aside.

2. Put chicken in a bowl with garlic, sesame oil, green onion, cornstarch, soy sauce, hoisin sauce, sugar, and sherry.

3. Heat wok or sauté pan and add peanut oil. Pour chicken mixture in and stir-fry for a minute. Add chicken broth, mushrooms, water chestnuts, and peas.

4. Cook while stirring until chicken is cooked and sauce is thickened.

5. Spoon filling into lettuce cups and sprinkle with almonds. Serve immediately.

Tandoori Chicken
Tandoori chicken is an Indian dish made from chicken that is marinated in yogurt, lime juice, and spices and is traditionally cooked in a clay oven. At home you can use a hot grill to achieve similar results.

Chicken Roulade with Mango, Spinach, and Red Bell Pepper

Serves 4

4 boneless, skinless chicken
   breasts, pounded thin
salt and pepper
8 fresh spinach leaves
4 slices mango
4 strips roasted red bell
   pepper
4 cups chicken broth

This is a fancy recipe to make for a dinner party using classic poaching technique. Any filling could be used, such as diced mushrooms or julienned carrots, leeks, and celery. Serve chicken roll cut on the bias to show the vibrant orange, green, and red filling. Rice and the coconut curry sauce below are the perfect complement to the chicken.

• • •

1. Lay chicken breasts out on plastic wrap and sprinkle them with salt and pepper.

2. Lay spinach on the middle of each breast; lay mango and pepper on top of spinach.

3. Roll each breast up so the mango and pepper are in the center. Wrap each breast individually in plastic wrap and foil. Twist the ends to make a tight sausage-like roll.

4. Combine chicken broth and 2 cups water in a 6-quart pot. Bring to a boil, and then reduce heat to simmer.

5. Drop chicken rolls into simmering liquid and poach for 10–15 minutes. Remove from liquid, peel off foil and plastic wrap, and cut each roll diagonally in half.

Coconut Curry Sauce

Combine 1 chopped shallot, 1 13.5-ounce can coconut milk (unsweetened), 1 teaspoon curry powder, and ½ cup chicken broth in a saucepan. Bring to a boil. Add ¼ cup cored, diced apple and ¼ cup diced banana. Turn down the heat and simmer until apples are tender. Purée in a blender, return to pot, reduce until thickened, and season with salt and white pepper.

How to Quarter a Whole Chicken

Place the chicken breast-side up on a clean cutting board.

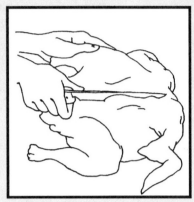

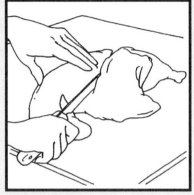

1 Cut in half along the breast bone with a sharp knife.

2 Pull the two halves apart. Break the ribs away from the backbone and finish cutting through the skin and meat with a knife to separate the halves.

3 Separate the thigh quarter from the breast quarter. Bend to locate the joint. Cut through the body above the joint and on through the joint to separate.

Serves 4

4 boneless, skinless chicken
    breasts
salt and pepper
4 fresh sage leaves
4 slices prosciutto
2 tablespoons butter
2 tablespoons olive oil

Chicken Saltimbocca

*This Italian classic is traditionally made with veal scallops
instead of the chicken in this recipe. Serve with Creamed Spinach (page 180)
and buttered fettuccine noodles for a complete meal.*

• • •

1. Pound the chicken breasts flat so they are the same thickness throughout.

2. Season chicken with salt and pepper.

3. Lay one sage leaf on each chicken breast and lay one slice of prosciutto on top of the sage leaf, covering the whole chicken breast.

4. Heat butter and oil in skillet.

5. Lay chicken in the skillet prosciutto-side down and sauté until crisp. Turn over and finish cooking on the other side.

Chicken Parmesan

Serve this chicken parmesan alone or with Caesar Salad (page 67),
Grilled Asparagus (page 183), and Focaccia (page 220) for a true Italian meal.

•   •   •

1. Preheat oven to 350°F. In a large bowl, combine breadcrumbs, Parmesan cheese, oregano, and pepper.

2. In a separate bowl, beat eggs with a whisk or fork. Put flour into another bowl.

3. Spread half of the tomato sauce on the bottom of a 9" x 13" baking dish.

4. Dip each chicken breast first in flour, then egg, then in the bread crumb mixture.

5. In a large sauté pan, heat the olive oil over medium-high heat. Fry the coated chicken breasts in heated olive oil, turning when bottom side of chicken is golden brown. Place browned chicken breast slices on top of the tomato sauce in the baking dish.

6. Cover chicken breasts with remaining tomato sauce. Top each chicken breast with a slice of mozzarella cheese and bake uncovered for 45 minutes.

Serves 4

4 boneless, skinless chicken breasts
½ cup flour mixed with 1 teaspoon salt
1 cup dry bread crumbs
1 cup grated Parmesan cheese
1 tablespoon dried oregano
¼ teaspoon pepper
1 egg
2 cups (1 16-ounce can) tomato sauce
½ cup olive oil
4 slices mozzarella cheese

Oven-Roasted Whole Chicken

*Quartered and served with Scalloped Potatoes (page 193) and a green salad,
this makes a satisfying bistro-style lunch or dinner any day of the year. Baked
Apples (page 272) make a nice dessert to finish the meal.*

• • •

1. Preheat oven to 400°F. Season inside of bird with salt and pepper, then
   put bay leaf and onion inside. Tuck wings under the back of the bird.

2. Mix together paprika, herbs, 1 teaspoon each salt and pepper, and rub
   the mixture all over the chicken's skin. Place chicken in a roasting pan,
   breast-side up.

3. Roast the chicken uncovered in the oven until you can move the legs
   easily and juices run clear, about 1½ hours.

Cornish Game Hen

*This small bird provides a perfect serving for one person. It can be stuffed with
poultry stuffing or other fillings such as green grapes, shrimp, or blueberries.*

• • •

1. Preheat oven to 400°F. Season inside of hens with salt and pepper,
   Place orange and onion pieces inside the hens.

2. Scatter leeks on the bottom of a roasting pan and set the hens on top
   of them. Rub breast skin with butter, and season with salt and pepper.

3. Roast until you can move the legs freely and juices run clear, about 40
   minutes.

Brine

*For a juicy bird, soak a whole chicken for 12 hours in this solution, then
rinse and roast the bird. Boil 1 gallon water; lower heat to medium-low.
Add ¾ cup salt, ½ cup sugar, and ¼ cup dark molasses; stir until dissolved and turn off heat. Chill brine before soaking the chicken.*

How to Cut Up a Whole Chicken

1 Place the chicken breast-side up on a clean cutting board. Cut through the skin and meat between the thighs and tail end of the body.

2 Grasp the legs in your hands and bend them back, while lifting the chicken, until the hip joints pop out.

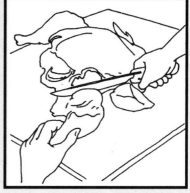

3 Cut the thigh from the body by cutting through the joint and remaining skin. The tip of the knife should point toward the tail end of the bird while making this cut.

4 Separate the legs and thighs. Bend the joint to locate it, then cut through it.

5 Cut the wings from the body. Pull the wings out slightly from the body and cut down through the body near the wing and through the joint, following its shape with the knife. Cut from the top down.

6 Separate the breast from the back. Hold the chicken up with its neck end on the board and cut through the joints along each side of the rib cage. Cut from the top toward the board.

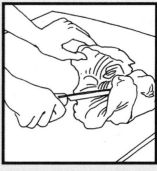

7 Place the breast skin-side down and cut through the white cartilage at the V of the neck. Grasp in both hands and bend the sides back to pop out the keel bone. Remove it. Cut the breast in half through the wishbone using the knife or kitchen scissors.

Serves 4

1 3-pound chicken, cut in 8
     pieces
1 cup all-purpose flour
1 teaspoon salt
1 teaspoon paprika
¼ teaspoon pepper
4 tablespoons butter
1 cup sliced onions
2 cups chicken broth
½ cup white grape juice
1 cup quartered mushrooms
1 bay leaf
½ cup heavy cream
salt and pepper to taste

Chicken Fricassee

*This is a comfort food recipe of braised chicken,
smothered in onions and mushrooms.*

• • •

1. On a dinner plate, mix together flour, 1 teaspoon salt, paprika, and pepper. Dredge chicken pieces in seasoned flour.

2. In a large skillet, melt butter over medium heat. Brown floured chicken pieces in butter. Remove from skillet; set aside.

3. Sauté the onions in the same pan, with more butter added if necessary. Pour the chicken broth and grape juice in the pan, stir, and then place the chicken back in the pan with the simmering sauce.

4. Add the mushrooms and the bay leaf. Cover and simmer for 45 minutes.

5. Take off the lid, remove the bay leaf, and stir in the heavy cream.

6. Simmer for 5 minutes. Season with salt and pepper to taste.

Duck Leg Confit

This is a way of cooking and preserving duck in fat so no air can get to the meat, thereby sealing out bacterial growth. Use this preparation on pizza and salad, in cassoulet (a traditional French dish composed of duck confit, sausage, and flageolet beans baked with a crust of breadcrumbs on the top), or warmed and served with parsnip purée, arugula, and prunes.

. . .

1. Mix salt, dried thyme, pepper, and allspice in a bowl.

2. Pack salt mixture over the entire surface of each duck leg, especially where the bone is, to draw out moisture. Put the duck legs in a glass dish, pour remaining salt mixture over them, and refrigerate for 24 hours. Turn legs every 6–8 hours.

3. Preheat oven to 275°F. Remove the duck legs from the refrigerator and wipe them clean of the salt mixture.

4. Pack legs tightly in a deep baking dish and pour the melted fat over them so they are completely covered with it. Add the bay leaves, juniper berries, and thyme.

5. Bake until the duck is tender when pierced with a fork, about 1½ hours. Remove duck from the fat; drain on a rack or on paper towels. Before serving, heat in a 400°F oven for 15 minutes. You also can take the meat off the bone and serve warm or cold.

Coq au Vin
Coq au vin is a traditional French dish made of chicken pieces stewed in red wine. Its original purpose was for tenderizing tough, old fowl. Do not use an aluminum pot when making it, because it will react with the wine and turn your chicken purple!

Serves 4

2 cups kosher salt
¼ cup dried thyme
2 tablespoons pepper
1 tablespoon ground allspice
8 duck legs
16 cups (8 pounds) duck or pork fat, melted (This is ordered from your butcher, even in grocery stores. It is measured after melting.)
2 bay leaves
2 sprigs thyme
2 juniper berries (found in the herbs section of the supermarket)

Serves 2

1 boneless whole duck breast
salt and pepper
1 shallot, chopped
1 tablespoon butter
1 fresh peach, chopped with
    peel on
2 tablespoons rice vinegar
1 tablespoon amaretto
    liqueur
½ cup chicken broth

Pan-Seared Duck Breast

Duck meat is good with fruit, and this recipe uses peaches in the sauce, which is finished in the same pan the duck was cooked in for enhanced duck flavor. Serve with Braised Red Cabbage (page 186) and polenta (page 104).

•   •   •

1. Preheat oven to 375°F.

2. Score the skin on duck breast, season both sides with salt and pepper, and sear it, skin-side down, in a sauté pan over medium-high heat for 3 minutes. Remove duck breast from sauté pan and place it, skin-side up, in a baking dish. Put the duck in the oven to finish cooking for about 5 minutes.

3. In the same sauté pan, cook the shallots in butter for 2 minutes; add peaches, vinegar, and amaretto.

4. Cook to reduce liquid by half. Add broth, and cook for 5 minutes more. Adjust seasoning with salt and pepper.

5. Slice the duck breast and fan the slices on a plate. Spoon the peach sauce over the meat.

Creamed Turkey Legs

Served on split Biscuits (page 214), this is comfort food to have when you are missing the warm flavors of Thanksgiving and don't have time to roast a turkey with all the trimmings. Cranberry sauce on the side is a nice, tart addition.

• • •

Serves 4

2 turkey legs
2 tablespoons butter
2 tablespoons flour
1 cup milk
1 sprig thyme
½ teaspoon pepper
salt to taste

1. Preheat oven to 350°F. Place turkey legs in a roasting pan. Roast about 1 hour, until a meat thermometer shows that the internal temperature is 165°F.

2. Take the meat off the bone; discard the skin and bones. Cut or tear the meat into bite-size pieces.

3. Melt butter in a skillet. Add flour; stir and cook for a few minutes. Add milk and thyme, and stir until smooth.

4. Add turkey; simmer until sauce is thickened. If it becomes too thick, add more milk and cook a little longer.

5. Remove from heat. Remove thyme sprig, and season creamed turkey with salt and pepper. To serve, spoon over split biscuits or buttered toast points.

Phony Abalone

Here's a way to turn chicken into something that doesn't "taste like chicken." Pound boneless, skinless chicken breasts thin and soak them in clam juice (bottled) for 2 days. Bread the breasts, sauté, and serve with tartar sauce and lemon wedges.

Turkey Burgers

*Serve these non–red-meat burgers on a bun, in the usual manner
of a beef burger, with a side of Macaroni Salad (page 62) and Sweet Potato
Fries (page 198) for a delicious change of pace. They can also
be served bun-less as an entrée with vegetables.*

• • •

1. Combine all ingredients in a bowl and mix thoroughly.

2. Form mixture into 4 patties, taking care not to compress them too much.

3. Grill or sauté burgers until cooked through, about 5 minutes per side.

Buffalo Wings

*These fiery wings are great to serve on game-day or at summertime cookouts. For
a cookout, simply grill the wings instead of baking them. If some guests or family
members don't like spicy foods, toss half of the wings in barbecue sauce instead.*

• • •

1. Preheat oven to 375°F. Combine the flour and salt in a large bowl. Toss chicken wings in flour mixture.

2. Shake off excess flour and put the wings on a foil-lined cookie sheet. Repeat in batches if all wings do not fit on one cookie sheet.

3. Bake wings for 30 minutes; remove from oven. Turn wings over on the cookie sheet and bake another 15 minutes.

4. In a large bowl, combine butter, garlic powder, Worcestershire Sauce and cayenne pepper sauce.

5. Remove cooked wings from oven; toss in the large bowl with sauce. Return coated wings to cookie sheet; bake for 15 minutes more.

CHAPTER 12
Seafood

Serves 4

½ cup all-purpose flour
1 teaspoon salt
1 teaspoon lemon pepper
16 sea scallops
1 tablespoon olive oil
2 tablespoons butter
1 shallot, chopped
¼ cup chopped leeks (white
    and light green parts
    only—discard dark
    green part)
2 tablespoons diced red bell
    pepper
¼ cup white wine or white
    grape juice
¼ cup heavy cream
½ teaspoon grated
    lemon zest
salt and pepper to taste

Pan-Seared Sea Scallops

Sea scallops are a sweet, creamy delight when cooked properly. Take care not to overcook them, or they will become rubbery. This recipe for scallops in a light, lemony cream sauce is best served with linguine or fettuccine.

• • •

1. Mix together the flour, salt, and lemon pepper.

2. Dip the scallops in the flour to coat both sides, shaking off excess (a process called "dredging"). Heat a large sauté pan over medium-high heat.

3. Add oil to preheated sauté pan, then add the scallops. Sear the scallops in oil for about 3 minutes per side; they should get a nice crust on them.

4. Remove the scallops from pan to warmed plates.

5. In the same pan, sauté shallots, leeks, and red bell pepper in the leftover oil in the pan. Add wine or juice, and simmer to reduce liquid by half. Add cream and lemon zest; and reduce by half again. Season with salt and pepper. To serve, pour sauce over scallops.

Tartar Sauce
Tartar sauce is traditionally served with fish. It is a mayonnaise-based cold sauce with lemon and diced pickles or pickle relish.

Lemon-Scented Bay Scallops

*Tender bay scallops are baked in gratin dishes in this easy and delicious recipe.
Serve with Rice Pilaf (page 169) and Minted Peas (page 178).*

• • •

1. Preheat oven to 400°F.

2. Butter 4 individual gratin dishes with ½ tablespoon butter each.

3. Arrange ½ pound scallops in each gratin dish, then sprinkle them with lemon juice. Season scallops with salt and pepper.

4. Combine bread crumbs with lemon zest and parsley; sprinkle scallops with bread-crumb mixture.

5. Bake gratin dishes in the oven for 12 minutes.

Serves 4

2 tablespoons butter
2 pounds bay scallops
2 tablespoons lemon juice
salt and pepper
½ cup dry bread crumbs
1 tablespoon grated
    lemon zest
2 tablespoons chopped fresh
    parsley

Shrimp Tempura

*Serve these crunchy morsels as an appetizer with soy sauce for dipping, or serve as
an entrée with vegetables and rice. Some vegetables, such as asparagus, green
beans, and carrot slices, can be cooked in the same way as the shrimp in this recipe.*

• • •

1. Whisk beer into flour until smooth. Stir in salt.

2. Heat 4 cups vegetable oil in a 6-quart soup pot or a deep fryer to 375°F.

3. Dip shrimp individually in batter. Let excess batter drip off, and then carefully drop the shrimp into the hot oil.

4. Cook battered shrimp about 3 minutes. Remove from oil using tongs or a slotted spoon.

5. Drain on paper towels or brown paper; serve immediately.

Serves 4

¾ cup beer
¾ cup all-purpose flour
¾ teaspoon salt
4 cups vegetable oil for
    deep-frying
24 large uncooked shrimp,
    shelled

1 cup flour
1 teaspoon salt
1 teaspoon paprika
½ teaspoon pepper
4 cups vegetable oil for
    deep-frying
2 pounds thawed calamari,
    cut into rings
lemon wedges

Fried Calamari

*Calamari (squid) can be bought cleaned and frozen for this recipe.
All you need to do is thaw them, cut them into rings (if they are still in their
tubular shape), and flash fry them. Serve with Quick Aioli (page 34) or
Marinara Sauce (page 152).*

• • •

1. Mix flour with salt, paprika, and pepper.

2. Heat 4 cups vegetable oil in a 6-quart soup pot or a deep fryer to 365°F.

3. Toss a handful of calamari in flour mixture and shake off excess.

4. Deep fry until golden brown, about 3 minutes. Drain on paper towels.

5. Repeat with remaining calamari. Serve immediately with lemon wedges to sprinkle calamari with lemon juice.

Rémoulade Sauce
Rémoulade is a traditional French sauce that is served with fish and seafood. It is similar to tartar sauce, but also contains hardboiled egg, capers, Dijon mustard, parsley, and cayenne pepper.

Citrus Shrimp Brochettes

This recipe can be served on salad greens that have been dressed with citrus vinaigrette, or as an entrée with rice and vegetables.

• • •

1. Combine juices, oil, zests, salt, and pepper in a bowl or plastic bag.

2. Marinate shrimp in juice mixture for at least an hour.

3. Thread 6 shrimp onto two parallel skewers, so that 2 skewers go through each shrimp. Repeat 3 more times.

4. Grill skewered shrimp for about 3 minutes per side.

5. Serve warm.

Serves 4

¼ cup orange juice
¼ cup lemon juice
¼ cup lime juice
¼ cup olive oil
1 teaspoon orange zest
1 teaspoon lemon zest
1 teaspoon lime zest
salt and pepper to taste
24 uncooked shrimp, peeled
8 bamboo skewers,
    presoaked in water

Fish Tacos

Fish tacos are healthier than beef tacos because fish is not high in saturated fat, and red meat is. Another reason is that fish tacos don't typically have cheese, and they taste best with healthy toppings of cabbage and fresh Tomato Salsa (page 42).

• • •

1. Warm tortillas wrapped in paper towels in microwave. Discard paper towels and wrap in foil to keep them warm.

2. Cut the fish into strips, dredge in cornmeal mixture, and sear in olive oil for about 5 minutes. (If you like, you could grill the fish instead.)

3. Break the cooked fish into chunks; and put chunks in warm tortillas.

4. Squeeze a lime wedge on the fish, then top with cabbage, salsa, avocados, and sour cream.

Taco Tip
Sometimes soft tacos get a little too juicy and they fall apart while you are eating them. Try using two tortillas to help prevent this problem. It also makes a more filling taco.

Serves 4

8 corn tortillas
1 pound firm white fish such
    as halibut or snapper
½ cup cornmeal, seasoned
    with ½ teaspoon salt and
    ¼ teaspoon pepper
1 tablespoon olive oil
lime wedges
1 cup shredded purple
    cabbage
1 cup fresh Tomato Salsa
    (page 42)
¼ cup diced avocados
¼ cup sour cream

Serves 2

2 live 1-2 pound lobsters
8 tablespoons salt
5 tablespoons butter, melted

Boiled Lobster

Cooking live lobsters from the supermarket is cheaper than
if you were to order lobster at a restaurant, but it can be a bit of an experience!
Try rubbing the forehead of the lobster, applying pressure with your thumb,
to calm or hypnotize it before you place it in the boiling water.

• • •

1. Fill an 8 quart or bigger stockpot or soup pot ¾ full with salted water. Make sure that you have enough water to completely cover lobsters (use two pots if necessary). Add 1 tablespoon of salt per quart of water.

2. Bring to a boil and pick up the lobster by the top of the body and put it head first into the boiling water until it is completely under water.

3. Put the lid on the pot and boil for 18 minutes. Do not remove from water until the shell turns bright red.

4. Remove from the pot and serve hot or plunge in ice water for chilled dishes. To serve hot, use a nutcracker to crack the shell and pull or push out the meat inside. Dip hot lobster meat in melted butter.

Eating Lobster
Stay away from the tomalley, which is the lobster's liver (it is green). You may also want to avoid eating the red roe, or unfertilized eggs, that you will find in a female lobster, although it is not harmful and many lobster enthusiasts enjoy eating it.

Lobster Rolls

These are standard fare on the coast in New England, where they are served without pomp and circumstance from beachside lunch shacks. They are delicious, simple sandwiches of lobster salad served on special hot dog buns, usually split down the middle from the top. Purchase lobster from the grocery store fish counter. They will steam the lobster for you if you ask.

• • •

1. Butter the insides of the buns and toast them on a griddle or skillet.

2. Combine lobster meat, mayonnaise, celery, salt, and pepper, and mix well.

3. Spoon lobster salad onto toasted buns.

Serves 4

4 hot dog buns
2 tablespoons soft butter
1 cup cooked lobster meat chunks
¼ cup mayonnaise
¼ cup diced celery
salt and pepper to taste

Chilled Lobster Salad

This recipe can be scaled up for more people by using ½ lobster for each person. Lobsters can be cooked by the seafood department of most supermarkets.

• • •

1. Toss greens and lobster meat with vinaigrette, divide evenly, and arrange on plates.

2. Scatter cherry tomatoes around greens.

3. Mix together mayonnaise and basil. Spoon mayonnaise mixture onto plates for dipping.

Serves 2

2 cups arugula or baby mixed salad greens
1 cooked and shelled lobster, chilled
¼ cup Vinaigrette (page 71)
½ cup cherry tomatoes, cut in half
½ cup mayonnaise
5 chopped fresh basil leaves

1 1½-pound piece of halibut
1 teaspoon olive oil
salt and pepper
½ cup diced papaya
¼ cup diced red onion
¼ cup diced jalapeño pepper
¼ cup diced red bell pepper
2 tablespoons lime juice
2 tablespoons chopped fresh
    cilantro

Halibut with Papaya Salsa

*This is a light fish dish that is simple to make. The fish is baked
and the salsa is put together at the last minute. Serve this with roast fingerling
potatoes and sautéed green beans for a lovely, easily prepared meal.
Leftovers make good Fish Tacos (page 143).*

• • •

1. Preheat oven to 350°F.

2. Brush halibut with oil, sprinkle with salt and pepper, and bake in the oven
   for about 15 minutes, or until fish flakes when you test it with a fork.

3. Combine papaya, onion, peppers, lime juice, and cilantro. Season with
   salt and pepper.

4. Spoon salsa onto baked fish before serving.

Salsa Suggestions

*Salsa can be made with a variety of fruits, not just papaya. Try some of
the following in fresh salsa: mangos, nectarines, peaches, plums, per-
simmons, apples, pears, guavas, and bananas. You can also use different acids, such as flavored vinegars, lemon juice, grapefruit juice,
lime juice, or orange juice.*

Potato-Crusted Salmon

*This is a quick and easy way to make an elegant dinner entrée.
Serve it with Mashed Potatoes (page 188) and Lemon Dill Peas and Carrots
(page 177) any night of the week.*

• • •

1. Preheat oven to 350°F.

2. Place fish, skin-side down, on an oiled baking dish.

3. Mix honey with mustard and spread it on the flesh side of the fish.

4. Combine bread crumbs, potato chips, and dill. Sprinkle the mustard-coated fish with all of this mixture.

5. Drizzle melted butter on top of the crumb mixture; then bake fish for 20 minutes. To serve, lift fish off the skin and place fish on individual plates.

Serves 4

1 1½-pound side of salmon, skin-on
½ teaspoon honey
1 tablespoon Dijon mustard
½ cup dry bread crumbs
½ cup crushed potato chips
1 teaspoon dried dill
2 tablespoons butter, melted

Grilled Tuna

*Use this instead of the traditional tuna confit in the classic Nicoise Salad,
or try it in Fish Tacos (page 143). It also makes a nice sandwich on
sesame seed Focaccia (page 220) with ponzu sauce for dipping.
Ponzu sauce is a light, soy sauce–based condiment flavored with rice vinegar
and dried fish flakes that is used for dipping in Japanese cuisine.*

• • •

1. Brush tuna steaks with oil. Season with salt and pepper.

2. Grill on both sides for about 7 minutes total.

3. Serve with salsa on top.

Serves 4

4 Ahi tuna steaks
olive oil
salt and pepper
Tomato Salsa (page 42)

4 trout filets with skin on
1 teaspoon vegetable oil
salt and pepper
½ cup chopped pecans
½ cup dry bread crumbs
¼ cup butter, melted

Broiled Pecan Trout

*For variety, other nuts, such as almonds, macadamias, or hazelnuts,
can be substituted for the pecans in this recipe.*

• • •

1. Preheat oven to 400°F. Place fish, skin-side down, on a baking tray that has been rubbed with vegetable oil. Season with salt and pepper.

2. Combine nuts with bread crumbs; coat fish flesh with the mixture. Drizzle melted butter over nut crust.

3. Bake for about 10 minutes, then broil for a minute or so to brown the crust. Serve one filet per person (one half of each fish). Skin can be eaten or the flesh can be eaten easily off the skin.

Nicoise Salad
Nicoise salad is a classic composed salad (a salad that has distinctive individual parts as opposed to a tossed salad) that contains tuna, haricots vertes (tiny green beans), boiled new potatoes, hardboiled eggs, anchovies, tomatoes, and nicoise olives. It is named after Nice, the area in France where the olives come from.

Crab Cakes

Crab cakes can be served a variety of ways, even as a sandwich.
Tiny ones can go into a po'boy, or they can be served as hors d'oeuvres.
Rémoulade, tartar sauce, lemon butter sauce, and beurre blanc
are all different sauces that can be served with crab cakes.

• • •

1. Pick out and discard any shells or cartilage that may be left in crabmeat.

2. Combine crabmeat, mayonnaise, red bell pepper, green onions, lemon juice, and bread in a bowl until well mixed. Season with salt and pepper.

3. Put the egg in one bowl and bread crumbs in another. Shape crab mixture into patties or cakes and dip them first in egg, then in bread crumbs.

4. Fry the crab cakes in butter until browned on both sides.

5. Serve warm.

Serves 4

1 pound crabmeat (fresh from the grocery store fish counter or canned is fine)
½ cup mayonnaise
¼ cup diced red bell pepper
¼ cup sliced whole green onions
1 tablespoon lemon juice
1 slice white bread, soaked in milk and squeezed dry
salt and pepper
1 egg, beaten
2 cups dry bread crumbs
butter to sauté crabcakes in

Serves 4

1 pound crabmeat
½ cup dry bread crumbs
½ cup Béchamel Sauce
(page 207)
¼ cup heavy cream
1 teaspoon cayenne
pepper sauce
1 egg
1 clove garlic, minced
¼ cup chopped green bell
pepper
2 tablespoons butter
salt and pepper

Deviled Crab

*This is a crab casserole with a little bit of spicy heat, which is
where the name "deviled" comes from. Adjust the heat according to your own
taste by adding or subtracting cayenne pepper sauce.*

• • •

1. Preheat oven to 400°F. Butter a 2-quart baking dish.

2. Combine crabmeat, bread crumbs, béchamel sauce, heavy cream, cayenne pepper sauce, egg, garlic, and green bell pepper until thoroughly mixed.

3. Season with salt and pepper and put mixture into buttered baking dish.

4. Bake for 15 minutes, or until browned and bubbly.

Crab Louis

*Crab Louis is a salad featuring Dungeness crabmeat and Louis dressing,
which is sort of like a cross between rémoulade sauce and Thousand
Island dressing. It was invented in the late 1800s or early 1900s on the
West Coast, where Dungeness crab comes from.*

CHAPTER 13
Pasta and Pizza

½ chopped onion
2 cloves garlic, minced
¼ cup olive oil
1 28-ounce can crushed
    tomatoes
¼ cup chopped fresh basil
    leaves
pinch sugar
salt and pepper to taste

Marinara Sauce

This is a tomato sauce that does not cook for very long, so it retains the garden-fresh flavor of the tomatoes and herbs in it.

•   •   •

1. On medium-low heat, sauté the onions and garlic in oil until soft.

2. Add tomatoes and cook for about 5 minutes.

3. Add basil, sugar, salt, and pepper and cook for 10 minutes.

4. Adjust seasoning with salt and pepper if necessary.

Bolognese (Meat Sauce)

This is a tomato-based sauce with ground beef in it.
The meaty flavor permeates the sauce because the meat is simmered in it.
Serve this sauce on ravioli or spaghetti for a classic pasta meal.

• • •

Serves 4

½ large onion, chopped
2 cloves garlic, minced
2 tablespoons olive oil
1 pound ground beef
1 28-ounce can crushed
  tomatoes
1 teaspoon dried oregano
1 teaspoon dried basil
1 teaspoon salt
½ teaspoon pepper

1. Sauté onions and garlic in olive oil until soft.

2. Add ground beef to the pan and cook, stirring occasionally, until brown.

3. Pour in the crushed tomatoes and bring to a simmer.

4. Stir in the herbs, salt, and pepper, and then simmer uncovered for an hour.

5. Adjust seasoning with salt and pepper.

Ravioli

Ravioli are usually square pasta pillows stuffed with various fillings. Two perennial favorites are ricotta cheese and ground beef. Other pasta shapes are circles and half-moons, and other fillings can be pumpkin, spinach, prosciutto, and even raw egg yolks.

Serves 4

2 cloves garlic
⅓ cup pine nuts or walnuts
2 cups packed fresh basil
    leaves
½ cup olive oil
¼ cup grated Parmesan
    cheese
½ teaspoon salt
1 teaspoon plain yogurt

Pesto

*This basil sauce is traditionally made using a mortar and pestle
to pound it into a paste. This recipe uses a food processor for an easier
preparation, but you could also use a blender. Pesto can be used as a pasta
sauce, a sandwich spread, or a stuffing enhancement. It also is the perfect
condiment to stir into Minestrone (page 52).*

• • •

1. Preheat oven to 350°F. Lay the pine nuts or walnuts out in an even layer on an ungreased baking sheet pan; bake for 10 minutes. Set aside.

2. In a food processor, chop the garlic and nuts together to make a paste.

3. Add the basil and 2 tablespoons of the oil to the food processor and process with the nuts and garlic.

4. With the processor running and the pour hole on the top open, pour the rest of the oil in a thin stream into the basil mixture to form a purée.

5. Add the Parmesan cheese and salt, and process to blend.

6. Store with a teaspoon of plain yogurt stirred into the pesto to prevent it from turning black.

Alfredo

This creamy, cheesy sauce is most commonly served with fettuccine noodles. Dress it up by adding sautéed shrimp or sliced, grilled chicken to the finished pasta and sauce. Green spinach fettuccine noodles are delicious with this sauce, and the contrasting colors add visual appeal.

•   •   •

1. In a 12" pan, sauté garlic in butter and olive oil for 1 minute, then sprinkle with flour.

2. Stir and cook for 1 minute; then add milk and cook, stirring constantly, until sauce thickens and is bubbling.

3. Add cream and cook for a minute or two.

4. Add Parmesan cheese and stir to make a smooth creamy sauce.

5. Season sauce with salt and pepper. Serve over pasta.

Manicotti

The Italian word manicotti *means "little sleeves" in English. In pasta it refers to a stuffed tube of cooked pasta that is covered with sauce and baked. Ricotta cheese is the usual filling.*

Serves 4

2 cloves garlic, minced
4 tablespoons butter
2 tablespoons olive oil
1 tablespoon all-
    purpose flour
1 cup milk
½ cup heavy cream
1 cup grated Parmesan
    cheese
salt and pepper to taste

6 slices pancetta, chopped
1½ cups heavy cream
4 eggs
1 cup Parmesan cheese
¼ cup frozen peas
4 cups cooked linguini
    noodles
salt and pepper to taste
2 tablespoons chopped fresh
    parsley

Carbonara

This recipe is very rich, and although you wouldn't want to eat it every day, it is worth the occasional indulgence. Pancetta is an Italian bacon that is cured but not smoked. Regular bacon may be substituted for the pancetta.

• • •

1. Cook the pancetta in a sauté pan until crisp. Add cream and turn off the heat while you do the next step.

2. Separate egg whites from egg yolks by straining the white through your cupped fingers over a bowl. The bowl will catch the white, leaving the yolk in your fingers. Whisk the 4 egg yolks and Parmesan cheese together in a bowl; discard egg whites.

3. Ladle about ½ cup of the warm cream from the pan into the egg yolk mixture to temper it. This will bring the yolks to a temperature closer to the cream and bacon so the yolks will not curdle when you add them.

4. Pour the yolk mixture into the pan with the bacon and cream and stir to combine. Add peas and cook for a few minutes while stirring, then add cooked linguini and toss to coat with sauce.

5. Remove from heat, season with salt and pepper, and toss in chopped parsley.

Primavera

Primavera *means "spring" in Italian, and this pasta dish is loaded with fresh vegetables that would be available in spring. A light cream sauce (compared to Alfredo or Carbonara) is the vehicle for the veggies. Serve it with farfalle (butterfly or bow-tie shaped pasta) for a pretty presentation.*

• • •

1. In a 6-quart soup pot, sauté onions, carrots, and red bell pepper in oil until tender.

2. Add chicken broth, asparagus, and broccoli. Simmer uncovered for 5 minutes.

3. Add cream and peas; simmer for 5 minutes more.

4. Stir in Parmesan cheese and remove from heat.

5. Season with salt and pepper. Serve sauce over cooked pasta.

Cannelloni

The Italian term cannelloni *loosely translates to "hollow canes." It refers to either a pasta sheet or crepe that is rolled into a tube around a filling of meat or cheese or any combination of meat and cheese.*

Serves 4

½ cup diced onion
½ cup diced carrot
¼ cup diced red bell pepper
2 tablespoons olive oil
½ cup chicken broth
1 cup fresh asparagus spears,
    cut into 1" pieces
1 cup broccoli florets
½ cup heavy cream
½ cup frozen peas
½ cup grated Parmesan
    cheese
salt and pepper to taste

Serves 4

2 cloves garlic, minced
¼ cup olive oil
1 28-ounce can crushed
    tomatoes
1 teaspoon dried crushed red
    pepper
½ teaspoon dried oregano
1 cup oil-cured black olives,
    chopped coarse
5 anchovies, chopped
salt and pepper to taste
2 tablespoons drained capers
2 tablespoons chopped fresh
    parsley

Serves 4

5 cloves garlic, minced
¼ cup olive oil
½ cup homemade or panko
    bread crumbs
1 pound spaghetti, cooked
salt and pepper to taste
2 tablespoons grated
    Parmesan cheese
2 tablespoons chopped fresh
    parsley

Putanesca

This is a spicy and pungent tomato-based sauce made with capers, black olives, and anchovies. Serve it over cooked pasta such as spaghetti, linguini, or fettuccine, along with a green salad and crusty bread.

• • •

1. In a 6-quart soup pot, sauté garlic in oil for a few minutes.

2. Add tomatoes, red pepper, and oregano, and cook over medium heat for 10 minutes.

3. Add capers, black olives, and anchovies and cook for another 5 minutes.

4. Season sauce with salt (if necessary) and pepper.

5. Toss cooked pasta in the sauce, and top with chopped fresh parsley.

Aglio Olio

This is the simplest of all pasta dishes. The quality of bread crumbs matters, so try to make your own if possible by processing chunks of Italian or French bread in a food processor until you have bread crumbs. Lay them out on a baking sheet pan to air dry for one hour. They may also be toasted in a preheated 350°F oven for 10-15 minutes.

• • •

1. Sauté garlic in oil for a few minutes. Add bread crumbs and lightly brown them in the garlic oil over medium heat for about 5 minutes.

2. Toss cooked spaghetti with the garlic mixture; season with salt and pepper to taste.

3. Serve with Parmesan cheese and parsley sprinkled on top.

Gnocchi

Gnocchi are little pasta dumplings made from potatoes. They need to be cooked in boiling water for 5–10 minutes. Serve with any sauce (tomato, alfredo, pesto) or a mixture of melted butter and dry bread crumbs.

• • •

1. Scoop the cooked potato flesh out of the skin and put it through a potato ricer or food mill (or just mash it with a fork or potato masher).

2. In a bowl, lightly toss the flour and salt with the riced potatoes.

3. Make a well in the center of the potato mixture and put the egg in it. Gradually incorporate the potato mixture into the egg to make a dough that comes together. Roll dough into 1-inch-thick logs, and cut 1-inch pieces off the logs. These are your gnocchi dumplings ready to be boiled.

Tortellini

Tortellini are circles of pasta that have been topped with a meat or cheese filling, folded in half and then pinched into a ring. They resemble little belly buttons.

Serves 4

1 large potato (about 1 pound), baked
¾ cup all-purpose flour
½ teaspoon salt
1 egg, beaten

Serves 12

5 cups Tomato Sauce
  (page 205)
1 pound ground beef,
  browned and drained
1-pound box lasagna noodles
3 eggs
16 ounces ricotta cheese
2 cups shredded mozzarella
  cheese
½ cup chopped fresh parsley
½ cup grated Parmesan
  cheese
salt and pepper to taste

Lasagna

This is a crowd-pleaser, full of meat and cheese.
For a complete meal, serve with a green salad and garlic bread.
Leftovers can be wrapped in individual portions and frozen for 1 month.

• • •

1. Preheat oven to 350°F. Oil a lasagna (baking) pan and spread 1 cup tomato sauce on the bottom. Mix the remaining tomato sauce with the cooked ground beef. Set aside.

2. Cook the lasagna noodles in boiling water. (Be sure to take them out before they are completely done—about 1 minute before package instructions suggest—so they don't overcook when you bake the lasagna.) Place one layer of noodles over the sauce layer in the pan.

3. In a bowl combine the eggs, ricotta, and 1 cup mozzarella cheese until well blended. Stir in the parsley and salt and pepper to taste.

4. Spread half of the ricotta mixture over the noodles in the pan. Top the ricotta with a layer of noodles. Ladle 2 cups of the meat sauce over the noodles; top with another layer of noodles.

5. Spread the remaining ricotta mixture over the noodles. Top with the last of the noodles. Ladle the remaining meat sauce over the noodles.

6. Scatter the remaining mozzarella cheese over the sauce; sprinkle it with the Parmesan cheese. Bake for 1 hour and 25 minutes.

Spaghetti and Meatballs

This is a recipe for a favorite comfort food for all ages. The meatballs can also be used to make Meatball Sandwiches (page 99).

• • •

1. In a large pot, heat the tomato sauce to a simmer while assembling the meatballs.

2. To make the meatballs: Combine ground beef in a bowl with the remaining ingredients (except for the spaghetti).

3. Shape meat mixture into 2-inch balls and drop them into the simmering sauce.

4. Simmer uncovered for 1½ hours, stirring gently from time to time.

5. Serve over cooked spaghetti.

Penne

Penne is dried tubular pasta, usually with ridges, that has been cut diagonally so each piece has pointed ends like a quill pen tip. They are perfect for baking with sauce because they hold up and don't get mushy.

Serves 4

4 cups Tomato Sauce
   (page 205)
1 pound ground beef
1 egg
1 slice white bread, torn into
   pieces
¼ cup chopped onion
2 tablespoons chopped fresh
   parsley
2 cloves garlic, minced
¼ cup grated Parmesan
   cheese
1 pound spaghetti, cooked

½ cup semolina flour
½ cup all-purpose flour
½ teaspoon salt
1 egg, beaten
2 teaspoons water

Pasta Dough

*This is a recipe for homemade fresh pasta. It needs only a brief
3–5 minutes of cooking time in boiling water. A pasta machine
is best for rolling this dough thin enough.*

• • •

1. Combine flours and salt in a large bowl. Using your fingers, make a well in the center.

2. Combine egg with water and pour into the well in the flour mixture. Gradually bring the flour into the egg with a fork to form the dough. When dough comes together, press it together with your hands to form a ball and transfer it to a lightly floured surface. Knead dough for 10 minutes by folding dough and pressing it down with your hands, adding flour sparingly if dough is too sticky. Wrap in plastic.

3. Let dough rest 45 minutes before rolling as thinly as possible with a pasta machine or rolling pin. If you're using a rolling pin, slice pasta thinly with a sharp knife when your dough is about $1/16$" thick.

4. Cook pasta in salted boiling water for 3–5 minutes. You will know it is done when the pasta floats to the top of the water.

Herb Pasta Dough

This is fresh pasta dough with fresh herbs added.
The flavor is subtle and delicious. Use any herb you want instead
of or in addition to the rosemary in this recipe.

• • •

Serves 2

½ cup semolina flour
½ cup all-purpose flour
½ teaspoon salt
2 teaspoons minced fresh
   rosemary
1 egg, beaten
2 teaspoons water

1. In a bowl, combine flours, salt, and rosemary. Using your fingers, make a well in the center of the mixture.

2. Combine egg with water and pour into the well in the flour mixture. Gradually bring the flour into the egg with a fork to form the dough. When dough comes together, press it together with your hands to form a ball and transfer it to a lightly floured surface. Knead dough for 10 minutes by folding dough and pressing it down with your hands, adding flour sparingly if dough is too sticky. Wrap in plastic.

3. Let dough rest 45 minutes before rolling as thinly as possible with a pasta machine or rolling pin. If you're using a rolling pin, slice pasta thinly with a sharp knife when your dough is about 1/16" thick.

4. Cook pasta in salted boiling water for 3–5 minutes. You will know it is done when the pasta floats to the top of the water.

½ recipe Pizza Dough
(page 221)
1 tablespoon olive oil
1 10-ounce can tomato sauce
4 cups shredded mozzarella
cheese

Classic Pizza

Pizza is not nearly as difficult to make as you may imagine, and makes for a quick meal that will satisfy your whole family. Experiment with toppings like feta cheese, spinach, broccoli, cooked sausage, or grilled chicken.

• • •

1. Preheat oven to 475°F. Lightly flour a large surface. Using a rolling pin, roll the pizza dough out into a 12" circle, flipping the dough over occasionally so that it does not stick to your surface.

2. Transfer the circle of dough onto a lightly oiled pizza pan or cookie sheet.

3. Use a ladle or spoon to spread tomato sauce over the dough. Leave a 1" border of dough for the crust.

4. Sprinkle the cheese evenly over the sauce.

5. Bake for 15 minutes, or until cheese is melted and bubbly and the crust is lightly browned.

Hawaiian Pizza

*While the idea of serving ham and pineapple on a pizza may seem odd,
the combination makes for an unusual and delicious blend of flavors.
Both the pineapple and the ham are slightly sweet and work
well with the saltiness of the cheese.*

• • •

Serves 4

½ recipe Pizza Dough
  (page 221)
1 tablespoon olive oil
1 10-ounce can tomato sauce
3 cups shredded mozzarella
  cheese
4 slices ham, chopped
½ cup pineapple chunks
¼ cup sliced red onion
¼ cup diced green pepper

1. Preheat oven to 475°F. Lightly flour a large surface. Using a rolling pin, roll the pizza dough out into a 12" circle, flipping the dough over occasionally so that it does not stick to your surface.

2. Transfer the circle of dough onto a lightly oiled pizza pan or cookie sheet.

3. Use a ladle or spoon to spread tomato sauce over the dough. Leave a 1" border of dough for the crust.

4. Sprinkle the cheese evenly over the sauce.

5. Cover the cheese with the ham, pineapple, red onion, and green pepper.

6. Bake for 20 minutes, or until cheese is melted and bubbly and the crust is lightly browned.

Serves 4

½ recipe Pizza Dough
  (page 221)
¼ cup cornmeal
¼ cup olive oil
½ cup (half of 18-ounce can)
  canned tomato sauce
1 10-ounce can diced
  tomatoes, drained
2 cups shredded mozzarella
  cheese
½ cup sliced pepperoni

Chicago Pan Pizza

*This recipe is for a style of pizza made famous by the city of Chicago.
The Chicago-style deep-dish pan pizza, which originated in
Chicago in the 1940s, is a pizza with a deep crust surrounding layers of sauce,
cheese, and plenty of toppings.*

. . .

1. Preheat oven to 425°F. Coat the bottom of a 9" cake pan with half of the olive oil and all of the cornmeal.

2. Press dough in pan to cover the bottom and go all the way up the sides, like a pie crust.

3. Cover the bottom of the dough with cheese.

4. Cover the cheese with pepperoni.

5. Put tomato sauce on the pepperoni. Cover the top with the diced tomatoes. Drizzle with the rest of the olive oil.

6. Bake for 35 minutes, or until cheese is melted and bubbly and the crust is lightly browned.

CHAPTER 14
Rice and Beans

Serves 4

1 cup diced onion
8 tablespoons butter
2 cups arborio rice
3 cups chicken broth
3 cups water
6 tablespoons grated
    Parmesan cheese
¼ teaspoon pepper
salt to taste

Risotto

*Risotto is a versatile recipe that serves as a base for many side dishes.
After the rice is cooked you can add cheese or seasonal cooked vegetables,
such as mushrooms, butternut squash, or asparagus. Arborio rice must be
used for this recipe because it has more starch, which provides
the velvety texture to the finished dish.*

• • •

1. In a large pot, sauté the onion in the butter until translucent, about 5 minutes.

2. Add rice to onion and sauté for a few minutes.

3. In a separate bowl, combine water and chicken broth. Add ½ cup broth to rice mixture, stirring constantly over medium-high heat until most of the liquid evaporates. Repeat with the rest of the broth mixture in ½ cup increments. It will take about 20 minutes.

4. Remove from heat and stir in the Parmesan cheese, pepper, and salt.

Sticky Rice
Sticky rice is a rice containing higher amounts of gluten than long grain. It is usually cooked by steaming. When it is chilled it can be mixed with a little rice wine and used to make sushi rolls.

Rice Pilaf

This recipe is great for times when you want more than plain rice for a side dish. It is also good as a bed for stewed dishes. Try it with Chicken Fricassee (page 134), Broiled Pecan Trout (page 148), or Pot Roast (page 117).

• • •

1. Preheat oven to 350°F.

2. In a saucepan over medium heat, melt butter. Sauté the onion in butter until tender.

3. Add rice; sauté for 3–5 minutes with the onion.

4. Pour rice mixture into a 9" x 13" baking dish. Add chicken broth, salt, pepper, and bay leaf. Stir to incorporate.

5. Cover and bake for 45 minutes. Remove bay leaf before serving.

Persian Rice
Persian rice has dried fruits and nuts in it, such as apricots and pistachios, and it is cooked so that it sticks to the bottom of the pot and forms a crunchy delicious crust when turned out.

Serves 4

8 tablespoons unsalted butter
½ cup diced onion
1 cup long-grain rice
12 ounces low-sodium chicken broth
½ teaspoon salt
¼ teaspoon white pepper
1 bay leaf

Wild Rice

*Wild rice is a delicious alternative to regular white rice.
This recipe calls for more water than usual for rice, because more liquid
is needed to cook wild rice than white rice.*

• • •

1. In a large sauté pan, sauté the onion, carrot, and celery in the olive oil until tender.

2. Add the wild rice to the sautéed vegetables and stir over medium heat for a few minutes. This scratches the outer husk of the rice so that the liquid can be absorbed more easily.

3. Pour the rice and vegetables into a baking dish.

4. Add the broth, thyme, salt, and pepper; stir to incorporate.

5. Cover and bake for 45 minutes to 1 hour.

Wild Rice Salad

*This is made from the Wild Rice (above) while it is still warm.
The salad is then chilled and served cold. It is good for lunch as a side dish
with a sandwich, or as ⅓ of a salad trio plate with Potato Salad (page 63) and
Strawberry Spinach Salad (page 66).*

• • •

1. Mix everything together while the wild rice is still warm, so that the rice can absorb the most flavor.

2. Chill mixture.

3. Adjust seasoning. Serve cold.

Rice Stuffing

You can use this to stuff roast Cornish Game Hens (page 132) or trout.

• • •

1. Preheat oven to 350°F. Lay the almonds out in an even layer on an ungreased baking sheet pan; bake for 10 minutes. Set aside to cool. Chop cooled almonds.

2. Combine all ingredients.

3. Season to taste with salt and pepper.

4. Use to stuff poultry, pork, fish, or vegetables before baking.

Serves 4

2 cups cooked white rice
1 cup cooked Wild Rice
  (page 170)
¼ cup sliced whole green
  onions
¼ cup almonds
2 tablespoons diced smoked
  sausage
1 teaspoon sesame oil

Red Beans and Rice

*Red beans and rice are a Cajun specialty. This combination makes
an inexpensive and satisfying dinner.*

• • •

1. In a large saucepan, sauté celery, onion, green bell pepper, and garlic in olive oil.

2. Add ham, beans, thyme, cayenne pepper, water, and salt.

3. Simmer for 45 minutes.

4. Adjust seasoning. Serve over rice.

Serves 4

¼ cup diced celery
¼ cup diced onion
¼ cup diced green bell pepper
1 clove garlic, minced
1 tablespoon olive oil
¼ cup diced ham
2 cups red beans (canned)
½ teaspoon dried thyme
¼ teaspoon cayenne pepper
¾ cup water
salt to taste
2 cups cooked white rice

Refried Beans

Refried beans are easy to make, and taste fresher than the ones that are canned. You can use cooked dried beans or canned beans in this recipe.

• • •

1. In a large skillet, sauté onion and garlic in olive oil until translucent.

2. Mash the beans. Stir half of them into the onion mixture over medium heat.

3. Stir in half the water and then the remaining beans.

4. Stir in the rest of the water and the salt and cook for 10 minutes, stirring often.

5. Stir in sour cream before serving.

Dirty Rice

Dirty rice is a spicy Cajun dish from Louisiana that is often made with chicken livers or gizzards and served as a side dish with fried chicken, collard greens, and Coleslaw (page 64).

Boston Baked Beans

This is the long-baking version of baked beans, but it doesn't take a lot of prep time. There is a smoky, candied quality to this dish, which makes it a good barbecue side dish.

• • •

1. Preheat oven to 250°F.

2. Simmer beans uncovered in enough water to cover them for about 1 hour, until tender. Drain beans.

3. Combine all ingredients with beans and bake in a covered 4-quart baking dish for 4 hours.

4. Add water if the top of the beans becomes exposed during baking so that they won't become hard.

Black Beans

This recipe can be kept refrigerated for 3 days. For a colorful presentation, serve the black beans with sour cream, chopped cilantro, and diced red onions as a side dish, or use them in recipes such as burritos or Chili (page 47).

• • •

Serves 8

1 pound dried black beans
½ onion, diced
1 slice bacon
5 quarts water
1 jalapeño pepper, cut
   lengthwise in half
1 tablespoon cumin
1 tablespoon salt
1 tablespoon honey

1. In a 6-quart soup pot, cover beans with boiling water; let stand with pot uncovered for 10 minutes. Drain.

2. Sauté onion in a large pot with the bacon for 5 minutes. Add the soaked, drained beans. Add 5 quarts of water.

3. Add the jalapeño, cumin, salt, and honey. Bring to a simmer.

4. Simmer uncovered for 1½ hours, stirring occasionally.

5. To see if the beans are done, blow on a few in a spoon. When they are done, the skin will peel off when you blow on them.

Bean Counting
Here is a list of some of the colorful varieties of dried beans (and peas) available for cooking: calypso, cranberry runner, fava, garbanzo, flageolet, pinto, pink, red, black, white, black-eyed peas, lentil, lima, and kidney.

Serves 4

1 can pinto beans
¼ cup chopped bacon
¼ cup chopped onion
½ cup chopped tomatoes
1 tablespoon chopped
    jalapeño
2 tablespoons chopped
    cilantro
salt and pepper to taste

Ranch-Style Beans

These are the best beans to serve with your barbecue, and they are a departure from the usual baked beans that you can buy in a can.

• • •

1. Combine everything except salt and pepper in a saucepan and bring to a simmer.

2. Simmer for 45 minutes.

3. Season with salt and pepper to taste.

Serves 6

2 15-ounce cans baked beans
¼ cup dark brown sugar
2 tablespoons ketchup
1 tablespoon yellow mustard
¼ cup chopped onion
3 slices bacon

Quick Baked Beans

This is a quick way to make canned baked beans taste like Boston Baked Beans (page 172).

• • •

1. Preheat oven to 350°F.

2. Mix together everything except the bacon; transfer to an ungreased 3-quart baking dish.

3. Lay the bacon slices over the top of the bean mixture and bake for 45 minutes to 1 hour.

CHAPTER 15
Vegetables

2 cups peeled, sliced carrots
(½-inch slices)
2 tablespoons butter
1 tablespoon lemon juice
2 tablespoons Dijon mustard
1 tablespoon honey
½ teaspoon white pepper
salt to taste

Honey Mustard Carrots

This is a zesty way to give zing to your carrots. This dish works especially well as a springtime side dish. Try serving it with baked ham and Twice-Baked Potatoes (page 197) for a nice flavor combination!

• • •

1. Steam carrots until they are tender. You will know they are done when a knife tip will pierce them easily.

2. In a skillet, sauté the steamed carrots in butter briefly. Add the lemon juice.

3. Stir in the remaining ingredients over low heat.

4. Cook for a few minutes, until carrots are glazed with sauce. Remove from heat.

5. Adjust seasoning with salt.

Serves 4

2 cloves garlic, minced
1 pound mushrooms, sliced
6 tablespoons butter
1 teaspoon Dijon mustard
2 tablespoons white
grape juice
¼ cup chicken broth
1 teaspoon salt
½ teaspoon pepper
1 tablespoon chopped fresh
parsley

Sautéed Mushrooms

These mushrooms are a delicious topping for grilled steak or a steak sandwich. When the mushrooms are cooked whole, they make a good appetizer or side dish.

• • •

1. Sauté the garlic and mushrooms in 4 tablespoons of the butter for a few minutes.

2. Add mustard, juice, and broth. Simmer for 5 minutes.

3. Season with salt and pepper; swirl in the remaining 2 tablespoons of butter.

4. Cook over low heat to reduce the liquid by half.

5. Remove from heat and sprinkle mushrooms with parsley.

Lemon Dill Peas and Carrots

This recipe dresses up the old standby combination of peas and carrots by adding a fresh lemon taste that is complemented by dill.

• • •

1. Steam the carrots, then set aside.

2. Melt butter in a sauté pan. Add the carrots and peas.

3. Sauté peas and carrots for a few minutes, until the peas are cooked.

4. Stir in the lemon juice and sprinkle the dill and lemon zest over the vegetables.

5. Stir and season to taste with salt. Remove from heat.

Turned Vegetables

Turned vegetables are a fancy way to garnish a dish with vegetables that would ordinarily be diced or sliced and cooked. To turn carrots, for example, cut carrots into 2-inch chunks, and then carve each chunk with a paring knife into a shape resembling a football. Blanch and sauté the turned carrots in butter; season to taste before serving.

Serves 4

1 cup diced carrots, fresh or frozen
2 tablespoons butter
1 cup peas, fresh or frozen
1 tablespoon lemon juice
1 teaspoon dried dill weed
1 teaspoon grated lemon zest
salt to taste

2 cups fresh peas
2 tablespoons butter
2 tablespoons water
2 tablespoons chopped
    fresh mint
¼ teaspoon white pepper
salt to taste
4 butter lettuce leaves

Minted Peas

*This is a refreshing way to serve peas, especially in the spring.
They are served in their own lettuce cups.*

• • •

1. Sauté peas in butter and 2 tablespoons water until tender.

2. Season with mint, pepper, and salt.

3. Serve in butter lettuce leaves.

1 whole bulb of garlic,
    unpeeled
1 teaspoon oil
square of aluminum foil
    (about 10" x 10")
¼ teaspoon salt
1 2-inch sprig thyme

Roasted Garlic

*Roasted garlic is a good addition to Mashed Potatoes (page 188),
Quick Aioli (page 34), or Chicken Broth (page 208). It also makes a delicious
spread for crusty bread on a cheese plate.*

• • •

1. Preheat oven to 350°F. Cut off the tip of the garlic bulb. Toss the bulb in a bowl with oil, and then put it on the piece of foil.

2. Sprinkle the garlic bulb with the salt and place the thyme on it.

3. Fold up the foil to form a sealed packet and bake for 1 hour. When the garlic is done, you can turn it so the cut side is down and simply squeeze the roasted garlic out of its papery skin and into a bowl.

Almond Green Beans

This is a version of the classic Green Beans Amandine.
It works very well as a side dish with fish dinners.

• • •

Serves 4

¼ cup sliced almonds
2 tablespoons butter
2 cups green beans, fresh or
    frozen, cut lengthwise
    into thin strips with a
    sharp knife (French-cut)
2 tablespoons water
1 teaspoon salt
¼ teaspoon white pepper

1. Sauté the almonds in butter until lightly browned. Remove them from the butter and set them aside, leaving the butter in the pan.

2. Add the green beans and 2 tablespoons water to the pan and sauté until the beans are tender, about 5 minutes.

3. Add the almonds to the beans.

4. Sprinkle with salt and white pepper.

5. Remove from heat.

Green Onion Brushes

Green onion brushes are a festive (and edible) garnish. Decorate a crudités platter, a salad, or a sandwich with them. Slice each green onion lengthwise 4–6 times, all the way to the end of the green part, leaving 1 inch of the white part intact. Soak them in ice water until they curl. Keep them in water in the refrigerator until ready to use.

Serves 4

2 medium-large tomatoes
1 clove garlic, minced
½ cup dry bread crumbs
2 tablespoons olive oil
2 tablespoons grated
    Parmesan cheese
1 tablespoon chopped fresh
    parsley
½ teaspoon salt
¼ teaspoon pepper

Broiled Tomatoes

*This is a good vegetable side dish to serve with Real Macaroni and Cheese
(page 294) or Stuffed Peppers (page 113).*

• • •

1. Cut each tomato horizontally in half. Set tomatoes with their cut sides up in an enamel-coated cast iron baking dish (aluminum will react with the acid in tomatoes, and glass should not be used under a broiler).

2. Sauté the garlic and bread crumbs in olive oil for 1 minute.

3. Combine bread crumbs and garlic with cheese, parsley, salt, and pepper.

4. Top each tomato half with ¼ of the bread-crumb mixture.

5. Broil until crumb topping browns, then finish baking the tomatoes in a 350°F oven for about 30 minutes.

Serves 4

¼ cup diced onion
2 tablespoons butter
2 tablespoons all-
    purpose flour
1 cup milk
pinch of nutmeg
1 teaspoon salt
¼ teaspoon pepper
4 cups cooked spinach leaves,
    chopped
2 tablespoons grated
    Parmesan cheese

Creamed Spinach

*Creamed spinach is a classic, especially when served with steak. Serve it as a
side dish with bacon-wrapped filets of beef with Béarnaise Sauce (page 201)
and a loaded baked potato for a rich and satisfying meal.*

• • •

1. Sauté onion in butter until translucent.

2. Sprinkle onion with flour and cook over medium heat for a few minutes.

3. Stir in milk; cook, stirring frequently, until it starts to thicken.

4. Season the sauce mixture with nutmeg, salt, and pepper.

5. Stir in the spinach and cheese; heat through.

Ratatouille—Provençal Mixed Vegetables

This is a vegetable dish made of summer's bounty that originated in Provence, France. Eggplant, zucchini, red bell pepper, and garlic are semi-stewed with herbs and olive oil, resulting in a vibrant-tasting multicolored side dish.

• • •

1. Sauté the onion, peppers, and minced garlic in olive oil for 5 minutes.

2. Add the eggplant and zucchini, toss to coat with oil, and then add the fresh (or canned) tomatoes and herbs.

3. Cover and simmer for 30 minutes, stirring occasionally.

4. Season with salt and pepper.

5. Scatter the oil-cured tomatoes and whole, peeled cloves of roasted garlic on top before serving.

Baby Corn

Slice canned baby corn lengthwise and use it to garnish a taco salad or tamale pie. Add the whole ears of baby corn to a veggie platter with dip, or serve them along with salsa that is made with fresh corn kernels. Slice the ears crosswise and toss them into corn chowder or on top of a pizza made with fresh tomato slices and arugula pesto.

Serves 6

½ cup diced onion
¼ cup diced red bell pepper
¼ cup diced green bell pepper
5 cloves garlic, minced
¼ cup olive oil
2 cups diced eggplant
1 cup diced zucchini
½ cup diced tomatoes, fresh or canned
¼ teaspoon dried tarragon
½ teaspoon dried thyme
1 teaspoon dried basil
salt and pepper to taste
¼ cup diced oil-cured tomatoes
6 cloves Roasted Garlic (optional; page 178)

Serves 4

8 ½-inch-thick slices eggplant
(2 medium-sized
eggplants)
1 tablespoon salt
1 cup all-purpose flour
1 cup dry breadcrumbs
1 cup grated parmesan
cheese
1 tablespoon dried oregano
¼ teaspoon pepper
2 eggs
2 cups (1 16-ounce can)
tomato sauce
½ cup olive oil
8 slices mozzarella cheese

Eggplant Parmesan

Eggplant parmesan is a hearty vegetarian dinner that is especially good in the summer, when eggplant is in season. Try to find the freshest eggplant at a local farmer's market to provide the best flavor in this dish.

. . .

1. Preheat oven to 350°F. Sprinkle eggplant with salt and put in a colander to drain for 15 minutes.

2. In a large bowl, combine bread crumbs, parmesan cheese, oregano, and pepper.

3. In a separate bowl, beat eggs with a whisk or fork. Put flour into another bowl.

4. Spread half of the tomato sauce on the bottom of a 9" x 13" baking dish.

5. Wipe eggplant slices dry with a paper towel. Dip each eggplant slice first in flour, then egg, then in the bread crumb mixture.

6. In a large sauté pan, heat the olive oil over medium-high heat. Fry the coated eggplant slices in heated olive oil, turning when bottom side of eggplant is golden brown. Place browned eggplant slices on top of the tomato sauce in the baking dish.

7. Cover eggplant with remaining tomato sauce. Top each eggplant slice with a slice of mozzarella cheese and bake uncovered for 40 minutes.

Grilled Asparagus

Grilled asparagus makes a good appetizer for dipping in Quick Aioli (page 34), tossing in salads, or serving as a side dish to accompany grilled meats.

• • •

Serves 4

1 bunch fresh asparagus
2 tablespoons olive oil
1 teaspoon salt
½ teaspoon pepper
1 tablespoon balsamic
    vinegar (optional)

1. Bend one asparagus stalk near the cut end until it snaps. This will find the natural breaking point of the asparagus.

2. Using the snapped asparagus as a guide, measure and cut the other stalks at the same place and discard the woody ends, saving the parts with the tips on them.

3. Heat an outdoor grill, an indoor grill, or an indoor grill-pan with ridges.

4. Toss asparagus with oil, salt, and pepper (and vinegar if desired).

5. Grill for about 5 minutes, until tender and tips are crisp. Serve warm or chilled.

Fluted Mushroom Caps

Fluted mushroom caps are traditionally served on steak, but they can be used to garnish other things too, such as fish, risotto, or chicken breast. To make, snap the stem off the mushroom, cut notches around the cap with a paring knife, and braise in butter and chicken stock in a sauté pan until tender, about 5 minutes.

Serves 4

16 baby beets, fresh

1 tablespoon chopped
    shallots

2 tablespoons butter

1 tablespoon grated fresh
    gingerroot

2 tablespoons heavy cream

½ teaspoon salt

¼ teaspoon white pepper

Ginger Butter Beets

Serve these beets with anything from beef to fish to Risotto (page 168).
Try the recipe with golden or Chioggia beets when available.

•   •   •

1. Preheat oven to 350°F. Wash beets, remove and discard greens; wrap beets in foil to form a packet. Bake for about 45 minutes, until the beets can be easily pierced with a knife.

2. Let beets cool enough to handle and peel them. The outer skin should peel away easily with the help of a paring knife and your thumb.

3. Cut beets in quarters and set aside.

4. Sauté shallots in butter for a few minutes. Add gingerroot and cream and cook for a few minutes more.

5. Add quartered beets, salt, and pepper to the sauté pan. Cook over low heat until sauce is thickened and beets are hot. Serve immediately.

Onion Rings

These are big, puffy onion rings cooked in a beer batter. The alcohol cooks out of the batter, so they are fine for children to eat. Try one of these on a cheeseburger, a bunch of them as a side dish with Teriyaki Flank Steak (page 120), or use them in the holiday classic Green Bean Casserole (page 283).

• • •

1. Soak onion slices in 1 cup of the milk while you assemble the batter and heat the oil for frying.

2. Combine ¾ cup of the flour, salt, pepper, and baking powder. Whisk beer in gradually, followed by the remaining milk, and then the egg yolks.

3. Beat egg whites to stiff peaks. Fold them into the batter.

4. Drain the onion slices, dip each in flour (remaining 1 cup), then dip in batter.

5. Heat oil to 350°F. Fry onion slices in hot oil immediately after dipping them in batter, until they are golden in color. Drain on brown paper and sprinkle with salt.

Tomato Roses
To make a rose garnish out of tomato skin: Peel the skin, including ⅛ inch of the tomato flesh, in a spiral around the tomato. Gather the peeling and shape it into a rose by twirling and tightening it into a bud, letting the outer part fall looser to form the rose's petals.

Serves 4

2 large onions, sliced
1⅓ cups milk
1¾ cups all-purpose flour
1 teaspoon salt
½ teaspoon pepper
1½ teaspoons baking powder
6 ounces dark beer
2 egg yolks
2 egg whites
4 cups peanut oil

*1 large red cabbage,
    shredded
1 large onion, sliced
2 peeled, cored apples, sliced
2 tablespoons bacon fat
1 tablespoon sugar
1 cup red grape juice
1 cup red wine vinegar
2 teaspoons salt
1 teaspoon pepper*

Braised Red Cabbage

*This is an excellent side dish for Pan-Seared Duck Breast (page 136).
It lends an Alsatian touch to the table.*

• • •

1. Preheat oven to 350°F.

2. Layer cabbage, onions, and apples in a 9" x 13" baking dish or large roasting pan.

3. Heat bacon fat, sugar, juice, and vinegar in a saucepan to a simmer.

4. Pour hot liquid over cabbage. Sprinkle cabbage with salt and pepper; toss to combine.

5. Cover and bake cabbage in oven for 2–3 hours, until tender.

Radish Roses

To make a classic garnish, cut the tips off both ends of a radish to reveal the white flesh. Make four cuts straight down on the top of the radish about ½-inch deep, forming the outline of a square. Soak cut radishes in ice water to get them to open up like a rose. Store in water in the refrigerator until ready to use.

CHAPTER 16
Potatoes

Serves 4

3 large russet potatoes (about
   3 pounds)
4 tablespoons butter
⅓ cup milk
2 teaspoons salt
½ teaspoon white pepper

Mashed Potatoes

To prep ahead of time, cut up the potatoes and keep them in the water you will be cooking them in, in a pot on the stove. When the rest of the dinner is almost ready, turn on the heat and cook the potatoes. This way they will still be warm and will not need to be reheated to serve.

• • •

1. Peel potatoes and cut them into 2-inch uniform pieces.

2. Put potato pieces in a pot with 1 teaspoon of the salt and cold water to cover.

3. Turn heat to medium high and bring potatoes and water to a boil. Turn down heat to simmer and cook until the potatoes can be easily pierced with a fork, about 15 minutes.

4. Drain potatoes in a colander and let the steam dissipate for 5 minutes. The steam evaporates the excess water, which allows the potatoes to dry out and makes them fluffier when mashed.

5. Put cooked potatoes in a bowl and mash with a potato masher or an electric mixer. Add butter and milk, and mix to a creamy consistency. Season with salt and pepper.

Garlic Mashed Potatoes

There are several ways to incorporate garlic into mashed potatoes. In this version, you boil garlic cloves with the potatoes. Other methods are adding minced raw garlic, garlic sautéed in butter, or roasted garlic to the finished mashed potatoes.

• • •

Serves 4

3 large russet potatoes
  (about 3 pounds)
2 cloves garlic, peeled
4 tablespoons butter
⅓ cup milk
1 teaspoon salt, plus extra for
  seasoning
½ teaspoon white pepper

1. Peel potatoes and cut them into 2-inch uniform pieces. Put potato pieces and garlic cloves in a pot with 1 teaspoon of salt and cold water to cover.

2. Turn heat to medium high and bring potatoes, garlic, and water to a boil. Turn down heat to simmer and cook until the potatoes can be easily pierced with a fork, about 15 minutes. Drain potatoes in a colander and let the steam dissipate for 5 minutes. The steam evaporates the excess water, which allows the potatoes to dry out and makes them fluffier when mashed.

3. Put cooked potatoes and garlic in a bowl and mash with a potato masher or an electric mixer. Add butter and milk, and mix to a creamy consistency. Season with salt and pepper.

Serves 4

3 large russet potatoes (about 3 pounds)
4 tablespoons butter
⅓ cup milk
1 teaspoon salt, plus extra for seasoning
½ teaspoon white pepper
1 cup shredded Cheddar cheese

Cheddar Mashed Potatoes

Make these yummy potatoes with either white or yellow Cheddar cheese.

• • •

1. Peel potatoes and cut them into 2-inch uniform pieces. Put potato pieces in a pot with 1 teaspoon of salt and cold water to cover.

2. Turn heat to medium high and bring potatoes and water to a boil. Turn down heat to simmer and cook until the potatoes can be easily pierced with a fork, about 15 minutes. Drain potatoes in a colander and let the steam dissipate for 5 minutes. The steam evaporates the excess water, which allows the potatoes to dry out and makes them fluffier when mashed.

3. Put cooked potatoes in a bowl and mash with a potato masher or an electric mixer. Add butter and milk, and mix to a creamy consistency. Season with salt and pepper. Stir in Cheddar cheese.

Cabbage Cups
Scoop individual servings of mashed potatoes ahead of serving time into cabbage leaves; refrigerate. Heat them up at dinner time in a 350°F oven for 15 minutes, on a foil-lined baking sheet pan.

Sour Cream and Chive Mashed Potatoes

You can make these with fresh chives but dried are just fine, because they rehydrate easily in the final product and are more convenient to have on hand year-round. If you're using fresh chives, you can use the same quantity as dried.

• • •

1. Peel potatoes and cut them into 2-inch uniform pieces. Put potato pieces in a pot with 1 teaspoon of salt and cold water to cover.

2. Turn heat to medium high and bring potatoes and water to a boil. Turn down heat to simmer and cook until the potatoes can be easily pierced with a fork, about 15 minutes. Drain potatoes in a colander and let the steam dissipate for 5 minutes. The steam evaporates the excess water, which allows the potatoes to dry out and makes them fluffier when mashed.

3. Put cooked potatoes in a bowl and mash with a potato masher or an electric mixer. Add butter, sour cream, and chives, and mix to a creamy consistency. Season with salt and pepper.

Serves 4

3 large russet potatoes
(about 3 pounds)
4 tablespoons butter
½ cup sour cream
3 tablespoons dried chopped
chives
1 teaspoon salt, plus extra for
seasoning
½ teaspoon white pepper

3 large russet potatoes
(about 3 pounds)
4 tablespoons butter
⅓ cup milk
2 tablespoons grated
horseradish
1 teaspoon salt, plus extra for
seasoning
½ teaspoon white pepper

Horseradish Mashed Potatoes

*Freshly grated horseradish is best in this recipe, but prepared bottled
horseradish is more convenient and tastes delicious too.*

• • •

1. Peel potatoes and cut them into 2-inch uniform pieces. Put potato pieces in a pot with 1 teaspoon of salt and cold water to cover.

2. Turn heat to medium high and bring potatoes and water to a boil. Turn down heat to simmer and cook until the potatoes can be easily pierced with a fork, about 15 minutes. Drain potatoes in a colander and let the steam dissipate for 5 minutes. The steam evaporates the excess water, which allows the potatoes to dry out and makes them fluffier when mashed.

3. Put cooked potatoes in a bowl and mash with a potato masher or an electric mixer. Add butter and milk, and mix to a creamy consistency. Stir in horseradish and season with salt and pepper.

Scalloped Potatoes

You can make this without the ham for an equally delicious, but more neutral side dish for many things, including Oven-Roasted Whole Chicken (page 132).

. . .

1. Preheat oven to 350°F. Butter a 9" x 13" baking dish; set aside.

2. Slice the potatoes into ¼-inch-thick slices.

3. Put down a layer of ⅓ of the potato slices in the baking dish, then sprinkle half of the flour over them. Add half of the ham; then sprinkle ⅓ of the salt and pepper over this layer.

4. Add another layer of potatoes, the rest of the flour and ham, and ⅓ of the salt and pepper on top of the first layer. Top this layer with a final layer of potatoes and the final ⅓ of the salt and pepper.

5. Pour milk over the potatoes, then drizzle the melted butter and sprinkle the cheese over the top. Cover and bake for 1 hour, until potatoes are tender and can be pierced easily with the tip of a paring knife.

Rumbledethumps
Rumbledethumps is a dish that consists of mashed potatoes and shredded cabbage. It is also known by the name of Colcannon in Irish cuisine.

Serves 4

4 large russet potatoes, peeled
¼ cup all-purpose flour
2 ounces sliced ham, cut in bite-size pieces
1 teaspoon salt
½ teaspoon pepper
1 cup milk
¼ cup butter, melted
¼ cup grated Parmesan cheese

Serves 4

4 medium russet potatoes
(about 3 pounds)
2 tablespoons butter
2 tablespoons all-
purpose flour
¾ cup milk
1 teaspoon salt
½ teaspoon pepper
2 tablespoons chopped
parsley

Creamed Potatoes

Here is a side dish that is a nice change of pace from the usual mashed or baked potato. These diced potatoes in a creamy parsley-flecked sauce are a good selection to serve with a baked ham and Grilled Asparagus (page 183).

• • •

1. Peel and dice the potatoes and put them in a pot of cold salted water.

2. Bring potatoes and water to a boil; turn down heat and simmer for 10 minutes. Drain.

3. Melt butter in a sauté pan and stir the flour into it. Cook for 5 minutes, stirring with a wooden spoon.

4. Add milk slowly to the butter and flour mixture (roux) and stir with a whisk to make a creamy sauce. Cook over medium heat, whisking until sauce thickens. Season with salt, pepper, and parsley.

5. Add the cooked potatoes to the creamy sauce and stir gently to coat the potatoes. Remove from heat.

Baby Red Potatoes

Belted red potatoes, made by shaving the peel away from the middle of red potatoes, are tossed with mustard butter and green onions to make this attractive side dish.

. . .

1. Shave an inch-wide belt around the middle of each potato with a vegetable peeler.

2. Place potatoes in a large pot in enough cold water to cover. Boil potatoes for 15 minutes or until they can be pierced easily with the tip of a paring knife.

3. Drain potatoes and toss them with butter, mustard, and green onions. Season with salt and pepper.

Serves 4

3 pounds small red potatoes
4 tablespoons butter
2 tablespoons Dijon mustard
¼ cup sliced whole green onions
salt and pepper to taste

Oven-Roasted Red Potatoes

Serve these potatoes as a side dish for dinner, tossed in Vinaigrette (page 71) with a sandwich, or as an accompaniment to an omelet for breakfast.

. . .

1. Preheat the oven to 350°F.

2. Cut the potatoes in quarters. In a large bowl, toss potatoes with oil and seasonings.

3. Spread the potatoes out on a sheet pan and roast uncovered for 45 minutes.

Heap o' Taters
As part of a hearty breakfast, serve a big bowl of roasted potatoes with caramelized onions (see Grilled Vegetable Sandwich recipe on page 100), sour cream, and Tomato Salsa (page 42).

Serves 4

3 pounds small red potatoes
2 tablespoons olive oil
1 teaspoon salt
½ teaspoon pepper
½ teaspoon dried thyme

Serves 4

3 pounds sweet potatoes
2 tablespoons olive oil
1 teaspoon salt
½ teaspoon pepper
1 tablespoon minced fresh
    rosemary

Oven-Roasted Sweet Potatoes

This recipe can be combined with Oven-Roasted Red Potatoes (page 195)
to add depth of flavor and color.

• • •

1. Preheat oven to 400°F.

2. Peel sweet potatoes, dice into 1-inch pieces, and put them in a bowl.

3. Toss diced sweet potatoes with oil, salt, pepper, and rosemary.

4. Spread out seasoned sweet potatoes on a sheet pan.

5. Bake for 30 minutes.

Pommes Duchesses

Mashed potatoes are combined with beaten eggs and piped from a pastry bag into rosettes ahead of serving time for the fancy potato side dish Pommes Duchesses (Dutchess Potatoes). The rosettes are browned in the oven before serving.

Twice-Baked Potatoes

These potatoes are fun to make and they can be frozen before the second baking to be served in the future with BBQ, steak, or fried chicken. Twice-baked potatoes are perfect for a buffet or potluck.

• • •

1. Preheat oven to 350°F.

2. Scrub potatoes and poke holes in the skin with a fork or knife. Bake for 1 hour.

3. Cut baked potatoes in half lengthwise and scoop out the flesh into a mixing bowl. Save the skins for stuffing later.

4. Mix butter, sour cream, bacon, cheese, chives, parsley, salt, and pepper into the potato flesh in the mixing bowl.

5. Fill the potato skins with the potato mixture and arrange them on an aluminum-foil lined cookie sheet. Bake in the oven for 20 minutes.

Serves 4

2 large baking potatoes
4 tablespoons butter
½ cup sour cream
2 tablespoons cooked bacon, crumbled
1 cup shredded Cheddar cheese
1 tablespoon chopped fresh chives
1 tablespoon chopped parsley
1 teaspoon salt
½ teaspoon pepper

Caramelized Sweet Potatoes

These sweet and crunchy sweet potatoes are a side dish that can be served on Thanksgiving but are simple enough to make any day.

• • •

1. Preheat the oven to 350°F.

2. Peel sweet potatoes and slice them into ½-inch-thick rounds.

3. In a covered 4-quart pot, simmer 2 inches of water. Place a steamer basket in the pot; put sweet potato slices in the steamer basket. Steam sweet potato slices for 10 minutes.

4. Overlap the steamed sweet potato slices in one layer in a large baking dish.

5. Sprinkle the sweet potatoes with the brown sugar and pecans, then drizzle them with the melted butter. Bake uncovered for 45 minutes.

Serves 4

3 pounds sweet potatoes
1 cup dark brown sugar
½ cup chopped pecans
8 tablespoons butter, melted

Sweet Potato Fries

These are a tasty alternative to regular fries. Serve them with a dipping sauce made from honey, mayonnaise, and cinnamon. Mix small amounts of these ingredients together until you perfect your own sweet dipping sauce!

• • •

1. Preheat oven to 350°F.

2. Peel sweet potatoes and slice them into ½-inch-thick planks lengthwise. Stack the planks and slice them lengthwise into ½-inch-wide sticks.

3. Heat oil in a deep pot to 330°F.

4. Add 1 cup of the sweet potatoes to the hot oil; blanch for 3 minutes. Remove the potatoes from the oil, lay them out on a baking sheet pan, and repeat the process with the rest of the sweet potatoes.

5. Bake sweet potatoes for 30–45 minutes, until they become crisp.

Baked Sweet Potato Toppings
Good toppings for baked sweet potatoes are butter, cinnamon, brown sugar, and pecans.

CHAPTER 17
Sauces

4 egg yolks
1 tablespoon cold water
4 tablespoons melted butter
1 teaspoon lemon juice
pinch cayenne pepper
salt and white pepper to taste

Hollandaise Sauce

If the hollandaise needs to be warmed up, put it in a bowl set over simmering water and whisk a teaspoon of hot water into the sauce. Be careful not to let the sauce container touch the simmering water, because the hollandaise will curdle if it gets too hot.

• • •

1. Whisk egg yolks and water in a stainless steel or glass bowl over simmering water (making sure that the bowl is a bit larger than the pot containing the simmering water) and cook until mixture thickens to ribbon stage. (The ribbon stage is the point in cooking a liquid mixture when, if a whisk is dipped into the liquid and raised a few inches above the pot, the liquid forms a "ribbon.")

2. Slowly pour melted butter into yolks, drop by drop at first, whisking constantly. Continue whisking, pouring the butter in a thin stream, after the sauce starts to thicken.

3. Remove bowl from heat and whisk in the lemon juice and cayenne pepper.

4. Season sauce with salt and white pepper to taste.

5. Serve immediately or keep in a warm, but not too hot, place until ready to serve. (A jar set in warm water or a Thermos are two good options.)

Béarnaise Sauce

This classic sauce is traditionally served with filet of beef and artichokes, but don't let that limit you. The tarragon flavor in the sauce makes it a perfect partner for fish and vegetables. Béarnaise sauce is similar to Hollandaise Sauce (page 200).

• • •

Serves 4

2 sprigs (about 4" each) fresh tarragon
2 shallots, chopped
1½ teaspoons pepper
1 tablespoon tarragon vinegar
¼ cup white wine
3 egg yolks
1 teaspoon cold water
4 tablespoons butter, melted
salt to taste
cheesecloth

1. Strip the leaves from the tarragon stems, save the stems, and chop the leaves.

2. Cook the shallots, tarragon stems, pepper, vinegar, and white wine over medium heat until most of the liquid is evaporated. This is called the "reducing to marmalade" stage.

3. Put egg yolks and water in a stainless steel or glass bowl over simmering water, and whisk the shallot reduction into the yolks. Cook to thicken the mixture, stirring constantly, until the mixture is thick enough to cling to the back of a spoon.

4. Slowly add butter while whisking, at first drop by drop and then in a slow stream. Cook to thicken. Strain the sauce by squeezing it through cheesecloth. (A metal strainer will react with the vinegar.)

5. Stir the chopped tarragon into the finished sauce and season to taste with salt.

Béarnaise Variations

Sauces made by making additions to the classic Béarnaise include Sauce Foyot and Sauce Choron. Foyot is made by adding in a few drops of demi-glace and Choron is made by adding tomato paste or diced, peeled tomatoes (tomato concasse).

Onion Gravy

Serves 4

½ cup sliced onions
2 tablespoons all-
    purpose flour
1 cup beef broth
1 teaspoon salt
½ teaspoon pepper

*Serve this gravy with Mashed Potatoes (page 188)
and Meatloaf (page 122) for the best in comfort food.*

• • •

1. In a medium saucepan, sauté the onions in butter until the natural sugars in the onion turn light brown (caramelize). Sprinkle onions with flour; cook and stir for a few minutes.

2. Add beef broth and stir with a whisk over medium heat until thickened.

3. Season with salt and pepper.

Mushroom Gravy

Serves 4

1 cup sliced mushrooms
2 tablespoons butter
2 tablespoons all-
    purpose flour
1 cup chicken broth
1 teaspoon salt
½ teaspoon pepper

Serve this over Grilled Chicken Breasts (page 126) with Rice Pilaf (page 169).

• • •

1. In a skillet, sauté mushrooms in butter until they start to brown.

2. Sprinkle mushrooms with flour and cook them over medium heat for a few minutes.

3. Add chicken broth, whisk until smooth, and simmer until thickened. Season with salt and pepper.

Turkey Gravy

Make this gravy when you don't have turkey drippings from a whole roasted turkey. It is much more flavorful than anything you'll find in a can!

• • •

1. Preheat oven to 400°F. Place the turkey wings in a baking dish that will fit them both; add whole shallots to the pan. Bake for 1 hour, or until juices of turkey wings run clear.

2. Cover the roasted shallots and turkey wings with 3 cups cold water in a saucepan and heat to a simmer. Reduce heat; simmer for 2 hours. Strain broth; discard wings.

3. Simmer broth in saucepan and reduce to 1 cup. Put milk and flour in a jar with a lid and shake to make a slurry.

4. Whisk slurry into simmering broth; cook until gravy thickens, stirring frequently. Season with salt and pepper.

Serves 4

2 turkey wings
2 shallots, peeled
3 cups water
½ cup milk
¼ cup all-purpose flour
salt and pepper to taste

Beef Gravy

This is a simple brown gravy to serve with Mashed Potatoes (page 188) for a classic side dish.

• • •

1. Melt butter in a 1-quart saucepan. Stir in flour. Cook, stirring, over medium heat, until mixture forms a lightly browned paste.

2. Whisk in beef broth and simmer, whisking until it becomes smooth and thickened.

3. Stir in Worcestershire sauce, salt, and pepper. Remove from heat.

Serves 4

2 tablespoons all-purpose flour
2 tablespoons butter
1 cup beef broth
1 tablespoon Worcestershire sauce
1 teaspoon salt
½ teaspoon pepper

Demi-Glace

Demi-glace is an important component in the classical French sauce repertoire. It is made by reducing brown veal stock very slowly, resulting in a thick, potent, mahogany-colored sauce. You can also purchase demi-glace in the supermarket if pressed for time.

Serves 8

¼ teaspoon white wine
 vinegar
½ teaspoon lemon juice
1 egg yolk
1 cup vegetable oil
salt and white pepper to taste
pinch cayenne pepper

Mayonnaise

*Mayonnaise is extremely easy to make from scratch and has more
flavor than premade mayonnaise.*

• • •

1. In a bowl, whisk vinegar and lemon juice into the egg yolk.

2. Whisk oil into egg yolk mixture drop by drop at first, and then in a slow, steady stream until all has been incorporated.

3. Season with salt, pepper, and cayenne pepper.

Serves 8

2 cups (1 16-ounce can)
 tomato purée
1 teaspoon sugar
½ teaspoon salt
1 teaspoon dried oregano
½ teaspoon dried basil
½ teaspoon garlic powder

Pizza Sauce

*This pizza sauce is simple to make.
The recipe is enough for two 12-inch pizzas.*

• • •

Combine all ingredients and refrigerate until ready to use.

Tomato Sauce

Use this slow-cooked sauce to make spaghetti, Lasagna (page 160), Stuffed Peppers (page 113), or Meatball Sandwiches (page 99).

• • •

1. Sauté onion, bell pepper, and garlic in olive oil 15 minutes.

2. Add fresh tomato, tomato purée, crushed tomatoes, tomato paste, and 2 cups water.

3. Add remaining ingredients and bring to a boil.

4. Reduce heat until liquid is simmering and cook for 3 hours, stirring occasionally.

5. Adjust seasoning with salt.

Au Jus
Au jus is thin, flavorful beef broth that is most often served with hot beef sandwiches for dipping.

Serves 8

1 cup diced onion
½ cup diced green bell pepper
¼ cup chopped garlic
½ cup olive oil
½ cup chopped fresh tomato
3 cups (3 8-ounce cans)
     tomato purée
2 cups (1 16-ounce can)
     crushed tomatoes
1 cup (1 8-ounce can)
     tomato paste
2 cups water
1 tablespoon sugar
2 tablespoons dried oregano
2 tablespoons dried basil
1 tablespoon onion powder
1 teaspoon garlic powder
1 tablespoon salt
1 tablespoon pepper
1 teaspoon crushed red
     pepper
2 tablespoons chopped fresh
     parsley

Serves 4

2 cups ketchup
⅓ cup honey
⅓ cup dark brown sugar
2 tablespoons chopped garlic
¼ cup Worcestershire sauce
3 tablespoons cider vinegar
1 teaspoon paprika
¼ teaspoon dried oregano
¼ teaspoon dried thyme
1 teaspoon salt
1 teaspoon pepper

BBQ Sauce

There are many variations of BBQ sauce: tomato-based, vinegar-based, mustard-based, molasses, honey, brown sugar, hot and spicy, sweet and tangy, and more. This one is a tomato-based version suitable for all your BBQ basting needs.

• • •

1. Combine all ingredients in a saucepan and simmer for 15 minutes.

2. Let the sauce cool, and then store it in the refrigerator until ready to use.

Smashed Garlic
This simple procedure makes garlic easy to peel and chop or mince. Simply take an unpeeled clove of garlic and smash it with the side of a heavy knife or cleaver. The papery skin will split and come off easily. Discard the skin and you have a clove of garlic that is already in pieces. Just chop or mince and use!

Béchamel—Basic White Sauce

*Béchamel is one of the sauces of French classic cuisine.
It is a basic white sauce that has many uses, including
forming the base of Real Macaroni and Cheese (page 294).*

. . .

1. Poke the cloves into the quarter onion.

2. Put the milk in a saucepan with the onion and bay leaf, heat to scalding (not quite boiling), and then turn off the heat. Let the mixture steep for 15 minutes. Remove onion and bay leaf.

3. Melt butter in a saucepan. Add flour and cook, stirring, for a few minutes.

4. Gradually add the hot milk, whisking to smooth out lumps. Bring to a boil, reduce heat to simmer, and simmer until thickened, 10–20 minutes. Stir frequently during simmering to prevent sticking and burning on the bottom.

5. Season to taste with salt and pepper. Strain finished sauce to remove any lumps.

Beurre Blanc
There is more to Beurre Blanc, a white butter sauce, than just melted butter. A thickened mixture of white wine and shallots is required first; then a dash of cream is added and a large amount of butter is whisked in.

Serves 6

2 whole cloves
¼ onion
4 cups milk
1 bay leaf
2 tablespoons butter
2 tablespoons all-
    purpose flour
salt and white pepper to taste

Chicken Broth

*This is a flavorful base to use in soups and sauces, and it fills
the kitchen with a delightful smell.*

• • •

1. Put the chicken wings in a large pot. Cover them with the cold water.

2. Add the carrots, celery, onion, parsnips, leek, parsley stems, bay leaf, peppercorns, and thyme sprig.

3. Bring water to a simmer, skimming off the fat that comes to the top of the water for the next 15 minutes.

4. Simmer for 2–3 hours. Strain broth; refrigerate.

5. When stock has completely cooled, fat will have risen to the top and hardened. Remove this fat. Broth is now ready to be used in recipes. You may immediately freeze broth for later use, or keep it the refrigerator for 3 days for more immediate use.

Peanut Sauce

Peanut sauce can be served with chicken sate (grilled skewers of chicken), steamed vegetables, cooked noodles, or on a Grilled Chicken Sandwich (page 101).

• • •

Serves 6

½ cup creamy or chunky
    peanut butter
2 cups coconut milk (canned)
¼ cup Thai red curry paste
¼ cup sugar
¼ cup lime juice
salt to taste
¼ cup chopped peanuts

1. Heat the peanut butter and coconut milk in a saucepan over low heat, whisking to smooth out the peanut butter.

2. Add the curry paste, sugar, and lime juice. Continue to cook over low heat for 10 minutes, stirring to prevent scorching.

3. Remove from heat and season with salt to taste.

4. Add chopped peanuts and serve warm.

Soy Sauce

A popular condiment, soy sauce is made by brewing fermented soy beans, which results in a thin, brown liquid. It is very salty, so be sure to adjust the salt content in recipes to which you add soy sauce.

Serves 6

2 whole cloves
¼ onion
4 cups milk
1 bay leaf
2 tablespoons butter
2 tablespoons all-
purpose flour
salt and white pepper to taste
1 egg yolk
2 cups shredded Cheddar
cheese

Mornay—Cheese Sauce

This is a basic cheese sauce that can be served over vegetables, on open-faced sandwiches, or with pasta. Parmesan, Monterey jack, or any other cheese you prefer may be substituted for the Cheddar.

•   •   •

1. Poke the cloves into the quarter onion.

2. Put the milk in a saucepan with the onion and bay leaf, heat to scalding (not quite boiling), and then turn off the heat. Let steep for 15 minutes. Remove onion and bay leaf.

3. Melt butter in a saucepan; add flour. Cook for a few minutes, stirring constantly.

4. Gradually add hot milk; whisk to smooth out lumps. Bring to a boil, then reduce heat and simmer until thickened, 10–20 minutes. Stir frequently during simmering to prevent sticking and burning on the bottom. Remove from heat.

5. Season to taste with salt and pepper. Strain sauce to remove any lumps. Quickly whisk in the egg yolk and shredded cheese. Allow time for the cheese to melt, then stir to make a smooth sauce.

CHAPTER 18
Breads and Doughs

3 small or 2 large loaves

5½–6 cups all-purpose flour
1 package active dry yeast
¼ cup warm water
2 tablespoons sugar
1 tablespoon salt
1¾ cups warm water
2 tablespoons vegetable
  shortening

Basic White Bread

In this recipe, you can replace the 1¾ cups water with potato water.
Save the water in which you boil potatoes to use in making white bread.
Potato water improves the action of yeast. It also adds a subtle
flavor and keeps home-baked bread moist longer.

• • •

1. Place about one third of the flour in a large bowl and set aside. In a separate bowl, mix the yeast with ¼ cup warm water, stirring well.

2. Add the sugar, salt, and 1¾ cups water to the yeast. Add the mixture to the flour in the bowl and stir well.

3. Cut in the shortening, using a pastry cutter or your hands. Stir in as much of the remaining flour as possible.

4. Turn the dough onto a lightly floured work surface. Knead 8 to 10 minutes until smooth and elastic, adding flour as necessary.

5. Transfer the dough to a large well-greased bowl, turning to coat both sides. Cover with a damp cloth and place in a warm, draft-free area. Allow to rise until double in volume, about 1–1½ hours.

6. Punch the dough down and let rise a second time until almost doubled in bulk. Grease three 8" x 4" or two 9" x 5" bread pans.

7. Punch dough down a second time and divide into two or three loaves. Shape loaves and place into prepared bread pans. Cover and let rise until almost doubled.

8. Preheat oven to 350°F. Bake 20 to 30 minutes, or until golden brown. Remove from pans and allow to cool on a rack.

Whole-Wheat Bread

The process of making bread in this recipe, called the sponge process, was more popular about fifty years ago, when foodstuffs were less processed and the quality of yeast was less consistently reliable. The yeast works in a batter and the dough rises only once. The sponge process results in a loaf that is lighter but coarser grained.

• • •

1. Add yeast to the 2 cups warm water. Stir in the all-purpose flour, sugar, and salt. Beat the mixture by hand or with an electric mixer until smooth. Set the mixture in a warm place until it becomes foamy and bubbly, up to an hour.

2. To the ½ cup hot water, add the brown sugar and shortening; stir. Allow to cool to lukewarm. Add to the bubbly flour mixture, which is called a sponge. Stir in the whole-wheat flour and mix by hand until smooth, but do not knead.

3. Divide the dough into two lightly greased bread pans, cover, and set in a warm place until doubled in size.

4. Preheat the oven to 350°F and bake 50 minutes.

2 loaves

2 cups warm water
1 package dry yeast
3 cups all-purpose or bread flour
2 tablespoons sugar
2 teaspoons salt
½ cup hot water
½ cup brown sugar
3 tablespoons vegetable shortening
3 cups whole-wheat flour

Serves 8

3 cups all-purpose flour
4½ teaspoons baking powder
1½ teaspoons salt
1 tablespoon sugar
6 tablespoons cold butter
1¼ cups buttermilk

Biscuits

This biscuit dough can be cut into smaller rounds to make mini biscuits, too. Serve the warm biscuits with butter, honey, jam, sausage patties, or ham for breakfast, or serve them with dinner instead of dinner rolls.

• • •

1. Preheat oven to 400°F.

2. Combine flour, baking powder, salt, and sugar in a mixing bowl.

3. Cut butter into small pieces and add to dry ingredients. Mix butter into dry ingredients with a pastry cutter or with your fingers. This mixture should be a bit lumpy so biscuits turn out flaky.

4. Add buttermilk and mix with a wooden spoon to form the dough.

5. Roll dough on a floured board to 1-inch thickness. Cut dough into circles with a 2–3-inch round cookie cutter or a drinking glass. Place rounds on an ungreased baking sheet and bake 12 minutes.

Dinner Rolls

Warm dinner rolls are hard to beat as an accompaniment to any meal.
This dough can be shaped like clover, knots, or ovals.

• • •

Serves 12

1 packet yeast
3 tablespoons warm water
1 cup warm milk
5 tablespoons butter, melted
1 teaspoon salt
1 egg, beaten
3 tablespoons sugar
4 cups all-purpose flour

1. Combine yeast and water and let sit for 5 minutes.

2. Add milk, butter, salt, egg, and sugar to the yeast mixture. Mix well.

3. Stir in half of the flour with a wooden spoon or the paddle attachment to an electric stand mixer. Gradually add remaining flour and knead with a dough hook for 10 minutes. To knead by hand, fold dough over in half on top of itself and press it down and away from you. Give it a quarter turn and repeat for 10 minutes. Put dough in an oiled bowl. Turn dough over in the bowl so that oil coats the entire ball of dough. Cover bowl, and let rise in a warm place for 1½ hours.

4. Punch down dough, divide into twelve pieces, and roll each piece into a ball. Place dough balls on a greased baking sheet, cover, and let rise until doubled, about 1 hour.

5. Preheat oven to 350°F. Uncover rolls and bake for 15 minutes.

Parker House Rolls
These luscious dinner rolls are made by rolling dinner roll dough flat, brushing the rolls with butter, folding them in half, brushing them with butter on top, and then baking them. The Parker House was the restaurant in Boston where these rolls originated in the 1850s.

Serves 6

1 packet yeast
3 tablespoons sugar
pinch dried ginger
1⅓ cups warm water
1 egg
2 tablespoons of water (for egg wash)
3 tablespoons soft butter
1 teaspoon salt
¼ teaspoon baking powder
3½ cups all-purpose flour

Hamburger Buns

You should make hamburger buns from scratch at least once in your life to appreciate the difference. After that it's hard to go back! This dough can be shaped into hot dog buns too. Various toppings, such as sesame seeds, poppy seeds, or diced onions, can be sprinkled on the buns before baking them.

• • •

1. Combine yeast, ½ teaspoon of the sugar, ginger, and ⅓ cup of the water in a bowl. Let sit for 5 minutes.

2. Make egg wash by mixing egg with 2 tablespoons of water.

3. In a mixing bowl combine remaining water, butter, remaining sugar, salt, and baking powder. Using an electric mixer, mix in 1½ cups flour and then the yeast mixture. Add remaining flour and knead with dough hook for 10 minutes. To knead by hand, fold dough over in half on top of itself and press it down and away from you. Give it a quarter turn and repeat for 10 minutes.

4. Turn dough into an oiled bowl. Cover and let rise in a warm place for 1–2 hours (until doubled in bulk).

5. Punch down dough, divide it into six pieces, and shape into buns. Cover and let rise in a warm place for 1½ hours (until doubled in size).

6. Preheat oven to 350°F. Uncover buns, gently brush with egg wash, and bake for 20 minutes.

Making and Kneading Bread Dough

Begin by stirring about half the flour into the dissolved yeast. Beat about 2 minutes, using an electric mixer on medium speed. The dough will still be very batter-like in consistency.

Step 1 Mix in as much of the remaining flour as possible, using a wooden spoon. Some cooks prefer to use their hands for this step. The dough will "form" or become stiff enough to leave the side of the bowl. Turn onto a lightly floured work surface. (Lightly floured means you will use approximately 1 tablespoon for each cup of flour in the recipe before you have finished kneading.)

Step 2 Knead the dough by folding it over toward you and pushing down with the heels of your hands. Then turn the dough about an eighth turn and repeat. Continue this process until the dough is satiny and elastic and no longer sticks to the board, usually about 8 to 10 minutes. Some air bubbles or blisters will appear under the surface of the dough.

Step 3 Grease a large bowl well. Place the dough in it, turning a time or two to grease the dough's surface lightly. Cover with a damp cloth and allow to rise in warm place (about 75° to 80°F).

Step 4 Allow dough to rise until doubled in size, usually about 2 hours. Do not allow to over-rise; it will begin to collapse and the bread's texture will not be satisfactory. To test, press fingertips into the dough about ½ inch. If the imprint remains, the dough has risen the proper amount.

Step 5 Make a fist and punch down the dough in the center, then fold the edges over and down into the middle, and turn the dough over in the bowl. Punching down and kneading the bread again removes large air bubbles and creates a fine texture. If directed by a recipe, knead the dough a second time, usually no more than 2 minutes. Knead in the bowl, if it is large enough, or turn onto the work surface. (Some breads do not require a second kneading.) Return to the bowl, cover, and let rise a second time until almost but not quite doubled.

Serves 12

1 cup cornmeal
¾ cup cake flour
⅓ cup sugar
1 tablespoon salt
2¼ teaspoons baking powder
3 egg yolks
1 cup heavy cream
1¼ cups half-and-half
3 egg whites
14 tablespoons butter, melted

Corn Bread

Corn bread can be made with a variety of additions, such as pecans, corn kernels, diced red bell pepper, sliced green onions, bacon, or shredded Cheddar cheese. To make muffins, simply scoop the batter into 12 greased muffin cups and bake for 12 minutes, or until a toothpick inserted in the middle comes out clean.

• • •

1. Preheat oven to 350°F. Grease a 9" x 11" brownie pan, then dust it with cornmeal.

2. Mix together cornmeal, flour, sugar, salt, and baking powder in a bowl.

3. In another bowl, mix together egg yolks, cream, and half-and-half.

4. Mix together the dry ingredients with the wet ingredients and let sit for 20 minutes. Stir.

5. In a separate bowl, whip egg whites to soft peaks. Fold whipped egg whites into batter; then fold in melted butter. Pour batter into prepared pan and bake 20–25 minutes.

Honey Butter
This is good for slathering generously on hot corn bread or fresh-out-of-the-oven Biscuits (page 214). To make honey butter, mix 4 tablespoons of soft butter with 1 tablespoon of honey.

Banana Bread

*This recipe makes one loaf of moist banana bread,
which can be served warm, cold, or toasted and slathered with butter. Banana
bread makes a delicious Bread Pudding (page 253) if you substitute toasted
banana bread cubes for half of the bread called for in that recipe.*

• • •

1. Preheat oven to 350°F.

2. Combine sugar, honey, and butter in a mixing bowl. Beat with an electric mixer until fluffy and light yellow in color.

3. Add eggs and vanilla; mix well. Add bananas; mix well.

4. Combine flour, baking soda, and salt in a separate bowl. Add the flour mixture to the batter, mixing well. Fold in the pecans if you are using them.

5. Scrape batter into a greased loaf pan and bake for 1 hour 10 minutes, or until a wooden skewer inserted in the middle comes out clean. Cool on a rack.

Serves 6

¾ cup sugar
¼ cup honey
12 tablespoons unsalted
  butter, softened
2 eggs, beaten
1 teaspoon vanilla extract
4 very ripe bananas, mashed
2 cups all-purpose flour
1½ teaspoons baking soda
½ teaspoon salt
½ cup chopped pecans
  (optional)

2 packets yeast
1 teaspoon honey
2½ cups warm water
7 cups (2 pounds) all-
    purpose flour
3 tablespoons olive oil
1 tablespoon salt
olive oil for pan and top
    of dough
kosher salt for top of dough

Focaccia

*Focaccia can be used to make sandwiches or cut into strips
and used for dipping in Marinara Sauce (page 152). Focaccia can be baked
plain or with a variety of toppings, such as herbs (rosemary is especially good),
sesame seeds, onions, or tomato paste.*

• • •

1. Combine yeast, honey, and warm water in a stand mixer mixing bowl and let sit for 5 minutes.

2. Add 3½ cups of the flour, the olive oil, and salt. Mix for 2 minutes, then let sit for 10 minutes.

3. Add remaining flour; mix with dough hook for 5 minutes. Place dough in an oiled bowl. Cover and let rise for 1 hour in a warm place.

4. Punch down dough, then stretch and press it out onto a well-oiled 11" x 18" sheet pan. Cover and let rise in a warm place for 1 hour.

5. Preheat oven to 400°F. Uncover dough and drizzle with olive oil. Poke holes about every 3 inches all over the dough with your fingertips, sprinkle with kosher salt, and bake for 25 minutes. Cool on a rack.

Golden Raisin
Focaccia that has been baked with golden raisins in it is a perfect chicken sandwich foil. Plump the raisins in warm water and Marsala or sherry, and then poke them into the foccacia dough before baking.

Pizza Dough

Pizza dough can be used to make not only pizza, but also calzone, stromboli, and breadsticks. This recipe is enough for 2 medium-size round pizzas.

. . .

1. Combine yeast with the warm water, sugar, and ½ cup of the flour. Let sit 10 minutes.

2. Add olive oil, cool water, salt, and 1 cup flour. Combine with a wooden spoon.

3. Add remaining cup of flour; mix to form dough.

4. Knead dough on a floured board for 5 minutes, adding flour as needed to prevent sticking.

5. Place dough in oiled bowl; cover. Let rise for 1 hour in a warm place. Punch down dough and divide in half. Roll the halves into balls and let rise, covered, for 1 hour. Dough is then ready to roll or stretch into pizza rounds, top, and bake.

Serves 8

1 package yeast
3 ounces warm water
½ teaspoon sugar
2½ cups all-purpose flour
2 tablespoons olive oil
½ cup cool water
1½ teaspoons salt

2 ¼ cups pastry flour
4 ½ teaspoons sugar
¾ teaspoon salt
1½ cups cold unsalted butter
½ cup ice water

Pie Dough

This flaky pie dough recipe will make enough dough for two single-crust 9″ pies or one double-crust 9″ pie. If you can't find pastry flour, all-purpose flour may be substituted. Rolled-out dough circles can be made in advance and frozen or refrigerated until you are ready to use them.

• • •

1. Combine flour, sugar, and salt in a bowl.

2. Cut butter into ½-inch-thick slices.

3. Mix butter into dry ingredients with a pastry cutter or a knife and fork until butter is in pea-sized lumps.

4. Add ice water (ice cubes removed) to flour/butter mixture, stirring with a wooden spoon to combine and form the dough.

5. Divide dough in half and form into two balls. Wrap in plastic and refrigerate for 1 hour before rolling out into 10″ circles.

Blind-Bake
To blind-bake a pie crust, line a pie pan with pie dough, put coffee filters over the dough, and fill the filters with dried beans or pie weights. Bake at 350°F until set, about 25 minutes. Remove beans and coffee filters and bake crust about 10 minutes more, until crust is a light golden brown in color.

Homemade Pie Crust

1 Use a pastry blender to blend the ingredients.

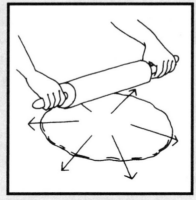

2 Flour the work surface. Using the rolling pin, roll the ball of dough from the center out in all directions.

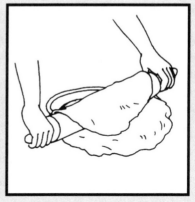

3 Roll the dough loosely around the rolling pin and transfer to the pie dish.

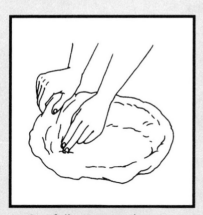

4 Carefully arrange the dough over the bottom and corners of the pie dish.

5 Pinch the dough on the rim of the pie dish. Trim away the excess dough with a knife.

6 To fix a tear in the dough, moisten a piece of extra dough and put it over the tear.

Serves 8

1¼ cups all-purpose flour
⅔ cup powdered sugar
3 tablespoons almond meal
¼ teaspoon salt
½ teaspoon baking powder
8 tablespoons cold unsalted
    butter
1 egg

Tart Dough

*This tender dough is perfect to form the crust for tarts, such as
the Fresh Fruit Tart (page 233) or the Lemon Curd Tart (page 228). You can purchase almond meal in the bulk bins of some grocery stores, or you can make
your own by finely chopping almonds in a food processor.*

• • •

1. Combine flour, sugar, almond meal, salt, and baking powder in a mixing bowl.

2. Cut butter into small pieces and mix it into the dry ingredients with a
   pastry cutter or a knife and fork until it is in pea-sized lumps.

3. Beat the egg and stir it into the flour/butter mixture with a wooden
   spoon to form the dough. Gather dough into a ball, wrap it in plastic
   wrap, and refrigerate it for 1 hour before you roll it out.

Serves 8

2 cups graham cracker
    crumbs
½ cup sugar
½ teaspoon salt
¼ cup butter, melted

Crumb Crust

*This crust can be used to form the base of cream pies, cheesecakes,
and ice-cream pies. Other cookies can be substituted for the graham cracker
crumbs, such as chocolate wafers, vanilla wafers, or gingersnaps.*

• • •

1. Preheat oven to 350°F. Combine crumbs, sugar, and salt in a bowl.

2. Add melted butter to crumb mixture; stir with a rubber spatula to
   combine.

3. Press mixture into a 9" pie pan. Bake for 12 minutes; cool before filling.

CHAPTER 19
Pies and Tarts

Serves 8

1 blind-baked 9" pie crust,
    made with a half recipe
    of Pie Dough (page 222)
2 cups pecans
½ cup dark brown sugar
½ cup sugar
1 cup light corn syrup
6 tablespoons butter, melted
3 eggs
1 teaspoon vanilla extract
½ teaspoon salt

Pecan Pie

*This pie is a Thanksgiving favorite for many people,
but you don't need the excuse of a holiday to bake it. It consists of pecans
and a gooey, candy-like filling baked in a prebaked crust. Whole pecans
or pecan pieces may be used, whichever you prefer.*

• • •

1. Preheat oven to 350°F.

2. Spread out nuts evenly in the pie crust.

3. Whisk together sugars, corn syrup, butter, eggs, vanilla, and salt to make filling.

4. Pour filling in crust over the pecans.

5. Bake for 50 minutes. Let cool before cutting.

Serves 8

1 Crumb Crust, made from
    chocolate wafers
    (page 224)
1 cup creamy peanut butter
8 ounces cream cheese,
    softened
1 tablespoon unsalted butter,
    softened
1 cup sugar
1 teaspoon vanilla extract
1 cup heavy (whipping)
    cream, whipped to
    soft peaks
¼ cup grated milk or dark
    chocolate

Peanut Butter Pie

*This is an irresistible pie you will want to make again and again.
Instead of topping it with grated chocolate, you can chill the pie and then
cover it with Chocolate Glaze (page 248). Also try substituting chocolate-
hazelnut spread for the peanut butter for a different flavor.*

• • •

1. Beat together the peanut butter, cream cheese, butter, sugar, and vanilla with an electric mixer until fluffy.

2. Fold the whipped cream into the peanut butter mixture. Turn the filling into the crust.

3. Top the filling with the grated chocolate.

4. Cover the pie, and chill it in the refrigerator for 4 hours.

Apple Pie

This is a delicious two-crusted pie suitable for any occasion.
A combination of Granny Smith and Golden Delicious apples
provides a nice texture and sweet-tart flavor.

• • •

1. Preheat oven to 350°F.

2. Line pie pan with one of the pie dough circles.

3. Mix apples in a bowl with cornstarch, sugar, and cinnamon.

4. Pile the apples into the dough-lined pie pan, and then dot them with the butter. Cover apples with the remaining pie dough circle. Crimp edges together to seal the crust. Cut 4 1-inch slits around the center of the pie to allow steam to escape during baking.

5. Brush the crust with water and sprinkle with sugar. Bake for 1 hour.

Decorative Dough
To decorate a pie crust, cut shapes, such as leaves or circles, out of scraps of pie dough. Affix them to the top crust with egg wash (1 egg mixed with 2 tablespoons water) before baking the pie. If the pie has only one crust, you can attach leaves to the crust on the rim in the same way. Glaze the top of the cutouts with more egg wash before baking.

Serves 8

Pie Dough, 2 rolled-out circles (page 222)
5 cups peeled, cored, apples, cut into ¼" slices
4 tablespoons cornstarch
½ cup sugar
1 tablespoon cinnamon
4 tablespoons butter, cut in pieces
2 tablespoons sugar, for sprinkling on top crust

1 blind-baked Tart Dough
    crust (page 224)
6 whole eggs
6 egg yolks
2 cups fresh lemon juice
1¾ cups sugar
1 cup plus 2 tablespoons cold
    unsalted butter
powdered sugar for garnish

Lemon Curd Tart

*Lemon curd is similar to a custard and is made using lemon juice
instead of cream. It is made into a tangy tart filling in this recipe. The finished
tart can be covered in raspberries, whipped cream, meringue, or caramelized
sugar like a crème brûlée. A combination of tangerine and lime juices may be
substituted for lemon juice to make another tasty tart.*

• • •

1. Whisk together eggs, egg yolks, lemon juice, and sugar. Stir occasion-
    ally with a rubber spatula in a mixing bowl set over simmering water
    until the mixture becomes thick. (Make sure the mixing bowl is slightly
    larger than the saucepan so the bottom of the bowl does not touch the
    water.) Remove the bowl from heat.

2. Cut up the butter and stir it into the thickened egg mixture until it
    melts.

3. Strain the mixture into the prebaked tart crust. Let the filling set and
    completely cool. Refrigerate tart.

4. Use a small sieve to dust the tart with powdered sugar before serving.

Lemon Meringue Pie

Lemon meringue pie has a filling that is a little less tart and concentrated than lemon curd, and it is topped with meringue that is lightly toasted.

• • •

1. Preheat oven to 300°F.

2. In a saucepan combine egg yolks, sugar, water, lemon juice, cornstarch, salt, and lemon zest. Whisk over medium heat for 20 minutes, until mixture thickens.

3. Remove saucepan from heat and whisk in the butter. Pour the filling into the prebaked pie crust.

4. Beat egg whites in a mixing bowl with an electric mixer, or by hand with a whisk, until they are foamy. Add cream of tartar and ¼ cup powdered sugar, and continue beating egg whites. Gradually add the remaining powdered sugar while beating the egg whites to stiff peaks to form the meringue topping.

5. Spread the meringue with a spatula over the warm lemon filling all the way to the edge of the crust to form a seal. Make decorative peaks in the meringue with the spatula. Bake the pie for 45 minutes to toast the meringue topping. Cool before serving. Refrigerate any leftovers.

Stiff Peaks

You'll know you have successfully created stiff peaks when the egg whites have been whipped to the point that a spoon can be dipped in the egg whites, pulled out, and the remaining "peak" sticks straight up and doesn't flop over to the side.

Serves 8

1 blind-baked half-recipe of
   Pie Dough crust (page 222)
6 eggs, separated
1 cup sugar
1½ cups water
½ cup fresh lemon juice
5 tablespoons cornstarch
¼ teaspoon salt
1 tablespoon grated
   lemon zest
2 tablespoons unsalted butter
6 egg whites
½ teaspoon cream of tartar
1½ cups powdered sugar

1 blind-baked half-recipe Pie
   Dough crust (page 222)
1 13.5-ounce can
   coconut milk
2 ½ cups heavy cream
pinch salt
1 tablespoon cornstarch
⅔ cup sugar
6 egg yolks
¼ cup sweetened, shredded
   coconut

Coconut Cream Pie

*This coconut cream pie filling has a creamy texture
with no chewy grated coconut in it.*

• • •

1. Preheat oven to 350°F. Spread shredded coconut on an ungreased cookie sheet. Bake for about 10 minutes, or until light brown.

2. Heat coconut milk, 1½ cups of the cream, salt, cornstarch, and ⅓ cup of the sugar in a saucepan over medium-low heat until the mixture simmers. Temper egg yolks with ½ cup of the heated cream mixture; then add yolks to cream mixture and cook, whisking, until mixture thickens. (Tempering brings the egg closer to the temperature of the hot liquid and helps to prevent curdling when it is added.) Strain filling into pie crust. Chill.

3. Whip remaining cream with remaining sugar to stiff peaks; spoon onto chilled pie. Sprinkle pie with toasted coconut.

Banana Cream Pie

*This banana cream pie has a satisfying and creamy filling
of vanilla custard and sliced bananas.*

• • •

Serves 8
_____

1 blind-baked half-recipe Pie
    Dough crust (page 222)
4 cups heavy cream
1 tablespoon cornstarch
⅔ cup sugar
6 egg yolks
1 teaspoon vanilla extract
2 bananas, sliced

1. Heat 3 cups of the cream, cornstarch, and ⅓ cup of the sugar in a saucepan over medium-low heat to a simmer. Temper egg yolks with ½ cup heated cream mixture; then add yolks to cream mixture and cook, whisking, until mixture thickens. (Tempering brings the egg closer to the temperature of the hot liquid and helps to prevent curdling when it is added.) Stir in vanilla. Strain filling into a bowl and set aside.

2. Lay half of the banana slices on the bottom of the crust. Spoon the filling on top of the bananas. Chill.

3. Whip remaining cream with the remaining sugar. Lay the remaining banana slices on top of the filling, and then top the pie with whipped cream.

Nut Crust
You can substitute ground nuts and 1 tablespoon of flour for cookie crumbs in the recipe for Crumb Crust (page 224) to make a nutty crust to use for pies such as lemon meringue, peanut butter, or chocolate cream.

Chocolate Cream Pie

The filling for this pie is a rich chocolate custard topped with sweetened whipped cream. For more chocolate, brush the bottom of the pie crust with melted milk, dark, or semisweet chocolate before filling, and top the whipped cream with grated chocolate of your choice.

• • •

Serves 8

1 blind-baked half-recipe Pie
 Dough crust (page 222)
4 cups heavy cream
4 ounces semisweet
 chocolate chips
1 tablespoon cornstarch
⅔ cup sugar
6 egg yolks

1. Heat 3 cups of the cream, chocolate chips, cornstarch, and ⅓ cup sugar in a saucepan over medium-low heat to a simmer.

2. Temper egg yolks with ½ cup of the heated cream mixture; then add yolks to cream mixture and cook, whisking, until mixture thickens. Strain filling into prebaked pie crust. Chill.

3. Whip remaining cream with remaining sugar to stiff peaks; spoon onto the chilled pie filling.

Butterscotch Cream Pie

Candied pecans make a nice garnish for this rich, creamy pie.

• • •

Serves 8

1 blind-baked half-recipe Pie
 Dough crust (page 222)
½ cup light brown sugar
2 tablespoons salted butter
4 cups heavy cream
1 tablespoon cornstarch
6 egg yolks
⅓ cup sugar

1. In a saucepan, cook brown sugar and butter together over medium heat for 5 minutes. Add 3 cups of the cream and the cornstarch. Heat to a simmer.

2. Temper egg yolks with ½ cup heated cream mixture; then add yolks to cream mixture and cook, whisking, until mixture thickens. Strain filling into prebaked pie crust. Chill.

3. Whip remaining cream with sugar to stiff peaks; spoon onto the chilled pie filling.

Fresh Fruit Tart

Take advantage of the ripest, most flavorful fruits of the season and showcase them in this attractive and tasty tart. Under the fruit is a cloud of Pastry Cream Filling (page 234) which is the same filling used in chocolate éclairs.

* * *

1. Heat the jam in a saucepan over low heat. Strain the jam and set it aside (keeping it warm). Discard solids that remain in the strainer.

2. Slice the peach, peel and slice the kiwi fruit, and hull and slice the strawberries.

3. Paint the bottom of the prebaked pie crust with the melted chocolate; chill a few minutes to harden it.

4. Spread the pastry cream over the chocolate to the edges of the crust.

5. Lay the fruit slices in concentric rings on top of the pastry cream, starting on the outside with the strawberries, then the peaches, then the kiwis, and then the blackberries. Brush the fruit with the jam.

Crust Sealers
To seal a blind-baked pie crust before filling it for a quiche or tart, you can brush the inside with egg white while the crust is still hot. This will help prevent sogginess. A layer of chocolate brushed on the bottom of a cooled pie crust will prevent sogginess and enhance the flavor for pies filled with pastry cream or mousse.

Serves 8

1 blind-baked Tart Dough crust (page 224)
¼ cup apricot or strawberry jam
1 fresh peach, pitted, not peeled
1 kiwi fruit
1 cup strawberries
4 ounces white chocolate, melted
1 recipe Pastry Cream Filling (page 234)
½ cup blackberries

Serves 8

2 cups milk
8 tablespoons unsalted butter
½ cup sugar
1 teaspoon vanilla extract
2 tablespoons all-
    purpose flour
1 tablespoon cornstarch
2 eggs

Pastry Cream Filling

*This classic pastry cream recipe is used in the Fresh Fruit Tart (page 233) recipe.
It can also be used as a filling for layer cakes, éclairs, and cream puffs.*

• • •

1. In a saucepan heat the milk, butter, and ¼ cup of the sugar to a simmer.

2. In a bowl whisk together the remaining sugar with the flour, cornstarch, and eggs to form a paste.

3. Temper the egg mixture with half of the heated milk mixture by gradually whisking the heated milk into the bowl.

4. Whisk the tempered egg mixture into the saucepan containing the remaining heated milk mixture and heat to a boil, whisking the whole time. Whisk in the vanilla.

5. Remove pan from heat and pour the mixture into a bowl. Cover the surface directly with plastic wrap and chill the pastry cream completely.

Cherry Pie

This recipe uses a double crust, but you can make a lattice crust instead by weaving strips of pie dough. Be sure not to use frozen cherries packed in syrup!

• • •

1. Preheat oven to 350°F. Line pie pan with one circle of pie dough.

2. Mix cherries with sugar and cornstarch and put them in the pie shell. Dot cherries with butter pieces.

3. Cover the cherries with the other pie dough circle, crimp the edges to seal, and cut slits in the top. Sprinkle with sugar and bake for 50 minutes. Cool before slicing.

Serves 8

2 rolled-out circles of Pie
    Dough (page 222)
5 cups pitted fresh or frozen
    cherries
¾ cup sugar
3 tablespoons cornstarch
2 tablespoons butter, cut in
    pieces
sugar for sprinkling on crust

Peach Pie

This recipe uses a double crust and fresh peaches. Variations could be a lattice crust (see instructions for Rhubarb Custard Pie on page 237), canned unsweetened peaches, or frozen unsweetened peaches.

• • •

1. Preheat oven to 350°F. Line pie pan with one circle of pie dough.

2. Mix peach slices with sugar and cornstarch and put them in the pie shell. Dot peaches with butter pieces.

3. Cover the peaches with the other pie dough circle, crimp the edges to seal, and cut slits in the top. Sprinkle with sugar and bake for 50 minutes. Cool before slicing.

Serves 8

2 rolled-out circles of Pie
    Dough (page 222)
5 cups peaches, peeled, pitted
    and sliced
¾ cup sugar
3 tablespoons cornstarch
2 tablespoons butter, cut in
    pieces
sugar for sprinkling on crust

Serves 8

2 rolled-out circles of Pie
    Dough (page 222)
5 cups fresh or frozen
    blueberries
1 cup sugar
¼ cup lemon juice
1 tablespoon grated
    lemon zest
4 tablespoons cornstarch
2 tablespoons butter, cut
    in pieces
sugar for sprinkling on crust

Blueberry Pie

*Blueberries and lemon are the classic combination that make up this pie
filling. This is an excellent pie to bake in the summer, when blueberries are in
season, and to serve with a scoop of vanilla ice cream.*

• • •

1. Preheat oven to 350°F. Line pie pan with one circle of pie dough.

2. Mix blueberries with sugar, lemon juice, lemon zest, and cornstarch,
   and put them in the pie shell. Dot blueberries with butter pieces.

3. Cover the blueberries with the other pie dough circle, crimp the edges
   to seal, and cut slits in the top. Sprinkle with sugar and bake for 50 minutes. Cool before slicing.

Pitting Cherries
*There are several ways to pit cherries, one of which is to insert an
unfolded paper clip into the end and twist around the seed, and then
pull it out. If you are using a manual cherry/olive pitter that works like
a paper hole punch, pit them inside a plastic bag to catch the splattering
juice, which stains.*

Serves 8

2 rolled-out circles of Pie
    Dough (page 222)
3 cups chopped rhubarb
2 cups hulled, sliced
    strawberries
1 cup sugar
¼ cup cornstarch
2 tablespoons butter, cut in
    pieces
sugar for sprinkling on crust

Strawberry-Rhubarb Pie

*The winning combination of strawberries and
rhubarb make up the filling for this pie.*

• • •

1. Preheat oven to 350°F. Line pie pan with one circle of pie dough.

2. Mix rhubarb and strawberries with sugar and cornstarch and put them
   in the pie shell. Dot fruit with butter pieces.

3. Cover the filling with the other pie dough circle, crimp the edges to
   seal, and cut slits in the top. Sprinkle with sugar and bake for 50 minutes. Cool before slicing.

Rhubarb Custard Pie

This is an old-fashioned favorite: a sweet-tart pie with a lattice top.
A double crust could be substituted if desired.
The custard does not have milk—just eggs.

• • •

1. Preheat oven to 400°F.

2. Cut one of the pie dough circles into ½-inch-wide strips and weave it into a lattice. Set aside the lattice. Line a pie pan with the other dough circle.

3. Combine sugar, flour, and nutmeg; beat this mixture into the eggs. Stir the rhubarb into the egg mixture.

4. Pour the rhubarb mixture into the pie shell, dot with butter pieces, and top with the lattice crust. Crimp the edges to seal.

5. Bake for 50 minutes. Cool before cutting.

Galettes

Try making galettes, such as the Apple Free-Form Tart (page 238), with other fruits—rhubarb, plums, pitted cherries, pears, or peaches. Add a few berries or candied orange slices to the apple version for another twist.

Serves 8

2 rolled out circles of Pie Dough (page 222)
1½ cups sugar
¼ cup all-purpose flour
¼ teaspoon nutmeg
3 eggs, beaten
4 cups chopped rhubarb
2 tablespoons butter, cut in pieces

Serves 8

1 recipe Pie Dough (page 222)
2 tablespoons all-
purpose flour
¼ cup ground almonds
¾ cup sugar
3 cups apples, peeled, cored,
and thinly sliced
3 tablespoons butter, melted

Apple Free-Form Tart

*This buttery free-form tart is also called a galette. It is a flat,
rustic tart that resembles a pizza, but the crust is a flaky, crunchy tart dough.
It is baked flat on a round pizza pan instead of in a tart pan with sides.
Baking it on a pizza stone in the oven will help achieve a crisper crust.
You can find ground almonds in bulk bins and in natural food stores, or you
can grind your own in the food processor.*

• • •

1. Preheat oven to 400°F.

2. Roll out pie dough to form a 16-inch circle. The edges don't have to be perfect. Put the dough circle on a 12- or 14-inch round pizza pan. Parchment paper underneath the crust is helpful but not necessary.

3. Sprinkle the flour, ground almonds, and ¼ cup of the sugar in the middle of the dough circle, radiating out to where the pizza pan ends. Scatter the apple slices over the flour mixture. Fold the edge of the dough partway back over the apples to form a 2-inch crust border all around the tart that covers some of the apples.

4. Brush the crust border with butter, and then drizzle the rest of the butter over the apples. Set the brush aside without washing butter off. Sprinkle the remaining sugar over the apples and on the crust border.

5. Bake for 45 minutes, until the pastry is crisp and the apples are tender and browned a bit. Using the brush that still has a bit of butter left on it, dab the apples with butter after the tart is removed from the oven.

CHAPTER 20
Cookies

Yield 2 dozen

*2 cups unsalted butter,
    softened*
1 cup dark brown sugar
1 cup sugar
2 eggs
1 teaspoon vanilla extract
2 cups all-purpose flour
1 teaspoon salt
1 teaspoon baking soda
*1 cup semisweet
    chocolate chips*

Chocolate Chip Cookies

*These cookies can also be made with chocolate chunks instead of chips.
Other variations include white chocolate chips and macadamia nuts, pecans,
or toffee bits. This dough can be rolled into a log, wrapped in plastic, and
refrigerated or frozen for future use.*

• • •

1. Preheat oven to 350°F.

2. With an electric mixer, cream together the butter, brown sugar, and sugar until fluffy.

3. Add eggs and vanilla; combine well. Scrape down the sides of the bowl.

4. Mix the flour, salt, and baking soda together in a bowl. Add the flour mixture to the butter mixture, mixing by hand with a wooden spoon to combine into a smooth dough. Stir in chocolate chips.

5. Using two spoons, drop dough in mounds onto an ungreased cookie sheet. Bake cookies 12 minutes. Cool on a rack.

Oatmeal Raisin Cookies

This recipe makes soft and chewy cookies perfect for dipping in milk. Golden raisins or currants may be substituted for the raisins with delicious results.

• • •

1. Preheat oven to 350°F.

2. With an electric mixer or by hand, cream together the butter, shortening, brown sugar, and sugar until fluffy.

3. Add eggs, water, and vanilla; combine well. Scrape down the sides of the bowl frequently during mixing.

4. Mix the oats, flour, salt, and baking soda together in a bowl then add it to the butter mixture, stirring well to combine into a smooth dough. Stir in the raisins.

5. Using two spoons, drop dough in mounds onto an ungreased cookie sheet. Wet your palm with water, and then press down on dough mounds to flatten them slightly. Bake cookies 12 minutes. Cool on a rack.

Yield 4 dozen

8 tablespoons butter, softened
¾ cup shortening
1½ cups dark brown sugar
1 cup sugar
2 eggs
5 ounces water
2 teaspoons vanilla extract
6 cups quick-cooking rolled oats
2 cups all-purpose flour
2 teaspoons salt
1 teaspoon baking soda
3 cups raisins

Yield 3 dozen

12 tablespoons soft butter
1 cup creamy or chunky
    peanut butter
1 cup dark brown sugar
½ cup sugar
2 eggs
2 teaspoons vanilla extract
2½ cups all-purpose flour
¼ teaspoon salt
1¼ teaspoons baking powder
½ teaspoon baking soda
½ cup sugar in a bowl

Peanut Butter Cookies

*These cookies are a favorite afterschool snack for children,
but that doesn't mean adults can't enjoy them too! Try rolling the dough in
coarse sugar before baking them to make them extra sparkly.*

• • •

1. Preheat oven to 350°F.

2. With an electric mixer or by hand, cream together the butter, peanut butter, brown sugar, and sugar until fluffy.

3. Add eggs and vanilla; combine well. Scrape down the sides of the bowl.

4. Mix the flour, salt, baking powder, and baking soda together in a bowl. Add the flour mixture to the butter mixture, stirring well to combine into a smooth dough.

5. Form dough into 1-inch balls by hand and place onto an ungreased cookie sheet. Dip a fork into the bowl of sugar and press a crosshatch mark into each cookie. Dip fork frequently into the sugar to prevent sticking. Bake cookies 10 minutes. Cool on a rack.

Peanut Butter Kiss
Instead of baking peanut butter cookies with fork crosshatch marks, press a chocolate kiss (foil removed!) into the top of each cookie before baking. It's an oldie but goodie.

Shortbread

This basic shortbread recipe can be embellished by adding nuts, ground coriander, cinnamon, candied ginger, or chocolate chips. There's really no need to though, since these cookies are buttery and divine in their plain form.

•   •   •

1. Preheat oven to 325°F.

2. With a wooden spoon or electric mixer, combine butter and sugar in a bowl and mix until slightly fluffy, but not whipped.

3. Add vanilla; mix well.

4. Add flour and salt. Mix to form a smooth dough.

5. Press dough into an ungreased 9-inch pie pan, prick all over with a fork, and bake for 20 minutes. Remove from oven and cut into 12 wedges immediately. Leave on pan to cool.

Pan Cookies
Press chocolate chip cookie dough, with or without the addition of nuts, dried apricots, raisins, or toffee bits, into an ungreased baking dish. Bake for 35–45 minutes at 350°F. Cool in pan. When cool, cut into bars.

Yield 12

8 tablespoons butter, softened
¼ cup sugar
½ teaspoon vanilla extract
1¼ cups all-purpose flour
½ teaspoon salt

Brownies

Yield 16

12 tablespoons unsalted
    butter, melted
1½ cups sugar
2 eggs
½ teaspoon vanilla extract
2 tablespoons water
¾ cup unsweetened cocoa
    powder
½ cup all-purpose flour
½ teaspoon salt
½ teaspoon baking powder
1 cup semisweet
    chocolate chips

This recipe uses both cocoa and chocolate chips to create a double chocolate brownie. You may add a variety of things to this batter before baking, such as chopped nuts, chopped candy bars, or dried fruits. The brownies can be sprinkled with powdered sugar or covered in Chocolate Frosting (page 259) after they have cooled.

• • •

1. Preheat oven to 350°F. Grease a 9" x 13" baking dish.

2. Mix together the butter and sugar in a mixing bowl.

3. Beat the eggs into the butter mixture; then stir in the vanilla and water.

4. In a separate bowl, combine the cocoa powder, flour, salt, and baking powder. Add this dry mixture to the wet mixture; stir to combine. Stir in the chocolate chips. Scrape the batter into the prepared baking dish, and smooth out the top of the batter.

5. Bake brownies for 30 minutes. Cool slightly in pan, and then cut into 16 squares. Serve warm or at room temperature.

Lemon Bars

Delicate and tangy lemon bars are a lunch-box and picnic favorite. Try substituting lime juice for half of the lemon juice for a twist on an old classic. Serve these with brownies for a great flavor combination.

• • •

1. Preheat oven to 350°F. Butter an 8" x 8" baking dish.

2. Combine 2 cups of the flour with the powdered sugar and salt in a bowl. Cut the butter into the dry mixture with 2 knives or a pastry cutter to make a crumbly mixture. Pat this into the bottom of the buttered pan. Bake this crust for 15 minutes. Remove from oven and set aside.

3. Combine eggs, sugar, 6 tablespoons of flour, lemon juice, and lemon zest with a whisk in a bowl and pour the mixture over the baked crust.

4. Bake filling and crust for 25 minutes.

5. Cool completely, cut into 16 squares, and dust with powdered sugar.

Ice-Cream Sandwiches

Cookies such as gingersnaps, chocolate chip, oatmeal raisin, and peanut butter make good homemade ice-cream sandwiches. Simply put a scoop of ice cream on one cookie, press another one on top of the ice cream, and roll the sides in crushed cookie crumbs, nuts, or mini chocolate chips.

Yield 16

2 cups plus 6 tablespoons all-purpose flour
1 cup powdered sugar
pinch salt
8 tablespoons unsalted butter, softened
2 eggs
2 cups sugar
3 ounces fresh lemon juice
1 tablespoon grated lemon zest
powdered sugar for garnish

*4 tablespoons unsalted
    butter, softened*
¼ cup sugar
1 egg
½ teaspoon vanilla extract
1 teaspoon baking powder
pinch of salt
1 cup all-purpose flour
½ cup whole almonds

Biscotti

Biscotti are perfect for dipping in coffee because they are dry (due to the second baking). You may substitute any nut you prefer for the almonds, and you may also add other flavorings such as almond extract, orange flower water, or cinnamon. Dipped in chocolate, these cookies are elevated to candy!

• • •

1. Preheat oven to 350°F. Lay the almonds out in an even layer on an ungreased baking sheet pan; bake for 10 minutes. Set aside. Keep the oven on for the biscotti.

2. Grease a baking sheet.

3. Cream the butter and sugar together with an electric mixer or by hand. Add egg and vanilla; beat to incorporate.

4. In a separate bowl combine the baking powder, salt, and flour. Add this dry mixture to the egg/butter mixture, and combine to make a smooth dough. Stir in almonds.

5. Scrape dough out onto the prepared baking sheet. Wet your fingers with water, and then form the dough into a broad, flat log. Bake for 30 minutes at 350°F. Remove from the oven and cool on the baking sheet for 5 minutes. Turn down the oven to 275°F.

6. Remove the log to a cutting board. Cut the log into ½-inch-wide slices and place the slices back on the baking sheet, cut sides facing up. Bake 15 minutes; turn cookies over and bake 10 minutes more. Remove from pan and cool on a rack.

Sugar Cookies

This recipe is for the kind of cut-out cookies that are especially popular around holiday time. You can also form the dough into a log and slice rounds, or roll the dough into balls before baking.

• • •

Yield 2 dozen

8 tablespoons butter,
    softened
1 cup sugar
1 egg
1 tablespoon heavy cream
½ teaspoon vanilla extract
½ teaspoon salt
1 teaspoon baking powder
1¾ cups all-purpose flour
colored sugar for decoration

1. Preheat oven to 300°F.

2. In a mixing bowl, with an electric mixer, cream together butter and sugar until fluffy. Add egg, cream, and vanilla; mix well. Scrape down the sides of the bowl.

3. In a separate bowl mix together the salt, baking powder, and flour. Add the dry ingredients to the butter mixture; mix to form a smooth dough.

4. Roll out the dough on a lightly floured surface to prevent sticking. Cut out shapes with cookie cutters or a drinking glass. Brush excess flour off the cookies and place them on ungreased cookie sheets. Sprinkle cut-outs with colored or white sugar.

5. Bake cookies for 9 minutes. Remove to rack to cool.

Chocolate Chunks
Make your own chocolate chunks for cookies by melting chocolate and spreading it out on the back of a sheet pan. Let the chocolate cool and set, then score it into squares and scrape it off with a metal spatula.

Yield 1 cup

¼ cup heavy cream
4 teaspoons butter, melted
1 teaspoon vanilla extract
½ cup powdered sugar
water as needed

Cookie Frosting

*Use this to frost sugar-cookie cut-outs. Decorate the frosted
cookies with nonpareils and colored sugar.*

• • •

1. Gently heat the cream over medium-low heat without bringing it to a boil or simmer; remove from heat.

2. In a bowl, combine the hot cream, butter, vanilla, and powdered sugar.

3. Thin with water or add more powdered sugar to achieve spreading consistency.

Yield 1 cup

½ cup heavy cream
½ cup semisweet
    chocolate chips

Chocolate Glaze

*While this rich glaze is warm, pour it over cookies on a rack with
a baking sheet set underneath to catch the drips.*

• • •

1. Gently heat the cream over medium-low heat without bringing it to a boil or simmer; remove from heat.

2. Add chocolate chips to the hot cream. Let sit for 5 minutes to absorb the residual heat and melt the chocolate.

3. Stir the chocolate and cream together to a smooth consistency.

Gingersnaps

*The combination of dried ginger and molasses creates a festive
cookie that snaps when you bite into it. Sandwich these cookies around
fresh peach ice cream for delicious ice-cream sandwiches. The "heat"
from the ginger contrasts with the cold ice cream nicely.*

• • •

1. Preheat oven to 350°F.

2. Using an electric mixer or a wooden spoon, cream together the butter and sugar in a bowl until slightly fluffy. Add egg, molasses, and vanilla; beat together. Scrape down the sides of the bowl.

3. In a separate bowl combine the flour, baking soda, salt, cinnamon, and ginger. Add this dry mixture to the butter mixture, and mix to form a smooth dough.

4. Roll the dough into 2-inch-diameter logs on a lightly floured surface. Wrap in plastic and chill for an hour.

5. Remove plastic and slice dough logs into ½-inch-thick slices. Place the rounds on a greased or parchment-paper-lined cookie sheet. Sprinkle sugar over the rounds and bake for 12 minutes. Cool on a rack.

Yield 3 dozen

*10 tablespoons unsalted
   butter, softened*
*¾ cup sugar (plus more for
   sprinkling)*
1 egg
¼ cup unsulfured molasses
½ teaspoon vanilla extract
2 cups all-purpose flour
1¾ teaspoons baking soda
¼ teaspoon salt
1 tablespoon cinnamon
*1 teaspoon ground dried
   ginger*

Yield 30

3 egg whites
½ cup sugar
½ cup applesauce
10 ounces unsweetened
   shredded coconut
2 tablespoons all-
   purpose flour

Coconut Macaroons

*Try to find dry, unsweetened coconut (desiccated) for these cookies.
This kind of coconut is often found in Asian grocery markets. Cut down the
sugar by ¼ cup if you must use sweetened coconut, or the cookies will seep
liquid because of the extra sugar (a process known as "weeping"). It is nice to
add chopped candied orange to this recipe for variety.*

• • •

1. Preheat oven to 350°F. Line cookie sheet with parchment paper.

2. Combine all ingredients together in a bowl.

3. Wet your fingers with water and form mixture into walnut-sized balls and place them on the prepared cookie sheet.

4. Bake for 20 minutes.

5. Cool, then peel cookies off the parchment paper.

Chocolate-Dipped Macaroons
Make your coconut macaroons fancy by dipping the bottoms in melted chocolate and then setting them on foil to cool and set up. You also can do the same using white chocolate.

CHAPTER 21
Desserts

Serves 8

½ recipe Biscuit dough
   (page 214)
sugar for sprinkling
4 cups (1 quart) whole
   strawberries
1½ cups sugar
3½ cups heavy cream
1 teaspoon vanilla extract
powdered sugar
8 sprigs mint (optional)

Strawberry Shortcake

This recipe is perfect for strawberry season, but frozen strawberries may be substituted for fresh if they are not available. Other fruit, such as nectarines and blueberries, may be used to make shortcake too.

• • •

1. Make the biscuit dough as directed in the recipe, substituting cream for the buttermilk. Before baking, brush the biscuits with some of the cream and sprinkle them with sugar. Bake according to the biscuit recipe. When the biscuits are cool, split them horizontally and set aside.

2. Hull and slice the strawberries and toss them in a bowl with 1 cup of the sugar. Gently mash some of the berries with your hands. Set aside.

3. In a bowl, whip remaining cream (2 cups), ½ cup of sugar, and vanilla to soft peaks, using an electric mixer or a whisk.

4. Assemble the shortcakes by placing one biscuit bottom on each plate. Top each biscuit bottom with a serving of strawberries. Put a dollop of whipped cream on top of the strawberries, and then top with the other biscuit half.

5. Garnish with a dusting of powdered sugar and a mint sprig.

Bread Pudding

Bread pudding is a versatile comfort food that can be served warm or cold for breakfast, dessert, or as a midnight snack. For endless variety, substitute different breads, such as Corn Bread (page 218), Banana Bread (page 219), Gingerbread (page 265), or fruitcake, for half of the bread in this recipe. Serve bread pudding with Crème Anglaise (page 268), whipped cream, or ice cream.

• • •

1. Preheat oven to 350°F. Generously butter a 9" x 13" baking dish.

2. Put the bread cubes in the buttered dish. Sprinkle the pecans and dried fruit over the bread cubes and toss them together lightly with your hands. Set aside.

3. In a bowl, mix together the egg yolks, eggs, milk, cream, sugar, and vanilla. Pour this custard mixture evenly over the bread cubes. Press down the bread cubes to submerge them in the custard and soak it up.

4. Drizzle the melted butter over the top of the bread-cube/custard mixture.

5. Bake for about 1 hour, or until the custard is set. Push down in the middle with your finger. The cream will be set and won't ooze if it is done. Serve with 2 tablespoons of crème anglaise per serving.

Hard Sauce

Hard sauce is traditionally served with steamed puddings, but it is delicious on warm bread pudding too. Simply whip these ingredients together: 4 ounces softened butter, 1½ cups powdered sugar, 1 teaspoon vanilla, 1 ounce orange juice, and 1 teaspoon orange zest.

Serves 12

12 cups stale bread cubes
1 cup chopped toasted pecans
½ cup chopped dried fruit (apricots, cherries, etc.)
5 egg yolks
7 whole eggs
2½ cups milk
3½ cups heavy cream
1 cup sugar
1 teaspoon vanilla extract
8 tablespoons butter, melted (plus more for dish)
1½ cups Crème Anglaise (page 268)

Serves 6

1 cup half-and-half
2 cups heavy cream
½ cup sugar
6 egg yolks
1 teaspoon vanilla extract
granulated sugar for
*   caramelizing*

Crème Brûlée

Crème brûlée is simply creamy custard with a crunchy, caramelized top.
You may omit the caramelizing and serve this recipe as plain custard, topped
with berries or grated chocolate.

• • •

1. Preheat oven to 325°F. Put 6 ramekins (4-ounce porcelain cups used for baking custards and soufflés) in a 2-inch-deep baking dish; set aside.

2. In a saucepan heat the half-and-half, cream, and sugar to melt the sugar. Stir in the vanilla. Remove from heat and slowly whisk the hot mixture into the egg yolks in a bowl. Strain the custard into a pitcher.

3. Pour the hot custard into the ramekins, dividing it evenly. Pour hot water into the baking dish around the ramekins to come halfway up the ramekins. Cover the baking dish tightly with foil.

4. Bake for 30 minutes, and then check to see if custard is set by carefully jiggling the pan. If the custard is not set, cover and bake for 10 more minutes. Check again; if necessary, cover pan again and bake another 10 minutes or so, until set. Remove from oven and uncover if necessary. When ramekins are cool enough to handle, remove them from the water to finish cooling. Refrigerate until completely chilled, about 4 hours.

5. To caramelize, sprinkle the top of each custard with about 1 tablespoon of sugar. Place ramekins on a baking sheet and use a propane torch to caramelize the sugar.

Propane Torches and Caramelizing
Propane torches can be found in hardware stores, and special propane
torches just for the purpose of caramelizing sugar can be found at cook-
ware stores. Be careful not to touch or get splashed by molten sugar as
you use the propane torch! Keep the flame close to the custard and
move it around for an even color.

Chocolate Mousse

*Top this luxurious classic with sweetened whipped cream,
a strawberry, raspberries, mint leaves, or chocolate shavings. For a fancier
presentation, put the chilled mousse in a pastry bag with a star tip and pipe it
into martini glasses. Substitute white chocolate for the semisweet,
and you will have White Chocolate Mousse.*

• • •

Serves 6

12 ounces semisweet
   chocolate chips
4 egg whites, at room
   temperature
2 whole eggs
4 egg yolks
¾ cup heavy cream

1. Melt the chocolate in a metal or glass bowl set over simmering (not boiling) water. When chocolate is melted, remove the bowl from heat and set aside.

2. Whip the room-temperature egg whites to stiff peaks with a wire whisk or electric mixer; set aside.

3. Crack the whole eggs into the egg yolks; beat well to combine. Stir the yolk mixture into the melted chocolate.

4. Fold the whipped egg whites into the chocolate/yolk mixture with a rubber spatula.

5. Whip the heavy cream in a chilled bowl. Whisk half of the whipped cream into the chocolate/egg mixture to lighten it. Then, gently fold the remaining whipped cream in, just to incorporate. Chill at least 2 hours before serving.

Chocolate Mousse Pie
Make chocolate mousse pie by filling a chocolate Crumb Crust (page 224) with chocolate mousse and topping it with whipped cream and chocolate curls made by running a vegetable peeler along a chocolate bar. You can make the whipped cream fancy by piping it with a star tip from a pastry bag.

1 cup butter
5 eggs
2 cups sugar
2 cups flour
1 teaspoon vanilla, almond,
    or citrus extract

Pound Cake

This classic recipe makes a pleasantly light cake that is wonderful by itself or covered in whipped heavy cream and seasonal fruit.

•   •   •

1. Preheat oven to 300°F. Butter a large bundt pan.

2. Using a whisk, cream the butter. Add the eggs, one at a time, beating 1 minute after each.

3. While beating continuously, gradually add the sugar, then flour, followed by your flavoring of choice.

4. Pour mixture into the bundt pan, and bake for 1½ to 1¾ hours, or until a toothpick or knife inserted in the middle comes out clean. Serve with strawberries or other berries if desired.

Cake Pan Tips

Tip 1 The best pans for cake baking are shiny metal. If using dark coated (nonstick) or glass pans, follow the manufacturer's directions: If the directions are not available, reduce the oven temperature by 25 degrees. Glass and dark pans absorb the heat instead of reflecting it.

Tip 2 To prevent sticking, grease both the bottom and the sides of the pan generously. Dust the bottom with flour; shake the pan to coat the bottom, then turn over and discard the excess flour.

Tip 3 For chocolate cakes, dust the baking pan with cocoa powder instead of flour.

Tip 4 Even if using a cooking spray, dust the pan with flour if the recipe instructs you to do so. Sprays containing flour are also available specifically for baking.

Tip 5 The bottom of the pan can also be lined with wax paper to help cakes release without sticking.

Tip 6 Solid shortening is the best choice for greasing pans. Butter browns or burns at a lower temperature, and will sometimes result in a browner "crust" on the bottom and sides of the cake.

several cake pans

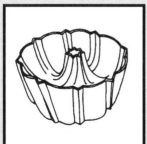
bundt pan

greasing the pan

flouring the pan

*16 tablespoons unsalted
    butter, softened*
2½ cups sugar
4 eggs
1 teaspoon vanilla extract
2¾ cups all-purpose flour
2 teaspoons baking soda
½ teaspoon baking powder
½ teaspoon salt
2 cups hot water
1 cup cocoa powder
Chocolate Frosting (page 259)

Chocolate Cake

*This chocolate cake is a classic three-layer cake that can be served with a
glass of milk, Crème Anglaise (page 268), whipped cream, or ice cream.
If you don't want to make a fancy layer cake you can bake this cake in
a 9" x 13" baking dish, frost it, and cut it into squares.*

• • •

1. Preheat oven to 300°F. Butter and flour three 9" round cake pans.

2. Combine hot water and cocoa powder; set aside to let cool.

3. In a large bowl, beat butter, sugar, eggs, and vanilla together for 5 minutes with an electric mixer.

4. In another bowl combine the flour, baking soda, baking powder, and salt. Add dry ingredients to the butter mixture in thirds, alternating with the cocoa mixture. Scrape down the sides of the bowl to make sure everything is well incorporated.

5. Divide batter evenly among the prepared cake pans. Bake for 20–25 minutes, until a toothpick inserted in the center comes out clean. Set pans on rack for 10 minutes, then turn layers out onto racks. If the layers stick in the pan, try carefully running a butter knife around the perimeter of the pan to loosen cake from the side of the pan.

6. When completely cool, frost tops of two cake layers with Chocolate Frosting (page 259); stack them; put third layer on top. Spread frosting on the top and sides of the layer cake.

Chocolate Frosting

*This is a dark, rich frosting for the Chocolate Cake (page 258)
or Brownies (page 244). It can also be melted and used as a glaze
for Sugar Cookies (page 247) or éclairs, or used as a fondue for
dipping strawberries and Pound Cake (page 256).*

• • •

1. Chop chocolates into small chunks and put them into a metal or glass bowl. Add water.

2. Set the bowl over simmering water. Stir occasionally to combine chocolate with the water as it melts.

3. Cut butter into chunks and stir it into the chocolate mixture.

4. When chocolate and butter have melted, remove the bowl from the simmering water and whisk the frosting to combine. It will be melted and liquid at this point. Set the bowl in a cool place (not the refrigerator) to set.

5. Stir the frosting occasionally while it is cooling to achieve a smooth, creamy consistency. This will take at least 6 hours. Before frosting a cake, whisk the frosting to fluff it up a bit.

White Chocolate Frosting

You can substitute white chocolate for semisweet chocolate and milk for the water in the Chocolate Frosting recipe to make rich white chocolate frosting. You can also alter the flavor by adding grated orange zest, almond extract, powdered espresso, or peppermint extract.

Serves 12

*16 ounces semisweet
chocolate chips
2 ounces unsweetened
baking chocolate
7 ounces water
1¼ cups unsalted butter*

½ cup all-purpose flour

2 tablespoons sugar

6 tablespoons butter, melted

½ cup ground almonds

24 ounces cream cheese (do not use whipped cream cheese), softened

2 cups sugar

2 tablespoons cornstarch

3 eggs

3½ cups sour cream

1 teaspoon vanilla extract

Cheesecake

This recipe is for a basic creamy cheesecake that can be served plain or with a variety of toppings and sauces, such as jam swirled on top before baking, Raspberry Coulis (page 270), or fresh fruit. Crumb Crust (page 224) may be substituted for the nut crust in this recipe.

• • •

1. Preheat oven to 350°F. In a bowl combine flour, 2 tablespoons sugar, melted butter, and ground almonds with a rubber spatula. Press mixture into the bottom of a springform pan that has been sprayed with cooking spray. Bake for 10 minutes. Remove from oven and set aside.

2. With an electric mixer, beat the cream cheese until fluffy. Add 1½ cups of the sugar and the cornstarch; cream together. Beat in eggs one at a time, scraping down the sides of the bowl after each one. Stir in 1½ cups of the sour cream.

3. Pour this batter into the springform pan and bake for about 1 hour. The middle of the cheesecake should jiggle slightly when finished. Remove from oven and cool at room temperature. Refrigerate and chill completely overnight.

4. With an electric mixer, whip 2 cups of sour cream with ½ cup sugar and the vanilla.

5. Top the chilled cheesecake with the whipped sour cream mixture; smooth the top. Let the cake set in the refrigerator, covered, for 1–2 hours before serving.

Apple Crisp

*This crisp topping turns any fruit into a warm, crunchy dessert,
but apple crisp is the classic. Serve it warm with a scoop of vanilla ice cream or
eat it cold for breakfast with a little cream poured over the top.*

• • •

1. Preheat oven to 350°F.

2. In a bowl, toss the apples with 2 tablespoons flour and ½ cup sugar. Turn the mixture into an ungreased 9" x 11" baking dish. Set aside.

3. In a bowl combine the nuts, 1¾ cups flour, brown sugar, sugar, cinnamon, and salt. Add the butter chunks and mix with an electric mixer to a sandy consistency. When this streusel-like topping clumps together when squeezed in the palm of your hand, it is ready to use.

4. Cover the apple mixture evenly with the topping and bake for 1 hour, or until the juices start to bubble up and caramelize. Test to see if the apples are done by inserting a knife in the middle. It should cut through easily.

5. Remove crisp from oven and cut around the sides to loosen. Cut into squares. Serve warm. This can also be baked ahead of time and reheated later.

Rhubarb Crisp
In the Apple Crisp recipe, substitute chopped rhubarb for apples and double the amount of sugar and flour. Rhubarb is more tart than apples and gives off more juice, which is why the sugar and flour must be increased.

Serves 8

8 cups peeled, cored, sliced apples, cut into ½-inch slices
2 tablespoons all-purpose flour
½ cup sugar
1 cup ground nuts (walnuts or almonds), ground in a food processor or chopped finely
1¾ cups all-purpose flour
½ cup dark brown sugar
¼ cup sugar
1 teaspoon cinnamon
½ teaspoon salt
12 tablespoons unsalted butter, cut in chunks

Serves 8

1 recipe Biscuits (page 214)
8 cups pitted, peeled, and
    sliced peaches
¼ cup all-purpose flour
¾ cup sugar
1 teaspoon almond extract
    (optional)
¼ cup heavy cream, plus an
    additional 1¼ cups for
    biscuits

Peach Cobbler

Fresh peaches are best for this recipe, although frozen will taste good too. If you only have access to canned, be sure to buy unsweetened and drain them first. Serve this cobbler warm with a scoop of vanilla ice cream, whipped cream, or a tablespoon of heavy cream drizzled over it. Try adding blueberries, raspberries, or blackberries to the peaches for a variation.

• • •

1. Preheat oven to 350°F.

2. Prepare Biscuit dough recipe (page 214), substituting cream for the buttermilk. Cut out the biscuit shapes and set them aside unbaked.

3. In a bowl toss the peaches, flour, sugar, and almond extract together. Turn the mixture into an ungreased 9" x 11" baking dish.

4. Bake the peaches for 25 minutes, remove from oven, and place the cutout biscuits on top of the hot peaches.

5. Brush the biscuit tops with cream. Return the cobbler to the oven to bake for another 25 minutes. Serve warm.

Apricot Soufflé

A soufflé is basically a warm pudding made from a pastry cream base with whipped egg whites folded in just before baking so it puffs up in the oven. A soufflé needs to be served immediately because it starts to deflate as soon as it has finished cooking.

• • •

Serves 6

4 tablespoons butter, melted
½ cup sugar
½ cup dried apricots,
    plumped in orange juice
    to cover for 15 minutes
4 egg whites, room
    temperature
¾ cup Pastry Cream Filling
    (page 234)
¾ cup heavy cream

1. Preheat oven to 400°F.

2. Brush six individual ramekins with melted butter. Coat the butter with sugar, dumping out the excess. Set aside.

3. Dice the plumped apricots and set them aside.

4. Whip the egg whites to stiff peaks. Fold the apricots into the pastry cream, then fold the egg whites into the pastry cream. Fill each ramekin to the top with the mixture and run your thumb around the rim to make a clean edge that will rise straight.

5. Bake the soufflés for 6 minutes. Serve immediately with cream on the side to pour into the top of the soufflés while eating.

Big Soufflé
To make one big soufflé instead of individual soufflés, bake the Apricot Soufflé recipe in a large soufflé dish for 35–45 minutes.

4 tablespoons unsalted butter
¾ cup dark brown sugar
fresh pineapple slices
(enough to cover bottom
of 9" round cake pan)
¼ cup dried cherries,
plumped in cherry or
pineapple juice to cover
for 15 minutes
2 egg whites, room
temperature
8 tablespoons salted butter
1 cup sugar
2 egg yolks
1 teaspoon vanilla extract
1½ cups all-purpose flour
2 teaspoons baking powder
½ cup milk

Pineapple Upside-Down Cake

This classic combination of caramel, pineapple, cherries, and butter cake needs nothing to embellish it, but if you must, top it with a dollop of whipped cream to make it fancy! Other fruits are delicious baked in the same manner. Try plums, apricots, or fresh cherries.

• • •

1. Preheat oven to 350°F.

2. Melt unsalted butter and brown sugar in a 9" round cake pan directly on top of a stove burner on low heat until the mixture starts to foam and the sugar starts to caramelize. Remove from heat.

3. Lay the pineapple and cherries on top of the caramelized sugar mixture and set aside. Whip the egg whites to stiff peaks and set aside.

4. In a mixing bowl, with an electric mixer, cream the salted butter with the sugar until fluffy. Beat in the egg yolks and vanilla. In a separate bowl, combine the flour and baking powder. Add the flour mixture to the butter/egg mixture in two parts, alternating with the milk. Fold the whipped egg whites into the cake batter, and then pour the batter over the fruit in the cake pan.

5. Bake for 50 minutes. Remove the cake from the oven, run a knife around the cake pan to loosen the edge, and then invert the cake onto a plate by first holding a plate face-down over the cake pan, then flipping the pan over. Leave the cake pan on top for 5 minutes to let the fruit naturally fall onto the cake. Remove the cake pan, and let the cake cool before cutting.

Gingerbread

*Warm gingerbread served with whipped cream is a classic.
This recipe can be made into individual cupcakes too. A simple dusting of
powdered sugar is enough garnish. This recipe can be used to
make Bread Pudding (page 253) too.*

• • •

Serves 9

1 cup sugar
1 cup vegetable oil
1 cup unsulfured molasses
1 cup boiling water
2 teaspoons baking soda
1 tablespoon ground dried
   ginger
½ teaspoon cinnamon
2½ cups all-purpose flour
2 eggs, beaten

1. Preheat oven to 350°F. Butter and flour a 9" x 9" baking dish.

2. In one bowl mix together the sugar, oil, molasses, and boiling water. Set aside.

3. In another bowl mix together the baking soda, ginger, cinnamon, and flour.

4. Whisk the wet ingredients into the dry ingredients. Mix in the eggs.

5. Pour the batter into the prepared pan and bake for 1 hour, or until the center springs back when lightly touched with a finger.

Gingerbread Muffins

Bake the Gingerbread batter in muffin tins and top them with the Black Bottom Cupcake filling (page 302) before baking them to make gingerbread muffins for a different treat.

6 egg yolks
½ cup sugar
1 cup fresh-squeezed
    orange juice
1 cup sliced strawberries
1 cup raspberries
1 cup blueberries
1 cup blackberries
8 sprigs mint
8 Shortbread cookie (page
    243) wedges

Sabayon with Fresh Berries

Sabayon is a light, foamy custard sauce that is a great partner for fresh berries in season. Sabayon is often made with alcohol, but this recipe uses fresh orange juice. Any liquid can be used instead of the juice. In this recipe sabayon is served chilled, but it may also be served warm. It can also be enriched and stabilized by folding whipped cream into the chilled version.

• • •

1. Whisk the egg yolks and sugar in a metal or glass bowl set over simmering water until the mixture is combined and warm.

2. Whip the orange juice into the yolk mixture ¼ cup at a time. It is important to keep beating so the yolks don't overcook and curdle.

3. When all of the juice has been incorporated, keep whisking until the mixture is very pale yellow and thick enough that if you run your finger through it, the mark should remain. This is the ribbon stage. The mixture will have expanded a lot in volume. Remove from heat, and store the sabayon on the refrigerator until it cools completely.

4. Whisk the sabayon occasionally while it is cooling to help retain the volume.

5. Divide berries evenly among 8 dessert cups and spoon the chilled sabayon on top. Garnish each serving with a sprig of mint and a shortbread cookie.

Caramel Sauce

*Homemade caramel sauce is far superior to the bottled version.
This recipe can be embellished with coffee, brandy, or orange liqueur,
added at the very end of the cooking process.*

• • •

Yield 3 cups

1½ cups sugar
½ cup water
1 cup heavy cream

1. Dissolve the sugar in water in a saucepan.

2. Without stirring, cook the sugar/water mixture over medium heat until it caramelizes to a golden brown color.

3. Carefully pour in cream (it will splatter) and heat to dissolve any coagulated caramel. Cook and stir until slightly thickened. Remove from heat; cool at room temperature. Thicken more as it cools.

Coffee Caramel
Substitute coffee for the water in the Caramel Sauce recipe for a mellow flavor change. You could also add Kahlua at the end of the cooking time for a kick at the end.

2 cups heavy cream
¼ cup sugar
¼ whole vanilla bean
5 egg yolks
ice-water bath

Crème Anglaise

This creamy vanilla custard sauce can be served with Bread Pudding
(page 253) or Chocolate Cake (page 258). If you have an ice cream machine,
you can freeze this mixture to make delicious vanilla ice cream.
If you can't find a vanilla bean, use 1 teaspoon vanilla extract.

• • •

1. Simmer cream, sugar, and vanilla bean (split, seeds scraped into cream) in a saucepan over medium heat.

2. Temper the egg yolks by adding ½ cup hot cream to them (this gently brings the temperature of the eggs closer to that of the hot cream); then add yolk mixture to the hot cream remaining in the saucepan.

3. Cook the mixture over medium-low heat, stirring constantly with a rubber spatula, until the sauce thickens enough to coat the back of a spoon.

4. Remove from heat. Strain the sauce into a bowl set in the ice-water bath.

5. Let the sauce cool completely in the ice bath, stirring occasionally to let steam escape. Refrigerate sauce up to 3 days.

Hot Fudge

Chocolate sauce is thin and creamy, but hot fudge is thick and sticky, making it perfect for topping ice cream.

• • •

1. In a saucepan over medium-high heat, heat and stir together the sugar, corn syrup, and water. Bring to a boil. Boil for 5 minutes.

2. Stir the cocoa powder and chocolate chips into the sugar syrup until the chips are completely melted.

3. Remove from heat, strain, and refrigerate.

Yield 3 cups

1 cup sugar
½ cup light corn syrup
1½ cups water
¾ cup cocoa powder
½ cup semisweet
   chocolate chips

Butterscotch Sauce

This sauce is a little sweeter than caramel sauce and is perfect for ice cream sundaes.

• • •

1. Combine brown sugar, cream, butter, and corn syrup in a saucepan. Stir over low heat until sugar has dissolved.

2. Increase heat to medium, and simmer 5 minutes.

3. Remove from heat and stir in vanilla (and Scotch, if desired). Cool and store in the refrigerator for up to 2 weeks.

Yield 1 cup

1 cup dark brown sugar
⅓ cup heavy cream
4 tablespoons butter
2 tablespoons light
   corn syrup
1 teaspoon vanilla extract
1 tablespoon Scotch whiskey
   (optional)

Yield 2 cups

1 cup sugar
½ cup water
4 cups fresh or frozen raspberries

Raspberry Coulis

This sauce can be served with almost any dessert, including Cheesecake (page 260), Chocolate Cake (page 258), and Bread Pudding (page 253). If you have an ice cream maker, this mixture can be stirred into Crème Anglaise (page 268) and then frozen to make raspberry ice cream.

• • •

1. Dissolve sugar in water over low heat in a saucepan. Cool completely.

2. Purée raspberries in a blender, then strain into a bowl.

3. Combine raspberry purée with chilled sugar syrup.

Strawberry Sauce

Strawberry sauce can be made in the same way as the Raspberry Coulis. Strawberry sauce can be stirred into Crème Anglaise and then frozen in an ice-cream maker to make homemade strawberry ice cream to go with your sauce.

CHAPTER 22
Fruit

4 apples, cored
4 cinnamon sticks
⅓ cup dark brown sugar
¼ cup chopped walnuts
1 teaspoon grated
    orange zest
¼ cup raisins
4 tablespoons butter, melted
⅔ cup apple cider or juice

Baked Apples

Baked apples are a homey dessert perfect for the time of year when the weather turns cold. Serve these warm treats with a scoop of vanilla ice cream or a drizzle of Crème Anglaise (page 268).

• • •

1. Preheat oven to 350°F. Lay the walnuts out in an even layer on an ungreased baking sheet pan; bake for 10 minutes. Set aside, leaving the oven at 350°F.

2. Place the apples upright and close together in a baking dish.

3. Put one cinnamon stick in the center of each apple where the core used to be.

4. In a bowl, combine the brown sugar, walnuts, orange zest, and raisins. Divide this mixture among the 4 apples, adding it to the centers with the cinnamon sticks. Drizzle the melted butter over the filling.

5. Pour cider into the baking dish around the bottom of the apples. Cover with foil and bake the apples for 30 minutes. Uncover and baste the apples with the liquid at the bottom of the dish. Return the apples, uncovered, to the oven for 10 minutes. Remove baked apples from the oven; serve warm with the basting liquid drizzled over them.

Poached Pears

Poached pears are an elegantly simple dessert. You can dress them up by dipping them in chocolate and serving them with vanilla ice cream as in the French classic Poires Belle Helene. You can also enjoy them sliced as part of a fruit compote with fresh figs and raspberries.

• • •

1. Rub the lemon juice on the pears.

2. In a saucepan combine the sugar and water and heat over low to dissolve the sugar. Add the lemon peel and vanilla bean. Simmer for 5 minutes.

3. Add the pear halves to the simmering liquid and place a piece of parchment paper over the surface of the liquid. Poke a few slits in the paper to let steam escape.

4. Simmer the pears for 20–25 minutes, until tender. (Poke them with a paring knife to test for tenderness.)

5. Remove from heat and let pears cool in poaching liquid. Refrigerate in liquid until ready to serve.

Serves 4

2 tablespoons lemon juice
4 ripe pears, peeled, halved
   and cored
½ cup sugar
2 cups water
1 2-inch strip lemon peel
1 whole vanilla bean, split
   lengthwise

4 firm, ripe bananas
4 tablespoons unsalted butter
½ cup dark brown sugar
¼ cup orange juice

Sautéed Bananas

This recipe is a version of the flambé dish Bananas Foster, but without the intoxicating liquor and dangerous flames! Served over vanilla ice cream or with French toast, this recipe will please your guests from morning to evening.

• • •

1. Peel the bananas and cut them in half crosswise, then again in half lengthwise. Set aside.

2. In a large sauté or frying pan over medium heat, melt the butter and brown sugar until the foam subsides, stirring to melt and brown evenly.

3. Add the bananas, cut-side down, to the bubbling sugar. Cook for 2 minutes.

4. Add the orange juice to the pan and cook for 2 minutes more.

5. Turn bananas over and cook another minute or two. Remove from heat and serve with the pan sauce drizzled over the bananas.

Serves 6

½ cup cubed cantaloupe
½ cup cubed
    honeydew melon
1 kiwi, peeled and cut into
    sticks
½ cup blueberries
½ cup green grapes
½ cup red grapes
½ cup sliced strawberries
½ cup fresh pineapple chunks
½ cup peeled mango chunks

Fruit Salad

Here is a nice combination of fruits, suitable for a brunch or lunch side dish. Feel free to substitute any of the fruits for your favorites or exclude any you don't care for.

• • •

Toss all the fruits together gently in a large bowl. Chill fruit salad before serving.

Fruit Compote
Poached Pears (page 273), figs, and raspberries are a nice combination to serve alone as a fruit salad compote or as a dessert with biscotti. Drizzle a little bit of the pear poaching liquid over the fruit before serving.

Baked Peaches

Serve this recipe with vanilla ice cream and Raspberry Coulis (page 270) for a variation on the classic Peach Melba. Baked peaches may be served warm or cold. You can purchase ground almonds in the bulk section of most natural food stores, or you can grind them yourself in a food processor.

• • •

Serves 4

4 ripe peaches
2 tablespoons lemon juice
8 tablespoons soft butter
⅓ cup sugar
1 egg
½ cup ground almonds
¼ cup dry bread crumbs
1 cup white grape juice

1. Preheat oven to 350°F. Butter a baking dish large enough to fit 8 peach halves snugly in one layer.

2. Cut the peaches in half and remove the pits. Place peach halves, cut sides facing up, in the prepared baking dish. Sprinkle the lemon juice over the peaches. Set aside.

3. In a bowl, cream the sugar and butter together until the mixture is fluffy. Beat in the egg; stir in the almonds and bread crumbs.

4. Place a scoop of the almond filling on top of each peach. Pour the white grape juice around the peaches, but not directly on them.

5. Bake peaches uncovered for 45 minutes, basting with the liquid at the bottom of the pan.

Serves 4

1 cup heavy cream
¼ cup buttermilk
12 ripe mission figs
¼ cup fresh mint leaves,
  thinly sliced into ribbons

Figs with Crème Fraîche and Mint

*This is a refreshing fruit salad of sorts. Thinly sliced prosciutto makes a nice
salty addition if you want to make it into an antipasto dish.*

• • •

1. To make crème fraîche: Combine cream and buttermilk, cover with
   cheesecloth, and set in a warm place for 3 days. Refrigerate after that.

2. Cut the stem tip off the figs; cut each fig into quarters.

3. Divide figs evenly among 4 salad plates.

4. Drizzle crème fraîche over the figs.

5. Scatter the mint ribbons over the figs.

Melon and Prosciutto
*The classic combination of salty and sweet make melon and prosciutto
the perfect appetizer. Simply peel, seed, and slice a cantaloupe into half
moons and drape pieces of thinly sliced prosciutto over each slice.*

Lemonade

Fresh-squeezed lemonade is a refreshing combination of tart and sweet flavors, and is perfect for a summer picnic or a trip to the beach.

• • •

Combine lemon juice, water, and sugar. Serve over ice.

Yield 1 quart

¾ cup fresh-squeezed lemon juice
4 cups water
½ cup sugar
ice cubes

Strawberry Lemonade

This recipe combines two of the best flavors of summer and is a favorite of kids.

• • •

1. Purée strawberries in the blender or food processor.

2. Combine lemon juice, sugar, and water, then stir in strawberry purée. Serve over ice.

Yield 5 cups

¾ cup fresh-squeezed lemon juice
½ cup sugar
4 cups water
½ cup fresh strawberries, hulled and sliced
ice cubes

Limeade

Yield 6 cups

¾ cup fresh-squeezed
     lime juice
4 cups water
½ cup sugar
1 cup lemon-lime soda
ice cubes

*Limeade is another refreshing citrus cooler
like lemonade, only a little more tart.*

• • •

Combine lime juice, water, and sugar; add lemon-lime soda. Serve over ice.

Cherry Limeade
To make refreshing cherry limeade, add maraschino cherry juice to fresh Limeade. Garnish with a maraschino cherry.

Tangerine Sorbet

Yield 1 quart

½ cup sugar
¼ cup water
3 cups tangerine juice
¼ cup lemon juice

Try to juice your own tangerines to add fresh citrus flavor to this frozen treat.

• • •

1. Combine sugar and water in a saucepan and heat, stirring, just until sugar dissolves. Remove from heat; chill.

2. Combine chilled sugar syrup, tangerine juice, and lemon juice.

3. Freeze in an ice-cream freezer according to manufacturer's instructions. If you don't own an ice-cream freezer, you can freeze the mixture, break it up into chunks, and blend it in a food processor or a blender. Refreeze and serve!

CHAPTER 23
Holiday Classics

1 blind-baked pie crust (half
    of Pie Dough recipe on
    page 222)
2 cups pumpkin purée
⅔ cup dark brown sugar
⅓ cup sugar
1 tablespoon all-
    purpose flour
½ teaspoon salt
1½ teaspoons cinnamon
½ teaspoon nutmeg
½ teaspoon ginger
¼ teaspoon allspice
¼ teaspoon ground cloves
1 cup heavy cream
⅓ cup milk
2 eggs
1 teaspoon vanilla extract

Serves 8

1 red onion, cut in big chunks
2–3 cups Stuffing (page 282)
1 10-pound turkey (giblets
    removed)
4 tablespoons butter,
    softened
salt
pepper

Pumpkin Pie

You can bake your own pumpkin and purée the flesh or you can use canned pumpkin for this recipe. If you use canned, make sure to get plain purée and not the kind with the pie spice already added to it.

• • •

1. Preheat oven to 350°F.

2. In a bowl, combine all the filling ingredients with a whisk.

3. Pour pumpkin filling into prebaked pie crust.

4. Bake 40 minutes. Cover crust with aluminum foil if it starts to get too dark while the filling is baking.

5. Cool before cutting.

Roast Turkey

Here is a recipe for the most important part of Thanksgiving. You may stuff the bird before roasting it, or bake the stuffing on the side.

• • •

1. Preheat oven to 325°F. Scatter onions on the bottom of a roasting pan.

2. Stuff turkey and place it on the onions. Massage butter on the skin of the turkey; season with salt and pepper.

3. Roast turkey, basting occasionally, for 3¾ hours, or until you can easily move the leg and the juices run clear.

How to Carve a Whole Turkey or Chicken

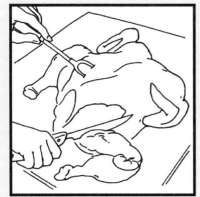

1 Place the bird on a clean cutting board and remove any stuffing. Begin carving by pulling the drumsticks to the side of the body. Cut through the thigh meat on the side of the body and through the leg joint.

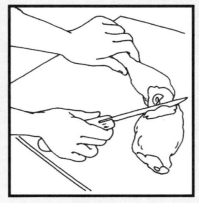

2 Cut the drumsticks and thighs apart at the joints.

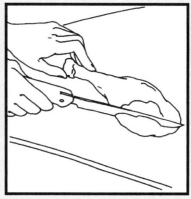

3 If you wish to cut the meat from the drumsticks, hold them by the tip and slice parallel to the bone.

4 Pull the wings away from the body and cut through the wing joints.

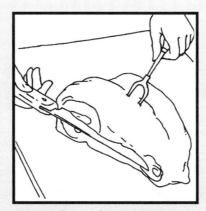

5 Just above the wing joints, cut horizontally through to the ribs. This cut will be the bottom of the breast meat slices.

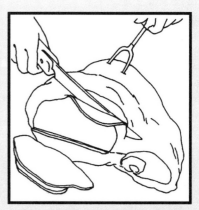

6 Beginning at the outer top of each breast side, slice down vertically to the horizontal cut, making slices of breast meat.

Yield 4 cups

2 cups Corn Bread cubes
    (page 218)
2 cups French bread cubes
¼ cup dried cranberries
½ cup chopped pecans
1 box Bell's seasoning
1 cup chicken broth

Stuffing

*Use this to stuff your roast turkey or bake separately
in a buttered casserole dish.*

• • •

1. Combine all ingredients together in a bowl.

2. Stuff turkey. Put any leftover stuffing in a buttered baking dish, cover with aluminum foil, and bake alongside the turkey. If you choose to bake the stuffing separately, bake at 350°F for 25 minutes.

Mashed Sweet Potatoes Praline

Make mashed sweet potatoes praline by whipping sweet potatoes with butter, milk, and eggs, and topping that with brown sugar and chopped pecans. Bake this dish for 30 minutes then broil it for a few more minutes to create a crunchy praline top.

Festive Mashed Potatoes

Serves 8

3 pounds peeled russet
    potatoes, cooked
8 ounces cream cheese,
    softened
4 tablespoons butter,
    softened
½ cup sour cream
½ cup milk
2 eggs, beaten
¼ cup minced onion
salt and white pepper to taste

This recipe is made the day before it will be served and then baked just before serving. It is a very rich version of mashed potatoes that is a nice change from the everyday puréed version.

• • •

1. Beat the hot potatoes until smooth.

2. Add cream cheese and beat again.

3. Add butter; beat until blended.

4. Mix in sour cream, then milk, eggs, onion, and seasoning. Put mixture into a buttered 9" x 13" casserole dish and refrigerate overnight.

5. Bake in a preheated 350°F oven for 45 minutes, until lightly browned.

Green Bean Casserole

This is a holiday tradition for many Americans. If you want to make this completely from scratch, substitute Onion Rings (page 185) for the French-fried onions; Béchamel Sauce (page 207) and sautéed fresh mushrooms for the mushroom soup, milk, and canned mushrooms; and fresh green beans for the canned.

• • •

1. Preheat oven to 350°F. Butter a 9" x 13" casserole dish.

2. In a bowl, whisk together the canned soup and milk. Season with salt and pepper.

3. Stir in the mushrooms, green beans, and 1 cup of the French-fried onions.

4. Turn bean mixture into prepared casserole dish and cover the top of it with the remaining French-fried onions.

5. Bake for 45 minutes.

Serves 6

1 can cream of
    mushroom soup
½ cup milk
salt and pepper to taste
1 small can sliced mushrooms
2 14-ounce cans green beans
2 cups French-fried onions

Serves 6

4 fresh yams or sweet
    potatoes, peeled
1½ cups fresh-squeezed
    orange juice
½ cup brown rice syrup
    (available in the corn
    syrup area of the grocery
    store)
pinch salt
½ teaspoon white pepper
4 tablespoons butter, cut in
    pieces

Candied Yams

*You can't have Thanksgiving without candied yams. This recipe does not
have marshmallows in it, but if you would like to include them, sprinkle
marshmallows on top of the yams during the last 10 minutes of baking time.*

• • •

1. Preheat oven to 375°F.

2. Cut the yams into quarters and put them in one layer in an ungreased
   9" x 13" baking dish. Set aside.

3. In a bowl combine the orange juice, brown rice syrup, salt, and pepper.

4. Pour the liquid mixture over the yams, and then scatter the butter
   pieces over them.

5. Bake, basting occasionally with the syrup, for 1½ hours, until yams are
   soft and candied to a golden sheen.

Marshmallow-Topped Sweet Potatoes
*Yet another sweet potato dish is made by mixing together 3 cups
mashed sweet potatoes, 2 ounces butter, 1 cup milk, 3 eggs, and 3 cups
mini marshmallows. Bake this dish at 350°F for 30 minutes or until the
marshmallows brown.*

Potato Casserole

*This casserole is perfect for a buffet or brunch at holiday time.
It is easy to prepare and very tasty. Potatoes O'Brien is a dish of
potatoes sautéed with peppers.*

• • •

1. Preheat oven to 350°F. Butter a 9" x 13" baking dish and set aside.

2. In a bowl whisk together the canned soup, sour cream, salt, and pepper.

3. Add the onions, cheese, and potatoes to the soup mixture; toss to combine.

4. Put the potato mixture in the prepared baking dish and sprinkle it with the crushed cereal. Drizzle the melted butter over the cereal.

5. Bake for 1 hour.

Onion Rings and Green Beans

For a twist on the classic Green Bean Casserole (page 283), simply combine sautéed fresh or frozen green beans with baked frozen onion rings. It's a quick fix for any time of the year when there are no holidays that require all the trimmings.

Serves 8

1 can cream of mushroom or
   celery soup
1 cup sour cream
1 teaspoon salt
¼ teaspoon pepper
1 cup diced onions
1 cup grated Cheddar cheese
1 bag frozen diced potatoes
   O'Brien (with bell
   peppers)
1½ cups crushed cornflakes
   breakfast cereal
8 tablespoons butter, melted

1 cup sugar
½ cup water
¼ cup orange juice
2 cups fresh cranberries
1 teaspoon grated
    orange zest

Cranberry Sauce

*This can be served in addition to the jelled, canned cranberry sauce
that some people enjoy with their Thanksgiving turkey.*

• • •

1. In a medium-size saucepan combine the sugar, water, and orange juice. Bring to a boil; reduce heat and simmer for 5 minutes.

2. Add the cranberries to the simmering liquid and stir over medium heat for 5 minutes, until the berries pop.

3. Stir the orange zest into the cranberries; remove from the heat.

4. Let the sauce cool to room temperature; then chill it in the refrigerator.

Lemon Baskets

Serve homemade cranberry sauce in hollowed-out lemon halves for an eye-catching holiday table. Oranges work well too, and complement the orange juice and zest in the recipe.

Indian Pudding

*Serve this cornmeal pudding warm with vanilla ice cream
for breakfast, dessert, or as a midnight snack.*

• • •

1. Preheat oven to 350°F. Butter a 9" x 9" baking dish and set aside.

2. Scald (heat to just under a boil—when steam starts to rise, reduce to low) 1 cup of the milk in a saucepan, add cornmeal, and stir over medium heat until it thickens. Remove from heat.

3. Add all the remaining ingredients, except the cream and 1 cup milk, to the cooked cornmeal. Stir to combine. Pour the mixture into the prepared baking dish.

4. Pour the cream and 1 cup milk over the top of the mixture to prevent a skin from forming during baking.

5. Bake uncovered for ½ hour. Stir the cream and milk on the top into the pudding; bake for ½ hour more.

Serves 8

5 cups milk
½ cup cornmeal
1 teaspoon vanilla extract
½ cup unsulfured molasses
1 teaspoon salt
1 cup sugar
16 tablespoons unsalted butter, cubed
1 teaspoon ground dried ginger
1 teaspoon cinnamon
1 cup currants
1 cup corn kernels, fresh if possible
1 cup golden raisins
1 cup heavy cream

Serves 4

½ cup butter, melted
1 cup soda cracker crumbs
    (crushed soda crackers)
½ cup dry bread crumbs
1 pint shucked oysters,
    drained, with juice
    reserved
¼ teaspoon salt
¼ teaspoon pepper
2 tablespoons heavy cream
2 teaspoons Worcestershire
    sauce
few drops cayenne
    pepper sauce

Scalloped Oysters

*If you don't have access to fresh oysters in the shell, it is perfectly
fine to use the kind that comes preshucked in a container from the grocery
store. Oysters were part of the original Thanksgiving meal
shared by the Pilgrims and Indians.*

• • •

1. Preheat oven to 425°F. Butter a 2-quart baking dish.

2. In a bowl toss together the melted butter, cracker crumbs, and bread crumbs. Spread half of this mixture on the bottom of the prepared baking dish.

3. Arrange the oysters on top of the crumb mixture. Sprinkle them with salt and pepper.

4. Mix the cream, Worcestershire sauce, cayenne pepper sauce, and 3 tablespoons oyster juice together. Pour this mixture over the oysters.

5. Sprinkle the remaining crumb mixture over the oysters. Bake for 25 minutes.

Oyster Stuffing
Enhance the Stuffing (page 282) for the holiday turkey by adding fresh or smoked oysters to it. Cut back a little on the chicken stock if using fresh oysters, and replace the cranberries with sliced green onions.

Roast Beef—Prime Rib

This succulent roast is traditionally served with Yorkshire Pudding (page 290) and horseradish cream. Horseradish cream is made by mixing 1 cup of sour cream with ¼ cup prepared grated horseradish. Leftovers from this classic holiday roast can be chilled and then thinly sliced for hot roast beef sandwiches.

• • •

1. Preheat oven to 450°F.

2. Rub the outside of the roast with the rosemary, salt, and pepper, leaving a crust.

3. Put the roast in a roasting pan and put it in the oven. Roast for 15 minutes.

4. Reduce the oven temperature to 325°F and continue to roast for 1½ hours. Check internal temperature with a meat thermometer; when it reaches 115°F, remove the roast from the oven. Let the roast stand for at least 15 minutes before carving to let the temperature rise and allow the juices to settle back into the meat,

5. Roast internal temperature will rise 10°F during the resting period after it is removed from the oven. Finished temperatures are 125°F for rare, 130°F for medium rare, and 135–145°F for medium.

Serves 8

18-pound boneless beef rib roast
2 tablespoons chopped fresh rosemary
¼ cup kosher salt
2 tablespoons cracked black pepper

Serves 8

½ cup beef fat (drippings
from the beef roast)
2 cups milk
4 eggs
1 teaspoon salt
2 cups all-purpose flour

Yorkshire Pudding

This is a batter that basically bakes into a beef-flavored popover.
It is the traditional partner to Roast Beef—Prime Rib (page 289). It can be baked
in the pan the roast was cooked in, or in muffin tins for individual puddings.

• • •

1. Preheat oven to 400°F. Divide beef fat evenly among 8 muffin tin cups.

2. Combine remaining ingredients in a blender or bowl with a whisk. Pour the batter into the muffin tin cups that have been prepared with beef fat.

3. Bake 15 minutes. Reduce the oven temperature to 350°F; bake 15 minutes more.

Yield 1½ cups

1 tablespoon butter
1½ cups dark brown sugar
1 tablespoon dry mustard
2 tablespoons all-
purpose flour
2 tablespoons orange juice
concentrate (frozen)
1 tablespoon water
whole cloves

Baked Ham Glaze

Spread this glaze on a ham that has been baked for 2 hours
at 250°F and cooled for 10 minutes.

• • •

1. Preheat the oven to 350°F. Melt butter in a saucepan. Stir in the brown sugar, dry mustard, and flour. Stir over medium heat for 2 minutes.

2. Add the orange juice concentrate and 1 tablespoon water. Stir over medium heat until glaze is smooth and thick. Remove from heat.

3. Score the ham by making shallow cuts into the ham in a grid pattern. Poke cloves into the intersections of the cuts. Spread ham with glaze. Bake for 30–45 minutes.

Ham Loaf with Pineapple

This is a good way to use leftover holiday ham. Be sure to save the ham bone for Split Pea Soup (page 59). Serve ham loaf with steamed asparagus with Hollandaise Sauce (page 200) and Scalloped Potatoes (page 193).

• • •

Serves 6

1¼ pounds ground ham
¾ pound ground pork
2 eggs
1 cup dry bread crumbs
½ cup buttermilk
¼ cup pineapple juice
1 pineapple ring

1. Preheat oven to 350°F.

2. Combine all ingredients except for the pineapple ring and form into a loaf.

3. Place the loaf in a loaf pan; place the pineapple ring on top.

4. Bake uncovered for 1 hour.

5. Cut into 1-inch-thick slices and serve warm.

Hobo Ham Loaf

Make the recipe for Hobo Stew (page 299), substituting Ham Loaf mixture for the ground beef mixture. Top the Hobo Ham Loaf with green and red bell peppers, red onions, and a pineapple ring instead of using potatoes, carrots, and onions. Wrap up the foil packets and bake in the same manner as Hobo Stew.

CHAPTER 24
Kids' Favorites

Serves 6

4 tablespoons butter
¼ cup all-purpose flour
1 teaspoon dry mustard
2¾ cups milk
1 teaspoon salt
⅛ teaspoon pepper
pinch cayenne pepper
3 cups shredded Cheddar
   cheese
16 ounces elbow macaroni,
   cooked and drained
1 cup dry bread crumbs

Real Macaroni and Cheese

*This is a kids' classic that is not just for kids! Serve it with
Broiled Tomatoes (page 180) and a green salad for a delicious meal.
This recipe can be divided into individual portions and frozen before it is
baked, and then baked at a later date for a quick weeknight dinner.*

• • •

1. Preheat oven to 350°F. Butter a 9" x 13" baking dish.

2. Melt the butter in a medium-size saucepan. Stir in the flour and dry mustard; cook (stirring) over medium heat for 2 minutes.

3. Add the milk and whisk over medium heat until mixture thickens, whisking constantly to prevent burning on the bottom. Stir in the salt, pepper, and cayenne pepper. Remove from heat.

4. Stir in the cheese and let the mixture sit for a minute. Stir again to smooth out the melted cheese.

5. Pour cooked macaroni into the casserole dish; add cheese sauce. Mix until macaroni is coated with cheese.

6. Sprinkle bread crumbs on top of the casserole and bake for 45 minutes, until browned and bubbly on the edges. Serve warm.

Oven-Fried Chicken Nuggets

These nuggets are not deep-fried but baked in the oven instead. They are still crunchy, and less oily. Serve these with dipping sauces such as honey, BBQ Sauce (page 206), honey mustard, Buttermilk (Ranch) Dressing (page 73), and ketchup.

• • •

1. Preheat oven to 350°F. Line a baking sheet with foil and set aside.

2. Melt butter and mix it with the mustard. Set aside.

3. Combine bread crumbs, Parmesan cheese, onion powder, paprika, salt, and pepper in a bowl. Set aside.

4. Toss chicken chunks in the butter mixture; then roll them around in the crumb mixture.

5. Arrange the coated chicken chunks on the foil and bake for 1 hour. Serve warm or at room temperature.

Dipping Sauce
To make a quick dipping sauce for chicken nuggets, mix equal parts of honey, Dijon mustard, and barbecue sauce together. Add a squeeze of ketchup for dipping French fries.

Serves 4

8 tablespoons butter, melted
2 tablespoons Dijon mustard
3 cups dry bread crumbs
1 cup Parmesan cheese
1 tablespoon onion powder
2 teaspoons paprika
2 teaspoons salt
1 teaspoon pepper
3 boneless, skinless chicken breasts, cut in chunks

1 pound ground beef
½ cup diced onion
¼ cup diced celery
¼ cup diced carrots
1 teaspoon minced garlic
1 tablespoon olive oil
1 teaspoon salt
½ teaspoon pepper
16 ounces elbow macaroni,
   cooked and drained
1 tablespoon chopped fresh
   parsley

Hamburger Macaroni

This concoction becomes cheeseburger macaroni if you add chunks of American cheese to it at the end. It becomes "goulash" if you add Tomato Sauce (page 205). Kids, young and old, love it!

• • •

1. In a large pot, brown the ground beef. Drain and discard the fat. Set aside the cooked meat.

2. In the same pot, sauté the onions, celery, carrots, and garlic in the olive oil until the onions and celery are translucent.

3. Add the ground beef back to the pot; season with salt and pepper.

4. Add the cooked macaroni to the pot. Stir over low heat to evenly heat the mixture.

5. Stir in the parsley, adjust seasoning with salt and pepper, and remove from heat.

Sloppy Joes

This recipe tastes even better when you put a slice of American cheese and potato chips in the sandwich, and serve it with pickles on the side.

* * *

1. In a frying pan, brown the ground beef. Drain and discard the fat. Set aside the cooked beef.

2. Sauté the onions, celery, bell peppers, and garlic in the oil until onions and celery are translucent.

3. Stir in the ground beef, tomato sauce, Worcestershire sauce, ketchup, salt, and pepper. Cook for 5 minutes.

4. Taste; adjust seasoning with salt and pepper. Remove from heat.

5. Serve hot on hamburger buns.

Loosemeats

A loosemeat sandwich is a sloppy joe that doesn't have the tangy sauce binding it together, just the "loose meat," onions, celery, and dry seasoning.

Serves 6

1 pound ground beef
½ cup diced onions
¼ cup diced celery
¼ cup diced green bell pepper
¼ cup diced red bell pepper
1 teaspoon minced garlic
1 tablespoon vegetable oil
½ cup (1 8-ounce can) tomato sauce
2 tablespoons Worcestershire sauce
1 tablespoon ketchup
salt and pepper to taste
6 hamburger buns

Serves 4

2 cups baked beans
2 cups sliced hot dogs
1 tablespoon ketchup
1 teaspoon mustard
1 teaspoon dark brown sugar

Beans and Franks

Hot dogs are always a favorite with kids, and beans are a classic complement to hot dogs. This casserole is an easy and quick way to combine the two! You can use the Quick Baked Beans recipe on page 174, or you can purchase canned baked beans at the supermarket.

• • •

1. Preheat oven to 350°F.

2. Combine all ingredients and put the mixture into an ungreased 9" x 13" casserole dish.

3. Bake for 45 minutes.

Serves 4

4 hot dogs
4 cups water
yellow mustard in a squeeze
    bottle

Octopus Dogs

Serve these with macaroni and cheese in the shape of seashells.

• • •

1. Heat the water in a saucepan until it simmers.

2. Starting 2 inches down from one end of the hot dog, make a cut through to the other end. Then make 4 cuts lengthwise to create 8 tentacles. The 2-inch uncut part of the hot dog is the head of the octopus.

3. Put the hot dogs in the simmering water for 5 minutes; remove and drain. The tentacles will separate and curl. Set each octopus on a plate and make eyes with dots of mustard.

Hobo Stew

Serves 4

1 pound ground beef
¾ cup dry bread crumbs
2 tablespoons Worcestershire
    sauce
1 tablespoon ketchup
1 tablespoon Dijon mustard
1 teaspoon onion powder
¼ cup Parmesan cheese
½ teaspoon salt
½ teaspoon pepper
1 cup peeled potatoes,
    large dice
½ cup sliced onion
½ cup sliced carrot
1 egg, beaten

*This campfire classic is revised for the oven. This recipe is easy for
kids to help with—they can assemble the mixture and an adult can transfer
the stew in and out of the oven. The "stew" is more like an individual
meatloaf with vegetables steamed together.*

• • •

1. Preheat oven to 350°F. Tear off 4 large squares of heavy-duty aluminum foil. Set aside.

2. In a bowl, combine the ground beef, bread crumbs, Worcestershire sauce, ketchup, mustard, onion powder, cheese, egg, salt, and pepper with your hands. Form the meat mixture into 4 oblong patties.

3. Set one patty on each foil square. Divide potatoes, onions, and carrots into four servings. Place one serving on top of each meat patty. Sprinkle the vegetables with salt and pepper.

4. Wrap each foil square up around the meat and vegetables into a tightly sealed packet.

5. Place the packets on a baking sheet. Bake for 45 minutes. Remove packets from the oven and carefully open them, avoiding the steam that will be released.

Campfire Cuisine
*The hobo stew can be cooked over a campfire instead of in the oven.
In fact, that is how it was originally made!*

Serves 4

1 can tomato soup
½ cup milk
½ teaspoon onion powder
1 teaspoon Worcestershire
  sauce
1 cup shredded American
  cheese
6 slices toasted bread, cut in
  half diagonally

Tomato Soup Rarebit

*This is like Welsh Rabbit, which is a cheesy snack made from cheese,
cream or beer, and seasonings, served over toast or crackers.*

• • •

1. Combine soup, milk, onion powder, and Worcestershire sauce in a medium-size saucepan. Heat until mixture is simmering. Add cheese and stir until melted. Remove from heat.

2. Arrange 3 toast triangles on each individual's plate.

3. Pour the sauce over the toast triangles.

Serves 1

2 slices bread
1 tablespoon butter, softened
2 slices American cheese

Grilled Cheese Sandwich

This is the perfect sandwich to dip in Tomato Soup (page 48).

• • •

1. Heat a griddle or skillet.

2. Butter one side of each piece of bread. Put the bread slices butter-side down on the hot griddle. Top each piece of bread with a piece of cheese.

3. Combine the two bread slices to make a sandwich, cheese-side in. When the bottom of the sandwich is golden brown, turn it over and cook the other side until golden. Remove from heat and cut into triangles.

Butterscotch Pudding

*Serve this treat topped with whipped cream and a
chopped toffee-chocolate bar.*

• • •

Serves 4

4 tablespoons unsalted butter
½ cup dark brown sugar
½ cup plus 3 tablespoons
    heavy cream
1½ cups milk
¼ teaspoon salt
3 tablespoons cornstarch
1 teaspoon vanilla extract

1. In a saucepan, cook the butter and brown sugar over medium heat until it bubbles. Add ½ cup of the cream to the sugar; stir until sugar dissolves.

2. Stir the milk and salt into the sugar mixture.

3. In a small bowl, dissolve the cornstarch in 3 tablespoons of cream. Stir this mixture into the milk/sugar mixture.

4. Cook, stirring constantly, over medium heat until the mixture thickens. Simmer for 1 minute; remove from heat.

5. Stir in vanilla and pour the pudding into a bowl or individual cups. Cover the bowl or cups with plastic wrap and chill the pudding.

Chocolate Crescents
Kids can make their own "pain au chocolat" (bread with chocolate) for breakfast by enclosing chocolate chips in crescent roll dough and baking them. These don't last long enough to get cool!

8 ounces cream cheese,
   softened
⅓ cup sugar
1 egg
pinch of salt
1 cup semisweet
   chocolate chips
3 cups all-purpose flour
2 cups sugar
½ cup cocoa powder
2 teaspoons baking soda
1 teaspoon salt
2 cups cold water
⅔ cup vegetable oil
2 tablespoons distilled
   vinegar
2 teaspoons vanilla extract

Black Bottom Cupcakes

*These chocolate cupcakes are filled with cream cheese and
chocolate chips before they are baked.*

• • •

1. Make the filling by combining the cream cheese, ⅓ cup sugar, egg, pinch of salt, and chocolate chips. Refrigerate until ready to use. (Can be made up to 3 days in advance.)

2. Preheat oven to 325°F. Put 12 fluted paper cups in a muffin tin and set aside.

3. Combine the flour, 2 cups sugar, cocoa powder, baking soda, and salt in a mixing bowl.

4. In a pitcher combine the water, oil, vinegar, and vanilla. Pour the wet ingredients into the dry ingredients and whip with an electric mixer for 3 minutes. Pour the batter evenly into the prepared muffin tin. Top each cupcake with 1–2 tablespoons of the cream cheese filling.

5. Bake for 28 minutes. Cool in the pan before serving.

Caramel Apples

These can be made with red or green apples, and the peanuts may be replaced by pecans, or omitted altogether. Serve these in fluted cupcake liners after the nuts and caramel have set.

• • •

Serves 6

1 pound caramels,
   unwrapped
¼ cup heavy cream
1 cup chopped roasted, salted
   peanuts
6 wooden skewers or frozen
   popsicle sticks
6 small apples

1. Melt the caramels in the cream in a saucepan over low heat.

2. Stir to make the caramel smooth. Remove from heat.

3. Spread the peanuts on a platter. Put the skewers in the apples.

4. Dip the apples into the melted caramels, and let the excess caramel drip back into the pan.

5. Roll the apples in the nuts, and set them on a platter with the stick pointing up. Refrigerate the platter for 5 minutes. Remove from the refrigerator after the caramel has set.

Hand Cookies

Have children trace their hands on rolled-out Sugar Cookie dough (page 247) using a clean wooden skewer or the handle-end of a silverware spoon. Help the children cut out the cookies, and then allow them to design decorations depicting rings and bracelets on the hand shapes using colored sugars and nonpareils. Bake according to directions for Sugar Cookies.

Serves 8

2 cups raisins

2 cups dry roasted peanuts

1 cup candy-coated
   chocolate (such as
   M&M's)

2 cups granola (page 89 or
   store-bought)

1 cup shelled sunflower seeds

Trail Mix

Bring this trail mix along when you go for a walk, hike, or road trip, or pack it in lunches. It's a convenient snack that will keep you going until dinner!

• • •

In a large bowl, combine all ingredients. Divide trail mix into individual portions and serve in paper cups or store in zippered plastic bags.

APPENDIX A
Substitutions

Emergency Substitutions

Baking Powder

1 teaspoon: ½ teaspoon cream of tartar plus ¼ teaspoon baking soda

Balsamic Vinegar

Sherry or cider vinegar (not white)

Beer

Apple juice or beef broth

Broth

1 teaspoon granulated or 1 cube bouillon dissolved in 1 cup water

Brown Sugar, Packed

Equal amount of granulated sugar

Buttermilk

1 teaspoon lemon juice or cider vinegar plus milk to make 1 cup; let stand 5 minutes

Cajun Seasoning

Equal parts white pepper, black pepper, ground red (cayenne) pepper, onion powder, garlic powder, and paprika

Chocolate

For 1 square unsweetened: 3 tablespoons unsweetened cocoa plus 1 tablespoon butter

For 1 square semisweet: 1 square unsweetened plus 1 tablespoon sugar

For 2 squares semisweet: ⅓ cup semisweet chocolate chips

Corn Syrup

For light or dark: 1 cup sugar plus ¼ cup water

For dark: 1 cup light corn syrup or 1 cup maple syrup, or ¾ cup light corn syrup plus ¼ cup molasses

Cornstarch

For 1 tablespoon: 2 tablespoons all-purpose flour

Dates

For chopped: equal amount raisins, prunes, currants, or dried cherries

Eggs

For 1 egg: 2 egg whites or 2 egg yolks; ¼ cup liquid egg substitute; or 2 tablespoons mayonnaise

Flour

For cake flour: 1 cup minus 2 tablespoons all-purpose flour

Flour, Self-rising

1 cup all-purpose flour plus 1 teaspoon baking powder and ½ teaspoon salt

Garlic

For 1 clove fresh: ⅛ teaspoon garlic powder

Half-and-Half

Equal parts milk and heavy cream

Honey

1¼ cups sugar plus ¼ cup water; equal amount corn syrup

Leeks

Equal amount green onions or shallots

Lemon Juice

For 1 teaspoon: 1 teaspoon cider vinegar or white vinegar

Milk

½ cup evaporated (not sweetened condensed) milk plus ½ cup water

Molasses

Equal amount honey

Mushrooms

For 1 cup cooked: 4-ounce can, drained

Mustard

For 1 tablespoon prepared: 1 teaspoon dry

Oil

Equal amount melted butter

Onion

For 1 medium: 1 teaspoon onion powder or 1 tablespoon dried minced

Poultry Seasoning

For 1 teaspoon: ¾ teaspoon sage plus ¼ teaspoon thyme

Prunes

Dates, raisins, or currants

Pumpkin Pie Spice

For 1 teaspoon: ½ teaspoon cinnamon plus ¼ teaspoon ground ginger plus ⅛ teaspoon ground allspice plus ⅛ teaspoon ground nutmeg

Red Pepper Sauce

For 4 drops: ⅛ teaspoon ground cayenne (red) pepper

Sour Cream

Plain yogurt or puréed cottage cheese

Tomato Products

For 1 cup juice: ½ cup sauce plus ½ cup water
For ½ cup paste: simmer 1 cup sauce till reduced to ½ cup
For 2 cups sauce: ¾ cup paste plus 1¼ cup water
For 1 cup canned: 1⅓ cups fresh, cut up and simmered 5 minutes

Wine

For white: apple juice or cider; white grape juice; chicken or vegetable broth; water
For red: apple cider; chicken, beef, or vegetable broth; water

Yeast

For 1 packet (2¼ teaspoons) regular or quick active dry: 1 compressed cake

Yogurt

Sour cream

Cooking Temperatures and Yields

Minimum Cooking Temperatures

Food	Internal Temperature
Fish, Beef, and Lamb	145°F
Pork, Eggs, Ground Beef	155°F
Poultry	165°F

Yields and Equivalents

Apples

1 medium, chopped = about 1 cup
3 medium = 1 pound
3 medium = 2¾ cups pared, cored, and sliced

Beans, Dried

1 cup = 2¼ to 2½ cups cooked

Butter

1 ounce butter or margarine = 2 tablespoons
1 stick butter or margarine = ¼ pound (4 ounces) or ½ cup
1 cup butter or margarine = 2 sticks or ½ pound (8 ounces)

Celery

2 medium stalks = ⅔ to ¾ cup

Cheese

1 pound American, Cheddar, Colby, Monterey jack, Swiss, or similar cheeses = 4 cups shredded
1 cup shredded = ¼ pound

Chocolate, Baking

1 ounce = 1 square
1 cup chocolate chips = 6 ounces

Cranberries

1 cup fresh makes 1 cup sauce
1 pound = 4 cups

Crumbs

1 cup cracker crumbs = 28 saltine crackers, 14 square graham crackers, or 24 rich round crackers

1 cup bread crumbs

soft = 1½ slices fresh bread

dry = 4 slices bread

¼ cup dry bread crumbs = ¾ cup fresh bread crumbs or ¼ cup cracker crumbs

1 cup vanilla wafer crumbs = 22 wafers

Eggs

1 cup = 4 large eggs

¼ cup liquid egg substitute = 1 egg

1 cup egg yolks = 10 to 12 egg yolks

1 cup egg whites = 8 to 10 egg whites

Fruits (see also Apples, Cranberries)

Bananas—3 large or 4 small = 2 cups sliced or 1⅓ cups mashed

Cherries—½ pound = 1 cup pitted

Grapes—1 pound = 2 cups halved

Peaches or Pears—1 medium = ½ cup sliced

Rhubarb— ½ pound = 2 to 4 stalks = 1 cup cooked

Strawberries—1 quart = 2 cups sliced

Garlic

1 clove fresh = ½ teaspoon chopped

Green Pepper

1 large = 1 cup diced

Herbs

1 tablespoon fresh, snipped = 1 teaspoon dried or ½ teaspoon ground

Lemon

juice of 1 lemon = about 3 tablespoons

grated peel of 1 lemon = about 1 teaspoon

Macaroni or Tube-Shaped Pastas

1 to 1¼ cups = 4 ounces = 2 to 2½ cups cooked

16 ounces = about 8 cups cooked

Mushrooms, Fresh

8 ounces = about 2½ cups sliced = about 1 cup cooked

Nuts

1 cup chopped = ¼ pound or 4 ounces

1 cup whole or halved = 4 to 5 ounces

Olives

24 small = 2 ounces = about ½ cup sliced

Onion, Green

1 sliced = about 1 tablespoon

8 sliced, white part only = about ½ cup

4 sliced, white part plus 4 inches green top = about ½ cup

Onion, Regular

1 medium, chopped = ½ cup

Orange

juice of 1 orange = ⅓ to ½ cup

grated peel of 1 orange = about 2 tablespoons

Potatoes

3 medium = 2 cups sliced or cubed

3 medium = 1¾ cups mashed

Rice

1 cup white rice (long grain) = about 7 ounces uncooked = 3 to 4 cups cooked

1 cup white rice (instant) = 2 cups cooked

1 cup brown rice = 3 cups cooked

1 cup wild rice = 3 to 4 cups cooked

Spaghetti and Noodles

8 ounces = 4 + cups cooked

1 pound (16 ounces) = 8 + cups cooked

Sugar, Powdered

1 pound = 4 cups

Whipping Cream

1 cup = 2 cups whipped

Index

THE EVERYTHING SERIES!

BUSINESS & PERSONAL FINANCE

Everything® **Accounting Book**
Everything® Budgeting Book
Everything® Business Planning Book
Everything® Coaching and Mentoring Book
Everything® Fundraising Book
Everything® Get Out of Debt Book
Everything® Grant Writing Book
Everything® Home-Based Business Book, 2nd Ed.
Everything® Homebuying Book, 2nd Ed.
Everything® Homeselling Book, 2nd Ed.
Everything® Investing Book, 2nd Ed.
Everything® Landlording Book
Everything® Leadership Book
Everything® **Managing People Book, 2nd Ed.**
Everything® Negotiating Book
Everything® Online Auctions Book
Everything® Online Business Book
Everything® Personal Finance Book
Everything® Personal Finance in Your 20s and 30s Book
Everything® Project Management Book
Everything® Real Estate Investing Book
Everything® Robert's Rules Book, $7.95
Everything® Selling Book
Everything® **Start Your Own Business Book, 2nd Ed.**
Everything® Wills & Estate Planning Book

COOKING

Everything® Barbecue Cookbook
Everything® Bartender's Book, $9.95
Everything® Chinese Cookbook
Everything® **Classic Recipes Book**
Everything® Cocktail Parties and Drinks Book
Everything® College Cookbook
Everything® **Cooking for Baby and Toddler Book**
Everything® Cooking for Two Cookbook
Everything® Diabetes Cookbook
Everything® Easy Gourmet Cookbook
Everything® Fondue Cookbook
Everything® **Fondue Party Book**
Everything® Gluten-Free Cookbook
Everything® Glycemic Index Cookbook
Everything® Grilling Cookbook

Everything® Healthy Meals in Minutes Cookbook
Everything® Holiday Cookbook
Everything® Indian Cookbook
Everything® Italian Cookbook
Everything® Low-Carb Cookbook
Everything® Low-Fat High-Flavor Cookbook
Everything® Low-Salt Cookbook
Everything® Meals for a Month Cookbook
Everything® Mediterranean Cookbook
Everything® Mexican Cookbook
Everything® One-Pot Cookbook
Everything® **Quick and Easy 30-Minute, 5-Ingredient Cookbook**
Everything® Quick Meals Cookbook
Everything® Slow Cooker Cookbook
Everything® Slow Cooking for a Crowd Cookbook
Everything® Soup Cookbook
Everything® Tex-Mex Cookbook
Everything® Thai Cookbook
Everything® Vegetarian Cookbook
Everything® Wild Game Cookbook
Everything® Wine Book, 2nd Ed.

GAMES

Everything® 15-Minute Sudoku Book, $9.95
Everything® 30-Minute Sudoku Book, $9.95
Everything® Blackjack Strategy Book
Everything® Brain Strain Book, $9.95
Everything® Bridge Book
Everything® Card Games Book
Everything® Card Tricks Book, $9.95
Everything® Casino Gambling Book, 2nd Ed.
Everything® Chess Basics Book
Everything® Craps Strategy Book
Everything® Crossword and Puzzle Book
Everything® Crossword Challenge Book
Everything® Cryptograms Book, $9.95
Everything® Easy Crosswords Book
Everything® Easy Kakuro Book, $9.95
Everything® Games Book, 2nd Ed.
Everything® Giant Sudoku Book, $9.95
Everything® Kakuro Challenge Book, $9.95
Everything® **Large-Print Crossword Challenge Book**
Everything® Large-Print Crosswords Book
Everything® Lateral Thinking Puzzles Book, $9.95
Everything® **Mazes Book**

Everything® Pencil Puzzles Book, $9.95
Everything® Poker Strategy Book
Everything® Pool & Billiards Book
Everything® Test Your IQ Book, $9.95
Everything® Texas Hold 'Em Book, $9.95
Everything® Travel Crosswords Book, $9.95
Everything® Word Games Challenge Book
Everything® Word Search Book

HEALTH

Everything® Alzheimer's Book
Everything® Diabetes Book
Everything® Health Guide to Adult Bipolar Disorder
Everything® Health Guide to Controlling Anxiety
Everything® Health Guide to Fibromyalgia
Everything® **Health Guide to Thyroid Disease**
Everything® Hypnosis Book
Everything® Low Cholesterol Book
Everything® Massage Book
Everything® Menopause Book
Everything® Nutrition Book
Everything® Reflexology Book
Everything® Stress Management Book

HISTORY

Everything® American Government Book
Everything® American History Book
Everything® Civil War Book
Everything® Freemasons Book
Everything® Irish History & Heritage Book
Everything® Middle East Book

HOBBIES

Everything® Candlemaking Book
Everything® Cartooning Book
Everything® **Coin Collecting Book**
Everything® Drawing Book
Everything® Family Tree Book, 2nd Ed.
Everything® Knitting Book
Everything® Knots Book
Everything® Photography Book
Everything® Quilting Book
Everything® Scrapbooking Book
Everything® Sewing Book
Everything® Woodworking Book

Bolded titles are new additions to the series.
All Everything® books are priced at $12.95 or $14.95, unless otherwise stated. Prices subject to change without notice.

HOME IMPROVEMENT

Everything® Feng Shui Book
Everything® Feng Shui Decluttering Book, $9.95
Everything® Fix-It Book
Everything® Home Decorating Book
Everything® Home Storage Solutions Book
Everything® Homebuilding Book
Everything® Lawn Care Book
Everything® Organize Your Home Book

KIDS' BOOKS

All titles are $7.95
Everything® Kids' Animal Puzzle & Activity Book
Everything® Kids' Baseball Book, 4th Ed.
Everything® Kids' Bible Trivia Book
Everything® Kids' Bugs Book
Everything® Kids' Cars and Trucks Puzzle & Activity Book
Everything® Kids' Christmas Puzzle & Activity Book
Everything® Kids' Cookbook
Everything® Kids' Crazy Puzzles Book
Everything® Kids' Dinosaurs Book
Everything® Kids' First Spanish Puzzle and Activity Book
Everything® Kids' Gross Hidden Pictures Book
Everything® Kids' Gross Jokes Book
Everything® Kids' Gross Mazes Book
Everything® Kids' Gross Puzzle and Activity Book
Everything® Kids' Halloween Puzzle & Activity Book
Everything® Kids' Hidden Pictures Book
Everything® Kids' Horses Book
Everything® Kids' Joke Book
Everything® Kids' Knock Knock Book
Everything® Kids' Learning Spanish Book
Everything® Kids' Math Puzzles Book
Everything® Kids' Mazes Book
Everything® Kids' Money Book
Everything® Kids' Nature Book
Everything® Kids' Pirates Puzzle and Activity Book
Everything® Kids' Princess Puzzle and Activity Book
Everything® Kids' Puzzle Book
Everything® Kids' Riddles & Brain Teasers Book
Everything® Kids' Science Experiments Book
Everything® Kids' Sharks Book
Everything® Kids' Soccer Book
Everything® Kids' Travel Activity Book

KIDS' STORY BOOKS

Everything® Fairy Tales Book

LANGUAGE

Everything® Conversational Chinese Book with CD, $19.95
Everything® Conversational Japanese Book with CD, $19.95
Everything® French Grammar Book
Everything® French Phrase Book, $9.95
Everything® French Verb Book, $9.95
Everything® German Practice Book with CD, $19.95
Everything® Inglés Book
Everything® Learning French Book
Everything® Learning German Book
Everything® Learning Italian Book
Everything® Learning Latin Book
Everything® Learning Spanish Book
Everything® Russian Practice Book with CD, $19.95
Everything® Sign Language Book
Everything® Spanish Grammar Book
Everything® Spanish Phrase Book, $9.95
Everything® Spanish Practice Book with CD, $19.95
Everything® Spanish Verb Book, $9.95

MUSIC

Everything® Drums Book with CD, $19.95
Everything® Guitar Book
Everything® Guitar Chords Book with CD, $19.95
Everything® Home Recording Book
Everything® Music Theory Book with CD, $19.95
Everything® Reading Music Book with CD, $19.95
Everything® Rock & Blues Guitar Book (with CD), $19.95
Everything® Songwriting Book

NEW AGE

Everything® Astrology Book, 2nd Ed.
Everything® Birthday Personology Book
Everything® Dreams Book, 2nd Ed.
Everything® Love Signs Book, $9.95
Everything® Numerology Book
Everything® Paganism Book
Everything® Palmistry Book
Everything® Psychic Book
Everything® Reiki Book
Everything® Sex Signs Book, $9.95
Everything® Tarot Book, 2nd Ed.
Everything® Wicca and Witchcraft Book

PARENTING

Everything® Baby Names Book, 2nd Ed.
Everything® Baby Shower Book
Everything® Baby's First Food Book
Everything® Baby's First Year Book
Everything® Birthing Book
Everything® Breastfeeding Book
Everything® Father-to-Be Book
Everything® Father's First Year Book
Everything® Get Ready for Baby Book
Everything® Get Your Baby to Sleep Book, $9.95
Everything® Getting Pregnant Book
Everything® Guide to Raising a One-Year-Old
Everything® Guide to Raising a Two-Year-Old
Everything® Homeschooling Book
Everything® Mother's First Year Book
Everything® Parent's Guide to Children and Divorce
Everything® Parent's Guide to Children with ADD/ADHD
Everything® Parent's Guide to Children with Asperger's Syndrome
Everything® Parent's Guide to Children with Autism
Everything® Parent's Guide to Children with Bipolar Disorder
Everything® Parent's Guide to Children with Dyslexia
Everything® Parent's Guide to Positive Discipline
Everything® Parent's Guide to Raising a Successful Child
Everything® Parent's Guide to Raising Boys
Everything® Parent's Guide to Raising Siblings
Everything® Parent's Guide to Sensory Integration Disorder
Everything® Parent's Guide to Tantrums
Everything® Parent's Guide to the Overweight Child
Everything® Parent's Guide to the Strong-Willed Child
Everything® Parenting a Teenager Book
Everything® Potty Training Book, $9.95
Everything® Pregnancy Book, 2nd Ed.
Everything® Pregnancy Fitness Book
Everything® Pregnancy Nutrition Book
Everything® Pregnancy Organizer, 2nd Ed., $16.95
Everything® Toddler Activities Book
Everything® Toddler Book
Everything® Tween Book
Everything® Twins, Triplets, and More Book

PETS

Everything® Aquarium Book
Everything® Boxer Book
Everything® Cat Book, 2nd Ed.
Everything® Chihuahua Book
Everything® Dachshund Book
Everything® Dog Book
Everything® Dog Health Book
Everything® Dog Owner's Organizer, $16.95
Everything® Dog Training and Tricks Book
Everything® German Shepherd Book
Everything® Golden Retriever Book
Everything® Horse Book
Everything® Horse Care Book
Everything® Horseback Riding Book
Everything® Labrador Retriever Book
Everything® Poodle Book
Everything® Pug Book
Everything® Puppy Book
Everything® Rottweiler Book
Everything® Small Dogs Book
Everything® Tropical Fish Book
Everything® Yorkshire Terrier Book

REFERENCE

Everything® Blogging Book
Everything® Build Your Vocabulary Book
Everything® Car Care Book
Everything® Classical Mythology Book
Everything® Da Vinci Book
Everything® Divorce Book
Everything® Einstein Book
Everything® Etiquette Book, 2nd Ed.
Everything® Inventions and Patents Book
Everything® Mafia Book
Everything® Philosophy Book
Everything® Psychology Book
Everything® Shakespeare Book

RELIGION

Everything® Angels Book
Everything® Bible Book
Everything® Buddhism Book
Everything® Catholicism Book
Everything® Christianity Book
Everything® History of the Bible Book
Everything® Jesus Book
Everything® Jewish History & Heritage Book
Everything® Judaism Book
Everything® Kabbalah Book
Everything® Koran Book
Everything® Mary Book

Everything® Mary Magdalene Book
Everything® Prayer Book
Everything® Saints Book
Everything® Torah Book
Everything® Understanding Islam Book
Everything® World's Religions Book
Everything® Zen Book

SCHOOL & CAREERS

Everything® Alternative Careers Book
Everything® Career Tests Book
Everything® College Major Test Book
Everything® College Survival Book, 2nd Ed.
Everything® Cover Letter Book, 2nd Ed.
Everything® Filmmaking Book
Everything® Get-a-Job Book
Everything® Guide to Being a Paralegal
Everything® Guide to Being a Real Estate Agent
Everything® Guide to Being a Sales Rep
Everything® Guide to Careers in Health Care
Everything® Guide to Careers in Law Enforcement
Everything® Guide to Government Jobs
Everything® Guide to Starting and Running a Restaurant
Everything® Job Interview Book
Everything® New Nurse Book
Everything® New Teacher Book
Everything® Paying for College Book
Everything® Practice Interview Book
Everything® Resume Book, 2nd Ed.
Everything® Study Book

SELF-HELP

Everything® Dating Book, 2nd Ed.
Everything® Great Sex Book
Everything® Kama Sutra Book
Everything® Self-Esteem Book

SPORTS & FITNESS

Everything® Easy Fitness Book
Everything® Fishing Book
Everything® Golf Instruction Book
Everything® Pilates Book
Everything® Running Book
Everything® Weight Training Book
Everything® Yoga Book

TRAVEL

Everything® Family Guide to Cruise Vacations
Everything® Family Guide to Hawaii

Everything® Family Guide to Las Vegas, 2nd Ed.
Everything® Family Guide to Mexico
Everything® Family Guide to New York City, 2nd Ed.
Everything® Family Guide to RV Travel & Campgrounds
Everything® Family Guide to the Caribbean
Everything® Family Guide to the Walt Disney World Resort®, Universal Studios®, and Greater Orlando, 4th Ed.
Everything® Family Guide to Timeshares
Everything® Family Guide to Washington D.C., 2nd Ed.
Everything® Guide to New England

WEDDINGS

Everything® Bachelorette Party Book, $9.95
Everything® Bridesmaid Book, $9.95
Everything® Destination Wedding Book
Everything® Elopement Book, $9.95
Everything® Father of the Bride Book, $9.95
Everything® Groom Book, $9.95
Everything® Mother of the Bride Book, $9.95
Everything® Outdoor Wedding Book
Everything® Wedding Book, 3rd Ed.
Everything® Wedding Checklist, $9.95
Everything® Wedding Etiquette Book, $9.95
Everything® Wedding Organizer, 2nd Ed., $16.95
Everything® Wedding Shower Book, $9.95
Everything® Wedding Vows Book, $9.95
Everything® Wedding Workout Book
Everything® Weddings on a Budget Book, $9.95

WRITING

Everything® Creative Writing Book
Everything® Get Published Book, 2nd Ed.
Everything® Grammar and Style Book
Everything® Guide to Writing a Book Proposal
Everything® Guide to Writing a Novel
Everything® Guide to Writing Children's Books
Everything® Guide to Writing Research Papers
Everything® Screenwriting Book
Everything® Writing Poetry Book
Everything® Writing Well Book